MUHAMMAD

MUHAMMAD

PROPHET *of* PEACE AMID
THE CLASH *of* EMPIRES

JUAN COLE

NATION
BOOKS
New York

Nation Books
116 East 16th Street, 8th Floor, New York, NY 10003
www.nationbooks.org
@NationBooks

First Edition: October 2018

Published by Nation Books, an imprint of Perseus Books, LLC, a subsidiary of Hachette Book Group, Inc. Nation Books is a copublishing venture of the Nation Institute and Perseus Books.

The Hachette Speakers Bureau provides a wide range of authors for speaking events. To find out more, go to www.hachettespeakersbureau.com or call (866) 376- 6591.

The publisher is not responsible for websites (or their content) that are not owned by the publisher.

Print book interior design by Six Red Marbles Inc.

Library of Congress Cataloging-in-Publication Data

Names: Cole, Juan Ricardo, author.
Title: Muhammad, prophet of peace amid the clash of empires / Juan Cole.
Description: New York : Nation Books, [2018] | Includes bibliographical references and index.
Identifiers: LCCN 2018007563 | ISBN 9781568587837 (hardcover) | ISBN 9781568587820 (ebook)
Subjects: LCSH: Muðhammad, Prophet, - 632— Biography. | Islam—Origin.
Classification: LCC BP166.5 .C65 2018 | DDC 297.6/3 [B] — dc23
LC record available at https://lccn.loc.gov/2018007563

ISBNs: 978-1-56858-783-7(hardcover); 978-1-56858-782-0 (ebook)

CONTENTS

ILLUSTRATIONS

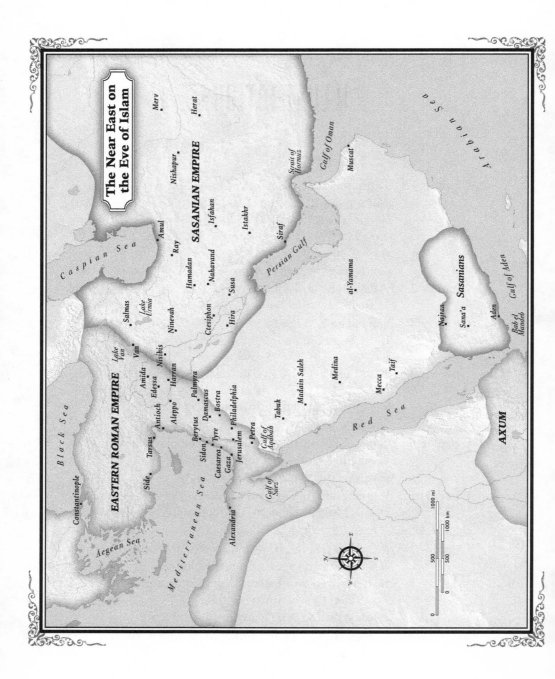

The Near East on the Eve of Islam

EASTERN ROMAN EMPIRE

SASANIAN EMPIRE

Sasanians

AXUM

Black Sea

Caspian Sea

Mediterranean Sea

Aegean Sea

Red Sea

Persian Gulf

Gulf of Oman

Arabian Sea

Gulf of Aden

Gulf of Aqaba

Gulf of Suez

Strait of Hormuz

Lake Van

Lake Urmia

Merv

Herat

Nishapur

Amul

Ray

Isfahan

Istakhr

Siraf

Muscat

Hamadan

Nahavand

Susa

Ctesiphon

Hira

Ninevah

Nisibis

Salmas

Van

Amida

Edessa

Harran

Palmyra

al-Yamama

Najran

Sana'a

Aden

Bab el Mandeb

Madain Saleh

Medina

Mecca

Taif

Tabuk

Petra

Antioch

Aleppo

Berytus

Damascus

Bostra

Tarsus

Sidon

Tyre

Caesarea

Gaza

Jerusalem

Philadelphia

Side

Constantinople

Alexandria

N

1000 mi

1000 km

500

500

0

0

PREFACE

THE NEW WORLD RELIGION OF ISLAM AROSE AGAINST THE BACKDROP of a seventh-century game of thrones between the Roman Empire and the Sasanian Empire of Iran that was fought with unparalleled savagery for nearly three decades. The imperial armies zigzagged bloodily across the Near East, the Fertile Crescent, Asia Minor, and the Balkans. Although the Qur'an makes it clear that this struggle between rival emperors, whom contemporaries called "the two eyes of the earth," formed an essential context for the mission of the prophet Muhammad, historians have only recently attempted explorations of the latter's life and thought with this framework in mind.[1]

This book puts forward a reinterpretation of early Islam as a movement strongly inflected with values of peacemaking that was reacting against the slaughter of the decades-long war and attendant religious strife. From the Crusades to colonialism, conflicts between Christians and Muslims led to a concentration among writers of European heritage on war and Islam, leaving the dimension of peace and cooperation neglected.[2] Both peace and war are present in the Qur'an, just as they are in the Bible, and both will be analyzed below, but the focus here is on peace.

This book studies the Qur'an in its historical context rather than trying to explain what Muslims believe about their scripture.[3] The Qur'an insists on liberty of conscience and forbearance toward

1

enemies, and it prohibits unprovoked, aggressive warfare. It promises salvation to all righteous monotheists and not just to followers of the prophet Muhammad. That many outsiders and a not inconsiderable number of adherents have associated it with none of these values, and indeed have often interpreted it as upholding the converse, demonstrates how badly it has been understood. The misapprehensions came about for many reasons, including the imperial ideologies of the later Christian Byzantine and Muslim Abbasid empires, difficulties in interpreting the text, and a failure to read it against contemporary Roman and Iranian texts, a procedure that allows us to compare and contrast its values and concerns with those of others living in that era.[4]

The Iranian invasion of Roman territory from 603 forward threatened the independence of western Arabia, where Muhammad was based. The Sasanian conquest of Jerusalem in 614 struck contemporaries as apocalyptic and provoked a mystical response from the Prophet. A close reading of the Qur'an shows that a profound distress at the carnage of the age led Muhammad to spend the first half of his prophetic career (610–622) imagining an alternative sort of society, one firmly grounded in practices of peace. The Qur'an repeatedly instructs Believers to "repel evil with good," pardon their persecutors, and wish peace on those who harassed them. These verses have as their greater context the outbreak of struggles among Christians, Jews, Zoroastrians, and a remnant of pagans, who were partisans in the clash of empires raging around them. Muhammad in these years resembles much more the Jesus of the Sermon on the Mount than is usually admitted.

Scholars have increasingly also tied the second half of Muhammad's career, 622–632, to the maneuverings of Rome and Iran, even suggesting that his move to Medina from his hometown of Mecca may have been connected to Roman diplomacy.[5] I argue that Muslims in the time of the Prophet were explicitly allied with the Christian emperor Herakleios (r. 610–641) and indeed that Muhammad saw his defensive battles against truculent pagans in places such as Badr and Uhud in West Arabia as protecting Roman churches in Transjordan and Syria, to the north. It is likely these militant Arabian pagans had allied with the Iranian king of kings.

In short, Islam is, no less than Christianity, a Western religion that initially grew up in the Roman Empire. Moreover, Muhammad saw himself as an ally of the West. The Prophet in those years of pagan attacks did not abandon his option for peace but moved toward a doctrine of just war similar to that of Cicero and late-antique Christian thinkers. He repeatedly sued for peace with a bellicose Mecca, but when that failed he organized Medina for self-defense in the face of a determined pagan foe. The Qur'an insists that aggressive warfare is wrong and that if the enemy seeks an armistice, Muslims are bound to accept the entreaty. This disallowing of aggressive war and search for a resolution even in the midst of violent conflict justifies the title "prophet of peace," even if Muhammad was occasionally forced into a defensive campaign. The Qur'an contains a doctrine of just war but not of holy war and does not use the word *jihad* with that latter connotation. It views war as an unfortunate necessity when innocents, and the freedom of conscience, are threatened. It strictly forbids vigilantism and equates premeditated killing of noncombatants with genocide, paraphrasing in this regard Jewish commentaries on the Bible in the Jerusalem Talmud.[6]

The Qur'an, read judiciously alongside later histories, suggests that during Muhammad's lifetime, Islam spread peacefully in the major cities of Western Arabia. The soft power of the Qur'an's spiritual message has typically been underestimated in most treatments of this period. The image of Muhammad and very early Islam that emerges from a careful reading of the Qur'an on peace-related themes contradicts not only widely held Western views but even much of the later Muslim historiographical tradition. This finding should come as no surprise. Life in medieval feudal societies did not encourage pacific theologies, and Muslims in later empires lost touch with the realities of the early seventh century. What if we read Jesus's life and thought only through the lens of Pope Urban II, who launched the sanguinary Crusades in the Holy Land with the cry, "God wills it!"?[7]

Even today, many scholars of early Islam seem unduly deferential to later medieval interpreters. Others radically reject all information in those sources, treating Muslim histories differently from Byzantine or Carolingian chronicles, once again condemning non-Europeans to being a people without a history. The Qur'an tells us about that history if we will listen to it, and it tells us what is plausible in the later biographies of the Prophet.[8]

§ 1 ♦

SANCTUARY

MUHAMMAD, THE SON OF ABDULLAH, HAVING BEEN CALLED TO THE audition of a lifetime, hurried through the filigree of Mecca's palm-leaf huts and humble mud-brick homes to the opulent coral stone mansion of Khadija bint Khuwaylid. The small town's wealthiest merchant, and its most eligible widow, was deciding whether to appoint the twenty-five-year-old to lead her next trading mission up to Damascus. If he received the commission, it would change his life, but many traders with more experience than he were likely in the running.[1]

5

Muhammad had been born in the West Arabian sanctuary city of Mecca, a zone of peace among feuding tribes. Muhammad's clan, the Hashim, served as caretakers and ministers of the Kaaba, a cube-shaped shrine to God the Most High, where they maintained concord throughout the year. The tribe of which it formed a part, the Quraysh, depended for their livelihood on the shrine to God and the penumbra of peace it cast over the Red Sea coastal region of the Tihama, in which Mecca was nestled. They traveled for commerce and held their own trade fairs that attracted merchants from all over the region. This rough neighborhood was bounded by the Roman Empire to the north and the Sasanian Empire (224–651 CE) of Iran to the south and east.[2]

Muhammad, an orphan, likely viewed peace and conflict through the lens of his disadvantaged start in life. Some traditions say that when Muhammad's mother was pregnant with him, his father, Abdullah, died of fever at Yathrib (later known as Medina) on returning from a trade journey to Gaza. That "Year of the Elephant," probably around 567, Mecca repulsed an invasion from Yemen.[3] When Muhammad was six, his widowed mother, Amina, took him to visit some of his relatives who lived in Yathrib. She died on the way back, leaving the little boy Muhammad bereft of both parents. Muhammad's grandfather Shayba "'Abd al-Muttalib" ibn Hashim took the boy into his own household. Reputedly tall, imposing in appearance, quick-witted, and a shrewd politician, 'Abd al-Muttalib had an arresting gray streak through his jet-black head of hair. The paramount chief of the Hashim clan, he served as custodian of the sacred well of Zamzam, which he had rediscovered. He provided its copious water to pilgrims who came to Mecca to worship at the city's shrine to God the Most High. Without providing a major water source, 'Abd al-Muttalib could not have hoped to attract a significant pilgrimage trade. Pilgrims brought in money and offerings of much-needed food from more fertile and prosperous areas—welcome gifts, given that hardscrabble

Mecca had limited agricultural lands. Arabia has been likened to a burlap cloak with golden hems—coarse within, as at Mecca, but flourishing along the coasts.

The Banu Hashim lacked the wealth and power of some other clans in the city, though as caretakers of the holy shrine they enjoyed high social status. Muhammad the orphan, as the least prestigious member of his clan, suffered some humiliations. He had to work as a shepherd for his grandfather. His uncles and cousins bullied him because he had no father to protect him, and he lacked a long-lived hero of the previous generation whose exploits he could celebrate in poetry. `Abd al-Muttalib used to spread a runner outside the Kaaba in Mecca where he would hold meetings. His many sons would gather and sit on it, waiting for him. Little Muhammad once came and plopped down, also eager for his grandfather to arrive. He was dismayed to find that his jealous uncles tried to wave him off, yelling, "Get off your father's carpet!" On one occasion `Abd al-Muttalib arrived to witness this scene and told them to cease.[4] Later on, the Qur'an would refer (*The City* 90:14–16) to "the steep path" of high ethics as requiring "feeding, during a famine, an orphan related to you, or a grubby vagrant." After two years, `Abd al-Muttalib also died, and Muhammad went to the household of his paternal uncle Abu Talib, who became the paramount chief of the Hashim clan.

Now, at age twenty-five, Muhammad had an opportunity to escape his relative poverty. When the modest camel trains assembled outside Mecca to go to Syria, Khadija's rivaled all the others combined—that is, she may have possessed half of the town's long-distance merchant capital.[5] Muhammad's uncle Abu Talib had recommended him when she asked for someone honest and reliable. Khadija, somewhat Muhammad's elder, would have met him in her receiving room with her circle of advisers. Making her decision, she underlined the responsibility she was vouchsafing to him: "I've

7

entrusted you with twice as many goods as any of your predecessors among your people."

She sent along her manservant Maysara, likely as much to keep an eye on her capital as to serve Muhammad. The young man had just gained a magnificent opportunity, but he had incurred daunting risks as well. Let us try to imagine what his hazardous journey through the world of the late sixth century was like.

The caravan may have set out from the small Arabian holy city in August 592. Citizens gathered beneath the lambent late-afternoon sun to see the traders off, having invested in the mission, ringing bells and beating tambourines. Muhammad and the other traders wore the white robes of merchant-priests of peace. They thereby signaled to any hostile tribesmen that they had no warlike intentions and traveled between sanctuaries under the protection of the Creator God. Members of the Hashim clan had a special advantage in this regard since they served as caretakers of the Kaaba and even coarse rural tribesmen respected their vocation. Bedouin children ran up to them, giggling and hawking fruit and water. Muhammad and his men would have passed through occasional adobe villages, roofs thatched with palm leaves, as they traversed the auburn steppe, interrupted by teal abal bushes and strewn with colorful loose chert.[6]

Such travelers rode through the night beneath a spangled sky. At dawn the sun slowly flared behind low basalt hills, tinting the twisted crags with rose and violet, then embossing them in brass. They halted when the heat of the day grew too oppressive, catching some sleep and waiting for nightfall. After several days of riding, the party would have reached the date-palm oasis of Yathrib. There, happy to see some limpid pools and fruit-laden date and jujube trees after days of eating dust, they would have stocked up on water, dates, and other refreshments for the precarious arid trek north. A vassal of Sasanian Iran from the local pagan Khazraj tribe then ruled this city, but the

Meccans had preserved their own neutrality between Iran and the Roman Empire.[7]

Muhammad would have visited with his relatives in Medina. His great-grandmother Salma was a Khazraji woman of the Najjar clan. The Banu Najjar, despite being such distant cousins, would have valued their connection to Muhammad's family, custodians of the sacred Kaaba. Medinans went on pilgrimage to the shrine of God in Mecca, though they also visited the temple they had erected to the goddess of fate, Manat.[8]

Then Muhammad and his convoy would have set off again north in the late afternoon. When voyagers passed over patches of white sand, the granules glinted in the relentless sun like miniature diamonds. Thirst and discomfort beset the travelers, as distant mirages of sweet water spitefully vanished on their closer approach. Occasionally, they might have startled ranging herds of spear-horned oryx, which scattered with dazzling speed. Keening desert gales assailed them like the breath of a dragon, and when a sandstorm came up, it pricked their skin as though with innumerable tiny needles. The Meccans would have been inordinately grateful for the occasional majestic cumulus cloud that offered them some respite from the irate summer sun.

Along the way, the merchants would have bought simple supplies from rural bedouins. We can gain an idea of this journey from the Piacenza Pilgrim, a Roman who traveled in the Near East in the 570s during Muhammad's childhood. He wrote of the Arabs, or "Saracens":

> Families of the Saracens and their wives came from the desert, and, sitting by the wayside with lamentations, laying down their bundles, begged for bread from those who passed by; and their husbands came, bringing skins of cold water from the interior of the desert, and gave it to us, receiving bread for it. They also brought ropes of roots, whose smell was delicious beyond all odours. They

had no permission to do this, because a prohibition [on commerce] was laid upon them, and they were celebrating a festival.[9]

The Pilgrim discovered that one of the holy months the Arabs considered sacrosanct, during which they prohibited fighting, was drawing to a close, and he heard that the chances of being attacked by the bedouins would increase.

Arabian society consisted of tribes, or large families. Each brother and each cousin could move out of the patriarchal residence and found a new clan, putting together a coalition in the extended family to vie for power or to raid the flocks of others. Some of these relationships were fictive. Occasionally, other clans joined a successful tribe, the way modern people join a political party, and by way of justification announced that they had discovered a common long-lost ancestor. Tribes engaged in a form of kinship politics and were not necessarily mobile. Most of those in the Hejaz, the northern stretch of the Tihama coastal region along the Red Sea, dwelled in towns and villages in the late sixth century, but a minority of pastoralists wandered with flocks to find patches of glaucous pasture. The two coexisted in an uneasy symbiosis: settled people provided agricultural goods and essential grain, and the nomads traded meat and dairy products for them.[10]

The trade route from Mecca to Roman Arabia appears to have revived in the last third of the sixth century. In part, this development reflected the unusual prosperity of Transjordan in this era. In part, it also derived from the Iranian invasion of Yemen in the early 570s, when they dethroned the previous Ethiopian Christian dynasty in alliance with local pagans and Jews. The Sasanians thus controlled the mouth of the Red Sea, the Bab al-Mandab, which opened Roman maritime commerce with Africa and Asia to interference and piracy, thus increasing the profitability of overland commerce. The Roman and Sasanian Empires had for centuries engaged in a globe-straddling contest for dominance, and throughout Muhammad's lifetime this imperial struggle would intensify in its savagery, powerfully shaping his world and his views on the desirability of peace.[11]

Roman historian Menander the Guardsman observed of the Arabs of this era, "There are a myriad Saracen tribes, for the most part anarchic desert-dwellers, some of whom are loyal to the Roman state, others to the Persian." Although a few Arab clans in the region had embraced Christianity, most Arabs of the Hejaz had remained pagans, stubbornly resisting the official religion of Constantine and his successors. This conservatism may have been in part a bid for neutrality between the Christian Roman Empire and the Zoroastrian Iranian empire, as with Mecca. Being noncommittal allowed them to move freely between the two. For others, their religious traditionalism reassured Iran about Arab allies since their conversion to Christianity might signal that they tilted politically toward Constantinople.[12]

During the blistering day, when the sand scorched their feet, travelers huddled miserably in sheepskin tents, awaiting the gloaming to start their journey afresh. They typically accomplished some of the trip at night. The nocturnal journey challenged the camel drivers and their steeds, bouncing their passengers unevenly as their mounts stumbled blindly across jagged lava fields and rock-strewn dry riverbeds.[13]

Such excursions depended on detailed Quraysh knowledge of the rugged countryside, of where the wells and oases lay and where robber bands might lie in wait. Occasionally, local tribes would have confronted Muhammad and the Quraysh, demanding that they pay out some of their goods for passage through that land. The Meccans are said to have bought off such hostile bedouins by offering carriage to them for their leather and other goods and a share of the profits on their return. Muhammad, a scion of the Banu Hashim, which specialized in settling feuds and keeping the peace around the Kaaba sanctuary, would have found himself forced to negotiate such challenges despite his youth and inexperience. If he failed, he could face raids and lose the whole value of his trading mission, ending his career as a long-distance merchant. If he did not bring back summer wheat from Syria, some of his friends might miss some meals.

❧

MUHAMMAD AND HIS camel train would have proceeded through the desert flatland between the jet carapace of hilly country to the east and the turquoise sea to the west. To fill the boredom, traders recited heroic poetry of their ancestors' battle days, glorying in raids, carnage, and swordplay, matching the rhythm of the verse to the gait of their steeds: "When I arise with my blade in vengeance / It slices at once—it's no dull orchard hatchet," an ancient bard boasted, characterizing his saber as being as "vicious as a darting snake's head." Muhammad, being of Banu Hashim and a peace builder, likely did not approve of the glorification of rough plunderers who preyed on innocents. Wealthy pagan temples in late antiquity before the hegemony of Christianity had often been a "resort" for the poor.[14] The Kaaba probably played a similar charitable role. At least later in life, Muhammad recited verses condemning "the one who drives away the orphan, and does not advocate for feeding the poor."[15] Freebooting warriors and the lay priests of the Kaaba devoted themselves to very different values, but Arabic poetry decidedly feted the raiders.

Muhammad's forebears had negotiated a set of alliances and informal treaties with most tribes of the Hejaz and Transjordan, which allowed a modest cavalcade to wend its way through their territory and involved payoffs, sharing of trading profits, marriage alliances, and respect for the Kaaba sanctuary of God and for the Quraysh as its guardians. The Qur'an (106:1–4) later referred to this network of treaty obligations, seeing it as a divine bestowal: "Because of his benevolence toward the Quraysh they were enabled to undertake the winter and summer caravans. So let them worship the lord of this shrine, who provided them with food to stop their hunger and gave them security against fear."[16]

Muhammad's great-grandfather Hashim ibn ʿAbd Manaf was said to have personally visited Roman authorities in Syria, likely in the early 490s, and negotiated tariff abatements and safe passage for the Meccan merchants who journeyed through the empire. He initiated the practice of bringing "bags of wheat" from Damascus. Meccans timed these annual treks north just after the summer grain harvest since they, wedged among obsidian lava beds and misshapen spatter cones, lacked that key dietary nutrient. Hejazis like Muhammad, who could not stand the cold of the Levant in December, instead went south to Yemen for winter wheat. Mecca, as a neutral city-state, could bring Indian Ocean goods up from the port of Aden and then take them to the Roman Near East. Because by treaty Iran limited the cities that could trade with Rome and charged its enemies in Constantinople a 25 percent tariff on desirable Asian luxury goods, Hejazis could offer these commodities at a discount by acting as a third party.[17]

The Quraysh brought back staples like grain as well as raisins, wine, and Damascene swords. The substantial expenses of overland caravan trade required carrying lightweight luxury items to make the voyage worthwhile. The Hejazis were known for their precious metals and called the mines near Medina the "Cradle of Gold." The Roman Empire had to pay large sums of gold annually to Iran to keep the peace after losing several key campaigns, an obligation that may have increased the profitability of the nuggets provided by the caravan trade. They probably also traded in leather, high-quality dates, ivory from Ethiopia, and Asian goods such as silk via Yemen. Occasionally, they may have brought wealthy Jews from Yemen up to Palestine, transporting their deceased loved ones in an ossuary for burial in the Holy Land.[18]

Muhammad's Meccan caravan would have arrived at Madain Salih, an old Nabatean oasis city also called Hijr. Arab tribes had invaded the Transjordan in the 300s BC, founding a kingdom there, Nabatea, where they introduced the worship of North Arabian gods. This Arab kingdom fell to Rome in 106 CE. The inhabitants continued to revere their own deities for centuries thereafter, though often in dialogue with Greek religion. The Qur'an called the Nabateans, the greatest of the Arab states of the ancient world, "'Ad," after a prominent ancient tribe of southern Transjordan.[19]

Bored Roman troops stationed at a base in Madain Salih before trade routes shifted had left Latin graffiti. By 592 sand drifted listlessly through its abandoned tall red sandstone buildings bearing enigmatic runes. The Nabateans had constructed a major graveyard there for aristocrats, which they believed the gods guarded. Tomb raiders are warned in an inscription that they will have to pay a fine to "Dushara and Hubal, and to Manotu." Dushara was the title of the chief of the gods among the Nabateans, who appears to have been especially important in this city. Hubal is a seldom-mentioned and apparently minor deity. Manotu is the Aramaic form of Manat, the Arab goddess of fate also beloved in Medina. Some Roman troops liked her so much that they took her back to Europe. At nearby Tayma one inscription called her the "goddess of goddesses." Another makes it clear that locals saw the graveyard at Madain Salih as a sanctuary, a place of peace: "The tomb and this inscription (wktbh) are inviolable according to the nature of inviolability among the Nabataeans...forever and ever."[20] The idea that a piece of writing could itself be a sanctuary of peace may have come down to the Arabs of Muhammad's own time and affected the way they perceived scriptures, whether the Bible or the Qur'an.

Some Arabs at Madain Saleh in the sixth century likely still worshipped Manat, who capriciously set people's fate. The northern Hejaz came to be dominated in the Roman period by the Thamud tribal federation, whom the Qur'an (*The Heights* 7:74) castigated for their stubborn paganism and their rejection of a native Arab prophet, Salih, whom God sent to them. It laments of the traditionalists in Madain Saleh, "The people of Hijr rejected the messengers."[21]

Muhammad and the rest of the column would have set off again, passing between friable sandstone hills to enter the prosperous Roman province of Third Palestine. Constantinople still administered this area and provided military security to this province from tribal raiding along the border known as the Arabian Line. For much of the sixth century, it had been aided in this task by Arab allies, the Jafnid paramount chiefs who commanded Roman-trained horsemen, as well as levies from the Ghassan, Kalb, and other tribes. Pastoral nomads proved useful to empires because their way of life made them a natural cavalry, and Roman generals in Europe deployed German tribes in the same way. In the Near East, drilled Arab cavalrymen had served as auxiliaries to the formal legions, fighting rural Arab pastoralists in return for gold from Constantinople. By 592, however, the alliance of the Romans with the Jafnids lay in tatters, placing Muhammad and his men at risk.[22]

The Jafnid elite had adopted Christianity, but the Arabs who fought for this dynasty included many devotees of the old gods. The Ghassan tribe, the backbone of the Jafnid-led force, claimed a common ancestry with the tribes of Medina, the city of Muhammad's paternal great-grandmother.[23] A branch of the Jafna lived in or around Medina, and likely some adventurous young men from Mecca and Medina had gone north as soldiers of fortune, serving the empire.

Muhammad and his band would have descended the escarpment, entering a field of dunes, the shadows in their slack like hyena stripes. When Muhammad and his band made camp long after midnight, they would have squatted around a campfire, its amber flames crackling in the stillness, cooking some supper. The Qur'an (*The Event* 56:71–73) later reminded its hearers among the Meccan caravanners, "Have you seen the fire that you made? Did you create the firewood or did we? We rendered it a reminder and a means of provisioning those strong enough to traverse the desert." They would have unpacked their beasts of burden and piled up their goods in a circle as protection from a raid and then slept with their swords close at hand. The snarling of jackals and wild saluki hounds around the camp might have startled Muhammad awake occasionally.

❧

MUHAMMAD AND HIS cavalcade would have made their way into Wadi Ramm in southern Transjordan. The people of this region, the Banu Judham (who succeeded the ancient `Ad tribe here), were largely Christian by this time. The archaeological record and literary sources make clear, however, "the continuity of the pagan population," especially on desert fringes where evidence of worship of standing stones is still found from the 500s and 600s. During an Arab revolt of the early 580s, according to a Christian contemporary of Muhammad, a group of pagan Arabs had kidnapped a young Christian man in the region just east of the Dead Sea. They were, Ioannes Moskhos (ca. 550–619) wrote, determined to take him to their priest and sacrifice him to their deity. A Father Nikolaos, however, prayed against them, and Moskhos alleged that a demon entered them and they tore one another apart. The liberated young man then took vows and became a monk. Nor did worship of the old gods continue in the Roman Empire only on its desert fringes. As late as 579, an inquisition launched by Tiberios II found that remnants of the pagan aristocracy in Heliopolis (Baalbak) routinely persecuted lower-class Christians and that Edessa notables held ceremonies for Zeus in their private homes.[24]

The remaining Arab traditionalists of Transjordan adored above all the great goddess Allat, who, inscriptions said, "is in Iram, forever," referring to the ancient name for this region, which also occurs in the Qur'an. They believed her to inhabit the featureless square god stones (or betyls) they set up. During the subsequent long centuries of Roman rule in this area, she came to be identified with the warrior-goddess Athena, associated with combat, protection, and, ironically, peace. People in Palmyra as well had erected a temple to her, wherein stood a statue of Athena and a sculpture of a gazelle sheltering between the legs of a lion with a first-century inscription, "Allat will bless whoever will not shed blood in the sanctuary." The tribes called on her to protect them from terrifying flash floods that could abruptly sweep down the flume of a desert wadi with fatal force, even if a cloudburst had opened up a fair distance away. In Roman times, an Arab named Akh ibn Sa`d celebrated one spring when his camels gave birth to foals and provided abundant milk, scratching into the stone, "So, Allat, give peace!" For Arabs, peace implied not only absence of deadly conflict but also safety and well-being. It clearly concerned individuals and not just the whole tribal collective. The surviving pagans likely regarded the shrines of Allat in Transjordan as tranquil sanctuaries, a belief that would have protected Muhammad and the other Meccans from raids.[25]

In the 570s, the Piacenza Pilgrim visited Mount Horeb in the Sinai and wrote,

> At one place upon the mountain, the Saracens have placed a marble idol of their own, as white as snow. There, also, dwells a priest

of theirs, dressed in a dalmatic and pallium of linen. When the time of their festival arrives, as soon as the moon is up (before its rays have departed from the festival) that marble begins to change colour; as soon as the moon's rays have entered in, when they begin to worship the idol, the marble becomes black as pitch. When the time of the feast is over, it returns to its original colour—a great object of wonder to us all.[26]

The Arabs held that their deities inhabited these square, featureless betyls.

Pagan Arabs believed that any major shrine to a deity created a safe zone around itself, prohibiting violence such as tribal feuds. Muhammad and his men were devoted to such a shrine in Mecca. In addition, they put aside four months of the year as sacred, during which they forbade raiding and fighting by the tribes. A Roman ambassador to the Arabs, Nonnosos, observed a few decades before Muhammad's birth that they "have a sacred meeting-place consecrated to one of the gods, where they assemble twice a year. One of these meetings lasts a whole month.... [T]he other lasts two months." He added, "During these meetings complete peace prevails, not only amongst themselves, but also with all the natives; even the animals are at peace both with themselves and human beings."[27] The ambassador confused two distinct sorts of sanctuary: the peaceful district around a temple and the sacred nature reserve, where hunting was prohibited. The precincts around the betyl stone of Allat in the Hejazi city of Taif served as a nature reserve. Mecca was both a sacred space of peace and an area where animals could not be harmed. Muhammad and his men, however, had left behind their realm of safety and entered the sometimes raucous tribal domains of the eastern Roman Empire.

Perhaps Christian converts living in Wadi Ramm blamed the decline of Nabatea and its fall to Rome on their predecessors' paganism and told young Muhammad and the Meccans of how the God of Abraham and Moses had punished the ancients. Certainly, that is the lesson the Qur'an drew, remarking of God, "He is the Lord of Sirius, who brought the ancient people of `Ad to ruin."[28]

Then the band might have stopped at Petra, one of the wonders of the world that must have astonished Muhammad every time he saw it, with its magnificent pink abandoned temples and monumental edifices carved right into the towering sandstone. A nineteenth-century Western traveler described one of the breathtaking buildings in this city: "This monument is sculptured out of an enormous and compact block of freestone, slightly tinged with oxide of iron. . . . What a people must they not have been who thus opened the mountain to stamp upon it the seal of their energy and genius!" He spoke of "the magical effect produced on the eye by the harmonious tints of the stone" from which the edifice was composed, "standing out as it does in a limpid rosy hue detached from the rough and somber colour of the mountain."[29] The Qur'an (Dawn 89:6–8) later commented, "Have you not seen how your lord dealt with `Ad, with Iram and its columns—the like of which had never been created in any land?" Petra had been, five hundred years before, the capital of the Nabatean kingdom. After pagan Rome conquered them, the locals had gradually identified their northern Arabian deities with Olympian figures like Zeus, Aphrodite, and Athena, and surely in doing so they influenced Mecca to their south as well.

Despite the rapid progress of Christianity after 312 CE, some people in Petra had still sung hymns to the warrior-goddess Allat in Arabic in the early fifth century, and some furtive such votaries likely remained in its precincts a century and a half later, when Muhammad may have visited it. Locals had also worshipped Manat, the goddess of fate, assimilating her to the Greek goddess Tyche and depicting her as holding a wheel of fortune.[30]

Nabateans of the Roman period carved a Greek inscription into the Qasr Bint in Petra that has been read as dedicated to Zeus Hypsistos, "God the Most High." Some worshippers of Zeus and his local manifestations, influenced by Judaism and Christianity, had moved toward a pagan monotheism, centered on the one unnamed god Theos "the All-High." Those All-Highers who kept their own rites but associated with Jews and Christians as fellow monotheists gained the epithet "Godfearers." Although most people in the Hejaz still worshipped an Arab pantheon, some of them likely adhered to a cult of a supreme deity, a reform of Greco-Roman paganism in dialogue with North Arabian ideas and the Bible.[31]

Muhammad, from parched Mecca, might have found Petra's pools and gardens, fed by an intricate set of canals and aqueducts, to be its most striking feature. In 592 the city served as the administrative center for the Roman province of Third Palestine. A Greek papyrus trove reveals sixth-century Petra to have been a rich agricultural center producing wheat, fruits from orchards, and wine. Roman Near Easterners still enjoyed great prosperity and could have barely imagined the economic tailspin into which the Huns and Germanic tribal invaders had plunged western Europe. For citizens in the East, the Roman Empire still had not fallen.[32]

The papyri also reveal Greek to have been the urban standard language, used by the city's Arabic speakers for formal purposes. Near Easterners in the sixth and seventh centuries had multiple identities and often spoke several languages, using each in a sophisticated way. They were not divided, as nineteenth-century Orientalism would have had it, into "Semites" and "Greeks." A long-distance merchant like Muhammad operated in a trilingual environment of Arabic, Greek, and Aramaic. Multilingual people switch back and forth between languages and adopt loanwords or use ideas from one language to imbue existing words in another with new meanings. Though he had come a long way from home, Muhammad was still often among Arabs. He would have found unusual words in their Neoplatonic and Christian Greek-inflected Arabic for conceptions such as divine love, wisdom, and salvation, which would have piqued his curiosity.[33]

Perhaps Muhammad and his caravan stopped off to trade in Jerusalem. They would not have been the only ones from the Red Sea littoral. The Piacenza Pilgrim, visiting in 570, said he saw men there "from the direction of Ethiopia," with slit ears and noses and wearing rings on both fingers and toes. After Emperor Constantine's conversion in 312, the rulers of Christian Rome had gradually rebuilt the city as a "New Jerusalem," razing colossal temples to Aphrodite and Zeus and maintaining, at least de jure, a long-standing ban on Jews. Constantine's officials made the Church of the Holy Sepulchre the city's spiritual center. Preachers and believing traders in the market would have told Muhammad and his party stories about Jesus Christ, who taught turning the other cheek and would one day return to bring a thousand-year reign of peace. It is said that even the pagan Meccans kept icons of Jesus and Mary in the Kaaba.[34]

After the Roman destruction of the second Jewish temple in 70 CE, the temple mount lay abandoned, an empty esplanade that may have still sported a crumbling statue of Zeus placed there by the old traditionalist Romans. Jewish tradition identified it with Mount Moriah, where God was held to have commanded the patriarch Abraham to sacrifice his son. The biblical story of Abraham had implied that he fathered pastoral nomads such as the Arabs through his son with Hagar, Ishmael. Genesis 16:12 says, "He shall be a wild ass of a man, with his hand against everyone and everyone's hand against him." The account in Genesis could, however, also be read to give the Arabs a high religious status as progeny of the patriarch. God appeared to Hagar and ordered her to return to the service of her mistress, Sarah, and he promised her he would "so greatly multiply your offspring that they cannot be counted for multitude" (Gen. 16:9–10). Jewish historian Flavius Josephus (d. ca. 100 CE) wrote that Ishmael had twelve sons, whose descendants "inhabited all the country from the Euphrates to the Red Sea and called it Nabatene. They are an Arabian nation." At least later in his life, Muhammad took this gene-alogy for the Meccans seriously, seeing the Kaaba as having been founded by Abraham and Ishmael after, he believed, they emigrated south to the Hejaz from Canaan. He viewed the temple mount as a place of cosmic spirituality linked mystically to Mecca.[35]

Leaving Jerusalem, Muhammad and the Quraysh would have turned northeast and passed through Philadelphia on their way to Bostra on the Hawran plateau. Bostra served as the capital of Roman Arabia, where a duke commanded Roman military units in the area. Muhammad knew from his scouts that security in this region had declined and that his band had to beware bedouin raiders. Having come so far, and spent so much money on this journey, he would face disaster, and perhaps a fatal tarnishing of his promising mercantile career, if tribesmen carried off his goods before he could reach his destination.

❧

THE ARRANGEMENT WHEREBY Constantinople in the sixth century depended on an allied Arab cavalry to supplement troops at the frontier had fallen apart, threatening the security of Muhammad's caravan. In better days, in 580, Tiberios II had brought the Jafnid phy-larch al-Mundhir III to his resplendent court in Constantinople in great pomp and allowed him to wear his own crown—a symbolic tri-umph for the Arabs that certainly reverberated in Mecca and Medina as well.[36] Al-Mundhir, not actually a king, had no realm. Rather, his troops and tribesmen enjoyed a special position in eastern Syria and Transjordan, where they served under the urban-based dukes of the Roman military units.

Tiberios fell out with al-Mundhir soon after he had bestowed on him the title of lesser king, suspecting him of colluding with the enemy during an abortive Roman-Arab expedition of 581 against the army of the Iranian emperor Hormezd IV (r. 579–590).[37] Tiberios brought al-Mundhir ignominiously to Constantinople that winter and put him and his family under house arrest.

John of Ephesos wrote that al-Mundhir's eldest son, Nuʿman, angered, gathered his forces and attacked a major Roman fort in Syria: "And, excepting the people whom they either took captive or slew, and what they burnt, everything else they plundered and carried away, gold and silver, and brass and iron...until the whole country of the East to the shores of the Mediterranean was in terror at them, and fled for refuge to the cities."

Then Nuʿman's tribal levies had surrounded Bostra's strong walls, demanding that the city's troops surrender al-Mundhir's armor and other property deposited there for safekeeping.

John of Ephesos observed, "And when the commandant, who was a man of note and fame, heard these things, he was very angry, and gathered his troops together, and sallied out, despising them as roving Arabs: and they set themselves in array against him, and overpowered and slew both him and large numbers of his men."

The Arab horsemen fought the Roman army using the imperial tactics in which they had long been trained, with devastating results. The citizens of Bostra then turned over al-Mundhir's property with alacrity.[38]

A medieval chronicler, Michael the Syrian of Antioch, maintained that in the aftermath, "The realm of the [Jafnid] Arabs was divided among 15 princes. Most of them joined in with the Iranians, and thereafter the realm of the Christian Arabs came to an end and ceased, as a result of the perfidy of the Romans."[39] Some of the Arab chieftains, however, clearly continued to be loyal to Constantinople.

A decade after that revolt, Muhammad may have held parleys with emissaries of the local Arab phylarch of that day, seeking safe passage. Medieval biographer Ibn Sa`d told a story that as they approached the city of Bostra, the party halted for a break. Muhammad sat beneath a tree. A local monk named Nestorios approached Khadija's agent Maysara breathlessly with a series of questions about the stranger. He declared, "No one but a prophet has ever sat beneath that tree."[40] The anecdote is, of course, a later Muslim apologetic. But stories that Meccan merchants such as Muhammad stayed in monasteries that doubled as inns and conducted amicable discussions with the monks are entirely plausible. Years later, Muhammad as an old man would recite verses of the Qur'an that praised Christians for their loving attitude, adding, "That is because they have among them priests and monks, and they are not haughty."[41]

Muhammad and his companions entered Bostra's great gates and passed under the Roman triumphal arch, proceeding along a colonnaded boulevard lined with two-story shops, in view of the spires of the domed grand cathedral. The caravanners would have found that Bostra, long an episcopal see, had a Christian majority—though some surrounding villages appear to have been pagan well into the sixth century.

The traders stayed in the Christian cloisters that often served as caravansaries and would have marveled at their fine mosaics and marble revetments. Some monasteries had been founded by the Arab phylarchs and may have been peopled by Arab Christian monks. These complexes were laid out as a quadrangle, with a church, a dormitory, hostels, a refectory for meals, and other buildings, linked by porticos. In Bostra monasteries dominated the center of the city. Despite his respect for its proponents, Muhammad found the Near Eastern Christian tradition too monastic and ascetic. The saints of this church, stylites, would sometimes erect a platform atop a pillar in the desert and climb up on it, living most of their time there.[42] The Qur'an (*Iron* 57:27) remonstrated that "as for monasticism, they invented it—we did not prescribe it to them."

Despite Emperor Maurikios's vehement championing of Christianity, it did not enjoy a monopoly on religious discourse or on monotheism. Some local Platonists and other highly cultured Syrians were devoted to what they saw as a single first principle, which could hardly be multiple.[43]

Only a few decades before Muhammad's journey for Khadija, the great Neoplatonic thinker from Damascus, Damaskios (d. ca. 550), had stayed with pagan friends in Bostra after fleeing Christian persecution in Alexandria. He wrote that his teacher Isidoros had moved away from the worship of statues of the gods (which had been prohibited) and instead was quickly "moving toward the gods themselves," who are concealed not in temples but in the mystery of the ineffable, through the power of love—and held that the gods were really only one.[44] Muhammad, as a young man from a non-Christian background with a thirst for spirituality, would have eagerly discussed religious ideas with Gentile monotheists as well as with friars.

The Meccans would have bathed at the public baths and taken their wares to the great monthlong fair, trading their handful of gold nuggets and small quantities of ivory, silk, jewelry, and decorated leather for grain, wine, armor, and worked metal tools and weapons. Muhammad is said to have doubled Khadija's investment.

The conditions of commerce were dictated not only by local dynamics, as with the rebellion of the Jafnids, but also by geopolitics. The outbreak of peace between Constantinople and the Iranian capital of Ctesiphon that prevailed in the 590s somewhat offset the dangers for Muhammad's mission created by the decline of the Arab federate system. Ironically, a coup in Iran's White Palace helped along this era of good feeling. The brothers-in-law of Hormezd IV assassinated him in 590 and then tried to ensconce his twenty-year-old son (their nephew) as shah. Their attempt to become regents of the young Khosrow II, and so the power behind the throne, backfired when another pretender, the senior general Bahram Chobin, emerged and took power.

Khosrow II, the heir apparent, fled to Constantinople, applying desperately to Emperor Maurikios (r. 582–602) for help in recovering his birthright. The Roman Augustus accepted these entreaties in return for territory that had been usurped by Iran. Maurikios gave his guest help in returning to power, and harmonious relations ensued in the 590s.[45] A Persian romance from that era gives a sense of how the Zoroastrian court in Ctesiphon probably celebrated the restoration. On such a festive occasion, the emperor "ordained that red rubies, royal pearls, and jewels be bestowed on the chief priest." Then the monarch "fell prostrate on his face, and offered much thanksgiving to Ohrmazd [God], to the immortal holy spirits, to the victory halo of the first kings, and to the triumphant, regal sacred fire."[46]

❧

MUHAMMAD AND THE Quraysh likely stayed in Bostra for a month, making their trades and enjoying city life. On such journeys, some reports suggest that they routinely went north to Damascus, for further commerce, before undertaking the nearly monthlong return journey to Mecca.

Merchants in the Hejaz often traveled during the four sacred months when tribes abstained from raiding and made a circuit to sanctuary cities with trade fairs that forbade fighting. Still, occasionally contentious tribes, jealous of their honor, broke these rules. A story is told that one day at a seasonal market in the central Arabian city of Ukaz, some visiting young men of the Kinana and Quraysh tribes were in a mood for love. They happened upon a lithe, beautiful young woman from the `Amer clan of the Hawazin tribe, sitting in the Ukaz market. She was talking to some bedouin boys. She had on a single long dress, wearing nothing beneath it. The young men from Mecca crowded around her and tried to flirt with her, but she would not give them a glimpse of her face.

One of them surreptitiously knelt behind her and managed to get a thorn into the hem of her robe and to attach it to her waist without her noticing. When she stood up, her backside was visible to all and sundry.

The young bucks guffawed and said, "You didn't let us see your front, but you granted us a view of your rear."

Mortified, she cried out, "O people of `Amer!"

Her tribesmen jumped to their feet and drew their swords, but the Banu Kinana stood their ground. A sanguinary battle ensued.

In order to make peace, the notable Harb ibn Umayya of the powerful `Abd Shams clan of Quraysh intervened and paid the blood money for those who had been killed in the fracas, as well as remitting a fine to Banu `Amer for the besmirching of the honor of their female relative. Several such melees had broken out during Muhammad's youth in the 580s, known as the "Sacrilegious Wars" because the Kinana fought them even in the sacred months.

In this instance, Harb was willing to spend some money to quiet things down because he did not want a dispute in Ukaz to come home to Mecca and spoil both its sacred tranquility and its commerce. In vendetta societies, payment of blood money is a key way of avoiding a feud and ongoing violence.[47]

As head of the Hashim clan, Muhammad's uncle Abu Talib maintained tranquility around the sanctuary. Once, when this paramount chief suspected a member of Hashim of committing a murder, it is said that Abu Talib came to the defendant and confronted him: "You have three choices: either you can pay a hundred camels for killing one of our people, or fifty of your kin can swear that you did not kill him, or if you refuse we'll execute you for his sake."[48] The Qur'an makes it clear that Muhammad also disapproved of feuding and undertook the vocation of peacemaking. *The Family of Amram* 3:103 says of God, "You were enemies, but he united your hearts—so that by his blessing you became siblings. You were on the brink of a pit of fire, and he delivered you from it."

❧

BACK IN MECCA, Muhammad's rising reputation as a canny merchant and manager of men impressed Khadija on a personal and not just a business level. A later biographer described her as "a resolute, disciplined and honorable woman" and said, "She was, in those days, the most distinguished in lineage among the Quraysh, the greatest of them in nobility, and the wealthiest of them. Every member of her clan wanted to marry her if he could, seeking her hand and lavishing her with gifts."[49]

He explained that Khadija had secretly sent a female emissary, Nafisa, to Muhammad on his return with a caravan from Damascus around 592.

Nafisa had asked him, "Muhammad, what holds you back from marrying?"

He said, "I do not have anything at hand to give in marriage."

Nafisa asked, "If you were provided the means and received an inquiry from an attractive, prosperous, and well-born woman of equal status, what would you say?"

He said, "Who is this?"

She said, "Khadija."

He asked, "How could that be possible for me?"

She said, "Leave that to me."[50]

And so they married. With Khadija's backing, Muhammad led summer trading missions to cities such as Bostra, Gaza, and Damascus, perhaps annually. Indeed, it seems likely that he would have maintained a summer-fall home in Syria and should be seen as a Damascene or Bostran as much as a Meccan. A late seventh-century author, Jacob of Edessa, wrote that "Muhammad went down for trade to the lands of Palestine, Arabia and Syrian Phoenicia." A medieval Christian chronicler speaking of the early seventh century wrote, "He used to go up from his town, Yathrib, to Palestine for commerce, buying and selling." Passages of the Qur'an suggest that he also regularly conducted winter commerce to the south in Yemen, with its Iranian garrisons and local pagans, Jews, and Christians.[51]

Muhammad did not take another wife until Khadija's death in 620. He then married two women in the early 620s, first the widow Sawda bint Zam`a and then Aisha bint Abi Bakr. I bring this up because Aisha lived to an advanced age and became the alleged source of many narratives about Muhammad's life.[52]

Aisha asserted that Muhammad became a spiritual seeker, dissatisfied with his traditional religion. She explained, "Then he began liking solitude, and he used to go off alone to the grotto of Hira. He would perform devotions, which are a form of nocturnal worship, for

29

many days before returning to his family. He would stock up on provisions, then later on return to Khadija, and stock up again in the same way." Meccans had a local custom of withdrawing occasionally to the wilderness, cutting themselves off from the world and engaging in prayer and rituals, seeking forgiveness for transgressions or escape from some travail. During this withdrawal they made charitable donations and freed slaves. Muhammad would spend a month of each year this way, distributing food to the poor and meditating, impatiently waiting for a sign.[53]

❧

THE IDEA OF the sanctuary looms large in Muhammad's story. The tribes honored Mecca as a shared sacred city where feuds had to be put aside and even the hunting of animals was banned. The city of peace, moreover, cast a long shadow. A common reverence for God and his tabernacle, the Kaaba, and respect for the clan that served as its custodian allowed the Quraysh to craft treaties with surrounding tribes, thus fostering the caravan trade that brought grain and other staples to Mecca.

Despite the waning of the Pax Romana, Muhammad likely formed a favorable impression of the order and security it still provided. In the three centuries after the establishment of the Roman Empire in 27 BCE, emperors became lenient to the conquered, and the provinces of the empire experienced relative tranquility. After Constantine's Christian revolution of the 300s, visionaries such as the historian Eusebius reworked the old notion of imperial harmony: "One universal power, the Roman empire, arose and flourished, while the enduring and implacable hatred of nation against nation was now removed." He then Christianized the motif: "And as the knowledge of one God, and one way of religion and salvation, even the doctrine of

Christ, was made known to all mankind; so at the self-same period, the entire dominion of the Roman empire being vested in a single sovereign, profound peace reigned throughout the world."[54] The empire in the late 500s hardly exemplified the ideals of Eusebius, but it offered more security than Muhammad's native Arabia, where only the law of the desert reigned in some regions.

By the late 500s the dream of a Roman peace faced severe challenges. Much of western Europe had come under the rule of warring German chieftains, and the economy of the West had collapsed. In the East, the threat of incursions by Sasanian Iran and its Arab allies always loomed, despite the 561–562 peace treaty. Sectarian factionalism roiled the institutions of the imperial faith. Emperors Tiberios II and Maurikios favored a Christology based on the 451 Council of Chalcedon, holding that Christ is of one substance with God but that he had two distinct natures, human and divine, in one person. They pursued a harsh policy of intolerance toward Near Eastern Miaphysites, who saw Christ as having only one nature (which is both human and divine). The clash between these factions underlay in part the disgrace of the Miaphysite al-Mundhir III and the fall of the Arab alliance.

The Qur'an (*The Table* 5:14) would later depict God as complaining, "We made a covenant with those who say, 'We are Christians,' but they forgot a portion of what they were reminded about. We therefore cast enmity and hatred among them until the Resurrection Day, and God will recount to them the things they did." Even Christian apologists such as Ammianus Marcellinus (ca. 330–395) admitted that "no wild beasts are so hostile to men as Christian sects in general are to one another."[55]

Although most of his biographers have treated him as a provincial holy man, Muhammad traveled widely. He would have been acquainted with Roman law, culture, and languages. Contrary both to later Muslim apologetics and to the assumptions of Western Orientalists, he was literate, as any great long-distance merchant would have been. He knew the Bible, probably in written Aramaic versions and oral Arab traditions, though possibly in Greek as well.[56] In his thirties, I suspect, Muhammad's inner thirst took him to Christian monasteries, eldritch shrines, Jewish synagogues, and Neoplatonist salons in Damascus and Bostra. Unexpectedly, his quest ended when its object came instead to him.

§ 2 §

PEACE IT IS

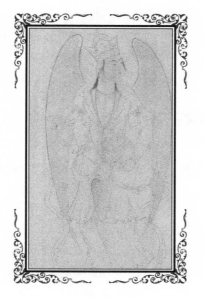

WHEN BY MY CALCULATIONS HE WAS THIRTY-FIVE, MUHAMMAD would have watched with horror the outbreak of an unprecedentedly savage world war in 603, which over two and a half decades wrecked two empires and ushered in a new world order. The armies of Sasanian Iran, having marched into the Roman Empire, sacked and sometimes torched entire cities, killing thousands and deporting tens of thousands of valued artisans to their capital, Ctesiphon. The Qur'an came to Muhammad in Mecca, a rare idyllic no-man's-land between battling titans but one threatened with being engulfed by the conflict.[1]

The generational struggle had some of its origins in a coup and years of bloody reprisals and instability in Constantinople. In 602 a general and adventurer broke a centuries-long tradition of peaceful Roman succession. Egged on by army units fighting in the Balkans who had suffered substantial salary arrears because the government was too strapped for cash to pay them, a General Phokas overthrew the elderly Emperor Maurikios. His soldiers captured and pitilessly murdered him, his family, and some of his retainers.[2]

The Iranian emperor Khosrow II considered this assassination of his old friend to be an act of war on Iran, and he immediately launched an invasion of Roman territory. By 604 Khosrow's troops had taken Dara in northern Mesopotamia, and then his armies rushed like flooding winter rivers into Asia Minor, the heartland of Phokas's realm. The resulting conflict led to the collapse of a Near Eastern order that had governed life in the region for a half millennium, one that had allowed Muhammad's commerce. While the Iranians had often challenged their rival's hold on the Near East, on the whole the successors of the caesar Trajan (r. 98–117 CE), under whom it was first conquered, could be expected to govern and tax this region and to provide bureaucracy and economic infrastructure.[3]

The sudden disintegration of this equilibrium stunned contemporaries and provoked a rash of apocalyptic speculations. Roman authors in Constantinople used biblical referents, calling the invading Iranians "Chaldeans," likening them to the empire in Mesopotamia of nearly a millennium before, which established hegemony over the Holy Land. Jews, who often felt better treated under Sasanian rule than by the Roman emperors, wrote religious poetry referencing other parts of the Bible that anticipated the defeat of "Edom" (the Roman Empire) at the hands of the "Assyrians."[4] The advance of a large invasion force alarmed the Syrians with whom Muhammad traded and raised questions for him about the future of the Hejaz, which was vulnerable to an Iranian takeover.

As Roman chroniclers told the story, the churlish Emperor Phokas had difficulty convincing his subjects of his legitimacy, and his coarse methods of rule alienated even members of his own family. Priskos, his son-in-law and count of the Excubitors (the Imperial Guard), secretly wrote to the respected governor of Roman Africa, the exarch Herakleios the Elder. He urged him to return from Carthage to the capital and to make a coup.

Instead, in 608 the governor sent his thirty-five-year-old son, Herakleios the Younger, with a fleet and North African Amazigh soldiers to take power. Herakleios's cousin Niketas the Patrician invaded by land and over the next two years secured Egypt and the Near East, in part because the population rose up against the unpopular Phokas. Meccan summer caravans must have been disrupted by Niketas the Patrician's campaign to take Syria from Phokas's land forces in 610. In the aftermath, Muhammad would have sent envoys seeking good relations with the new imperial authorities in preparation for resuming his commerce.

The revolt ended in October 610 when Herakleios's naval invasion force powered through the Aegean into the choppy, cerulean Sea of Marmara and managed to make a landing at the Harbor of Sophia in Constantinople below the Hippodrome. One of Phokas's enemies captured him and brought him before the new emperor, who was still on horseback amid his Libyan cavalrymen. Herakleios rebuked the usurper for his mutiny. A contemporary chronicler said of Phokas, "And his right arm was removed from the shoulder, as well as his head, his hand was impaled on a sword, and thus it was paraded along the Mese [boulevard], starting from the Forum."[5]

No doubt to the trepidation of Muhammad and his Syrian friends, the coup in Constantinople had no effect on the Iranian armies still marching from Mesopotamia in 610. In that year, the minions of the shah took the eastern Roman city of Edessa, known as a bulwark of Christian piety. A late seventh-century chronicler wrote, "And (the Persians) made themselves masters of the river Euphrates and of all the cities of Antioch, and they plundered them and left not a soldier surviving at that epoch."[6]

This period of brutal warfare set people to thinking of how peace might be attained. The three power centers of the eastern Roman Empire were imperial officials (both in the capital and in the provinces), bishops, and monks, and each had its own vision of concord.[7] Bishops acted in local congregations to mediate disputes. Monks sought harmony with the divine through solitary faith, propitiation, and intense worship. The government pursued peace, when it cared to, through treaties and bargains and sometimes through defensive warfare.

"Negative peace," or the mere absence of conflict, has been contrasted with the "positive peace" of active policies intended to foster reconciliation over time.[8] State diplomacy, as with the exchange of envoys, and treaties such as that of 561–562 between the Roman Empire and the Sasanians represented efforts of "positive peace" intended to lay the groundwork for avoidance of violence. Imperial authorities in Constantinople and Ctesiphon signally failed to find a formula for peace of either sort in the early seventh century. As a result, spiritual leaders such as bishops and monks in that era often turned inward, concentrating on the spiritual serenity of the soul even as the creeping flames of conquest licked at their cathedrals and monasteries. In the Hejaz as well, the unfolding Roman-Iranian conflict, with the Holy Land as one of its prizes, had a profound impact. This dark cloud hanging over the world certainly formed a key context for the Qur'an's view of peace.[9]

❧

DECADES AFTER HIS death, Muhammad's third wife, Aisha bint Abi Bakr, resided in her coral stone villa in Medina, a venerable silver-haired widow. She held regular salons where she recalled for her nephew 'Urwa ibn al-Zubayr (c. 645–715) and others of the next generation the stories she had heard in her youth about what had happened in Mecca in 610.[10]

She is said to have related that at night, Muhammad was increasingly disturbed by inspirational dreams: "The beginning of revelation to God's messenger was in the form of righteous dreams while he was sleeping. Whenever he saw a vision, it came like daybreak." She said she heard an anecdote from an early companion of the Prophet, who asked him what the experience of encountering the divine was like. He told her that the Prophet had replied, "Sometimes it comes like the tolling of a bell, and that is the hardest on me; then it leaves me and I am aware of what he said. And sometimes it appears to me as an angel in the form of a man and addresses me, and then I am conscious of what he says."[11]

Aisha asserted, "I saw him when revelation was descending on him on an extremely frigid day, and when it left him sweat was streaming from his brow."[12]

During his monthlong annual retreat to the black basalt cave of Hira', he had a vision of a spectral being. The first time he saw the angel, she said, the apparition demanded that Muhammad "read."

He replied, "I cannot read!"

The angel grabbed him and squeezed him until he could barely stand it, then released him and made the same demand.

He again said, "I cannot read!"

The angel embraced him roughly for the third time, then conveyed from God these words:

> Read in the name of your Lord, who created—
> created the human being from a clot.
> Read, and your Lord is most generous,
> who taught by the pen,
> taught human beings what they did not know.[13]

Muhammad, Aisha said, departed for home in terror at the encounter with the divine envoy.

When he saw his wife, Khadija, he implored her, "Cover me! Cover me!" She put a blanket over him, and he lay there until his fear subsided.

He told her what had happened and said, "I am afraid for myself."

Khadija attempted to reassure him: "God would never disgrace you!"[14]

It has long been recognized that this account of the interchange between the angel and Muhammad is patterned on Isaiah 29:11–12.[15]

Isaiah says,

> And the vision of all this has become to you like the words of
>   a book that is sealed.
> When men give it to one who can read, saying, "Read this,"
> he says, "I cannot, for it is sealed."
> And when they give the book to one who cannot read,
>   saying, "Read this,"
> he says, "I cannot read."

In the Aisha narrative, the angel unseals the book by giving to the prophet Muhammad the ability to recite or read out the revelation of God after his initial inability. The prophet Muhammad or early Believers drew on this biblical imagery to explain the significance of the first revelations.[16]

Aisha or her sources invoked the ancient prophet Isaiah (fl. eighth century BCE) because he also wrote at a time when a powerful army from Mesopotamia was trudging toward the Holy Land.[17] Isaiah was saying that with the Kingdom of Israel under Neo-Assyrian pressure—and later foreign rule—the literate and the illiterate among the Jews could not understand his visions: the book was sealed up by virtue of foreign occupation and collaboration. That Muhammad or his companions quoted these verses to explain his own epiphany implied that his contemporaries were also spiritually blind and deaf in the face of an onslaught from the East. It has been pointed out that ordering the illiterate to read or the literate to read a sealed book is paradoxical. That enigma is intended to take the hearer out of the present and point to a future day, on which idolatry will end or war will be abolished (Isa. 2:4) or hostile nations will be defeated. A criticism of great kingdoms is implied as well. In the Greek Bible or Septuagint, the chapter ends (Isa. 29:24) by promising, "And the stammering tongues shall learn to speak peace."[18] The typical greeting of Muhammad's followers, "Peace be upon you," may thus have messianic overtones. The angel's afflatus reversed the darkness of the era described in Isaiah 29 and held out hope for a new age, through the unsealing of a book of scripture to "the deaf" and the consequent triumph of the oppressed.

The books of Isaiah and Daniel have a kinship with one another. Both speak of visions, and they contain the only two passages in the Bible to mention sealed prophetic books (Dan. 12:4, 9). Both critique the great empires of their day, and both were appealed to by Christian writers as having prophesied the rise of Jesus in the time of the Roman Empire. It is therefore not surprising that the Aisha narrative appears also to paraphrase the book of Daniel when it asserts that Muhammad was afraid for himself. Daniel 7:15 says, "As for me, Daniel, my spirit was pained in the midst of my body, and the visions of my head affrighted me." At the end of Daniel 8, the prophet is said to have taken to his bed as if ill: "And I, Daniel, was overcome and lay sick for some days." Muhammad reacted similarly, and Khadija covered him with blankets. Along with distress, however, the experience of revelation was said ultimately to have brought inner peace (for instance, Dan. 10:16–19).[19]

In Mecca, after the first revelation, Khadija took her husband to her wizened cousin Waraqa, the son of Nawfal, who had converted to Christianity and had learned how to read the Gospels in their original language.

Muhammad described his experience to his wife's relative: Waraqa said, "This is the Law (*nomos*) that was revealed to Moses."[20]

The words attributed to Waraqa about the nature of prophecy may have been intended to echo Paul's letter to the Galatians (3:19), which spoke of the law being given to Moses through an angel. The Greek word *nomos* can also mean in Christianity the moral instruction given by Christ, especially the command to love one's neighbor, and in some forms of the tradition Waraqa recognizes the new messenger as the Jesus of his people who brought a precept.[21]

These accounts of Muhammad's revelatory experience would have marked him, for audiences of that day, as unmistakably a holy man. The biography of the Christian Saint Sabas the Sanctified, a Syrian monk who founded several monasteries outside Jerusalem in the late 400s, contains many of the same symbols.[22] Muhammad met such men on his travels north, though perhaps only a few as truly pious. It is said that Sabas was praying into the wee hours in the desert when an angel appeared to him in dazzling robes. The angel led him to an elevated cave in the east side of a gorge and instructed him to reside there. Arab bedouins who visited him, marveling at his self-denying way of life, had to be lifted by ropes. They then began bringing him bread, cheese, dates, and other gifts. When he was forty-five, after years of wrestling with demons, he began devoting his efforts instead to gathering followers and engaging in positive peacemaking, urging that swords be beaten into ploughshares (Isa. 2:4). By a miracle, a wild ass discovered a spring near his cave from which visitors could drink.

Such Syrian monks were portrayed (not always accurately) as mediators of disputes and builders of concord among farmers and bedouins. The more otherworldly monks concentrated on inner spiritual peace, attempting to overcome the maelstrom of emotions. Transjordan and Northern Hejaz had monasteries, and such Christian institutions offered models to the Arabs.[23]

It is not that Muslims borrowed the story elements that hagiographers marshaled in profiles such as that of Saint Sabas. Rather, everyone in the greater Mediterranean at that time told such stories with the vocabulary of these symbols. The narrative about Muhammad is distinctive, of course, despite containing a cave, an angel, a devotional life, a mission that began in his forties, a sacred well, a concern for mediating conflict, and bedouin admirers who brought gifts to the Kaaba. Muhammad was a great merchant rather than an ascetic and urged positive engagement with the world. Supernatural demons and struggles against them play no role in the story of his life. He was no mere saint but a messenger of God who sought to revolutionize the spirituality of humankind. Still, the Qur'an's earliest visions of peace are personal and heavenly, as were those of contemporary bishops and monks who despaired of profane harmony.

Back in Mecca, `Urwa reported that his aunt Aisha had said that the end of Muhammad's conversation with Waraqa turned ominous. "I wish I could still be alive when your people expel you."

Muhammad, alarmed, asked if that was really what would happen to him.

"Yes," Waraqa replied firmly. "Whenever a man has brought what you are bringing, he was treated with hostility."

The wise old cousin is said to have promised his support, but he died a few days later.

THE ACCOUNT IN the Qur'an that most resembles the Aisha revelation narrative is chapter 97, *The Night of Power*. This tableau also depicts a descent of angels and the Holy Spirit to earth. According to Muslim tradition, this short address comments on the tremendous experience of divine revelation that encompassed the prophet Muhammad for the first time around 610.[24] It says:

> In the Name of God, the Merciful, the Compassionate.
> [1]Behold, we revealed it on the night of power.
> [2]What will make you understand the night of power?
> [3]The night of power is better than a thousand months.
> [4]The angels and the spirit descend then, with the permission
>   of their Lord, in every affair.
> [5]And peace it is, until the breaking of the dawn.

The phrase "we revealed it" has traditionally been taken as a reference to the beginning of Muhammad's divine call. This visitation of the holy is above all mysterious and hard to comprehend for human beings. The Qur'an wonders, "How can I get you to understand it?" As with Daniel's visions, the meaning of revelation requires interpretation. In this chapter it is not an angel that explicates but the voice of God himself. The precious night on which the revelation first descended, it is asserted, surpasses in value a thousand months. The Qur'an then explains this descent of supernatural potency as an advent of angels and the Holy Spirit. While angels had by the time of Muhammad become universal touchstones among pagans, Christians, and Jews, they enjoyed a special place in apocalyptic literature, from the book of Daniel to Revelation and later commentaries on those works. In the late-antique period, people saw angels as God's means of communicating to the human world while remaining transcendent himself.[25]

Likewise, the notion of the Holy Spirit, an aspect of the divine, was ubiquitous in the Near East.[26] Moreover, many ancient authors asserted a connection between the Holy Spirit and peace. Paul wrote in Galatians 5:22, "The fruit of the Spirit is love, joy, peace, patience, kindness, generosity, faithfulness, gentleness, and self-control." Along with the angels, then, the Holy Spirit is a mysterious presence sent by God into the temporal world, to promote well-being and harmony.

The final verse of *The Night of Power* comes as a surprise. It builds on what came before but abruptly takes a fresh and unexpected turn. "And peace it is, until the breaking of the dawn." In this phrase, what exactly is being equated to peace? In the Arabic, *it* is feminine, and the only referent in this short chapter that makes sense is *night*, which is a feminine noun. We may understand the verse to say, "And this night of power is peace, until the coming of daybreak."

The night of power symbolizes the revelation's first irruption into the mundane world and so is a part that stands for the whole. If this night is peace, then so is the revelation, that is, the Qur'an itself. The sentiment here recalls Romans 14:17: "For the kingdom of God is not food and drink but righteousness and peace and joy in the Holy Spirit."

People of this era viewed angels as bearers of spiritual tranquility. Archbishop John Chrysostom (349–407) preached in Constantinople in 399 that every person has an angel. That realization, he said, should make the faithful behave with propriety, as if they were walking around in the company of a teacher. This belief explains the litany recited by those (called "catechumens") who wanted to convert to Christianity and were receiving instruction in preparation for their baptism. John Chrysostom explained, "Wherefore we bid them ask for the angel of peace, teaching them to seek that which is the bond of all good things, peace; so that they may be delivered from all fighting, all wars, all seditions."[27]

The revelations then ceased for a while, it is said, causing Muhammad consternation and anxiety.

AFTER A FEW months, later in 610, Muhammad again heard the voice of the divine, assuring him that God had not abandoned him. The traditions say that he initially kept the passages secret from all but a circle of close family members and friends, who shared them in hushed voices with trusted intimates. The first person to believe in Muhammad and his verses was his upright and intelligent wife, Khadija. The second was his teenage cousin `Ali, the son of Abu Talib (who was like a son to him since he and Khadija had brought him to live in their house and he later married their daughter Fatima). Likewise, Muhammad's freedman and client Zayd, a Christian captured from the Kalb tribe on the Syrian frontier, accepted the new faith. Then Muhammad brought in his boon companion, the thin, sallow-cheeked merchant Abu Bakr, who in turn proselytized his wide circle of intimates, people like Talha ibn Ubaydullah, "the Generous," who would perish at the hands of militant pagans; Sa`d Ibn Abi Waqqas, the future conqueror of Iran who would die in China as a diplomat; and `Uthman ibn `Affan, who would rule much of the Old World.[28]

After Muhammad had spent three years forming a secret society in Khadija's courtyard, according to one early historian, "God commanded his messenger to make known what had come to him and to disclose to the people his cause and to summon them to him." Even that preaching did not cause very much of a stir in Mecca, where no one could visit the Kaaba for worship without navigating a sea of seers and oracles and self-taught monotheists preaching from their carpets in the square. 'Urwa's student Muhammad ibn Shihab al-Zuhri (d. ca. 741) is alleged to have said that in this early public period of the Prophet's ministry, around 613, "The youth and men and lower classes that wanted to, answered God, so that the number of Believers multiplied. The Quraysh pagans did not arise in rejection of what he said. And when he passed by them when they were sitting around talking, they would point at him and say, 'that boy from 'Abd al-Muttalib's clan is speaking from the heavens.'"[29]

Muhammad's teachings assuaged a pervasive thirst for new religious ideas in western Arabia. Later Muslim chroniclers contended that the Prophet was not alone in his search for a spiritual alternative to Meccan paganism. They said that many Hejazis of that era became Gentile monotheists (*Hanif*). Indeed, some medieval Muslim authors asserted that Muhammad's ancestor Qusayy ibn Kilab (d. 480), who came from Syria to establish Quraysh control of the shrine to Abraham at Mecca, which he rebuilt, rejected the gods in favor of a form of monotheism. Later historians allege that some of Muhammad's contemporaries came to a realization that the polytheist Meccans had not understood the religion of Abraham. They concluded that the black stone at the Kaaba around which they circumambulated could not harm or benefit anyone and could not see or hear. An older Meccan contemporary of Muhammad named Zayd ibn 'Amr, for instance, is said to have declined to become either a Jew or a Christian but left the religion of his people, eschewing idols and animal sacrifice, saying, "I worship the lord of Abraham." He visited Damascus, suggesting that some of his ideas came to Mecca via a religious group active there. Some other seekers who adopted such a Gentile monotheism ended up converting to Christianity in the end.[30]

These Meccan Hanifs resemble what we know of the Godfearers in the Roman Empire, pagans who moved toward the worship of Zeus alone or of a figure they called "the Most High God."[31] Some of these former polytheists found they had a great deal in common with Jews and associated with them, though they kept their own form of monotheism and did not convert. Perhaps Hejazi merchants made the acquaintance of such a Godfearer group in Damascus during annual visits to that city. Some Meccans may have seen God as the chief deity and creator and the other supernatural figures around him as lesser beings—a belief called henotheism. This way of thinking became so popular in the 200s CE and after in the Roman Empire that some have described that era as the "second paganism." The Prophet recited verses acknowledging that the Meccans believed in God: "If you ask them who created them, they will certainly say, 'God.'"[32]

Sometime after he began preaching publicly in 613, the traditions say, Muhammad openly took a position bound to cause a great deal of trouble in his hometown. Perhaps in 614, he came out and denied the very existence of the pagan gods. Was it at the sacrificial slab before the mysterious Kaaba, around which pagans had placed their square, featureless betyls (standing stones) that they thought were inhabited by the lesser gods and goddesses? The Qur'an (*The Genies* 72:18) insists that only God be worshipped at the Kaaba. The early Qur'an chapter *Sincerity* (112:1–4) epitomizes the message Muhammad brought to the Meccans about the divine some four years into his mission: "Say: He is God, one; God, the unshakeable. He is unborn, and does not give birth, and nothing else is like unto him." This scintillating gem is the simplest and most beautiful statement of monotheism in the world religions. Note that in denying that God is born or gives birth, *Sincerity* 112 maintains that the Supreme Being has no gender and is not a "father." Some scholars have seen this chapter as echoing biblical themes, but its portrayal of God as "ungenerated" and "unshakeable" strikes me as more philosophical than the Bible and sounds Neoplatonic.[33]

The more hidebound Meccans reacted angrily. In part, Muhammad offended their traditionalism. In part, it may be that they feared that, in adopting the one God and speaking of Moses and Jesus, he was preaching some form of Christianity aligned to the Roman Empire and that by taking this stance, he would anger the minions of Khosrow II, with whom their commerce to the south and east gave them ties. Sasanian garrisons bristling with Zoroastrian warriors glowered up at Mecca from Yemen, as they waited for the order to expand Iran's westernmost colony to the north.

❧

WORSHIPPERS GATHERED AT cockcrow before the Kaaba as the lilac-gray sky brightened into amber above eerie lava hills. They circumambulated the inscrutable stone tablets of their primeval divinities, cantillating, "We are at your service—let our offenses go unpunished, lead us towards the clearest guiding light, and let us enjoy long lives."[34]

On one such occasion, the prophet Muhammad arrived to reverence the one God, Lord of the shrine, ignoring the lifeless betyls set up around it and the susurrus of their fervent votaries. He stood to the south of the Kaaba, facing both it and Jerusalem to the north. His presence and demeanor enraged the pagans. `Urwa ibn al-Zubayr was told,

"They leaped upon him as one man and surrounded him, saying, 'Are you the one who said such-and-such denouncing our gods and our religion?'

"The messenger said, 'Yes, I am the one who said those things.'

"And I saw one of them grab up his cloak.

"Then Abu Bakr the Truthful stood up to them, weeping and saying, 'Would you kill a man for saying God is my Lord?' "

`Urwa is said to have heard this account from the early Believer `Amr ibn al-`As (d. 664), having asked him about the way the Quraysh in this period treated the Prophet.[35]

He said, "Then they left him. That is the worst I ever saw Quraysh do to him."

The story implies that the Believers and the Meccans both accepted God, though the latter saw him as part of a divine family, and that Abu Bakr proved successful in calming them by pointing to this commonality.[36] Such an incident may be referred to in the Qur'an (*The Genies* 72:18–19): "The shrine belongs to God; do not call upon anyone else there alongside him. And when the Servant of God stood up there supplicating him, they virtually swarmed around him."

Abu Talib, the leonine chieftain of the Hashim clan, is said to have received strong pressure from the Quraysh to stop Muhammad from his monotheistic preaching, but decided to protect his nephew. Most later sources maintain that while Muhammad dearly loved his uncle Abu Talib, the latter never accepted the new faith, saying, "I must remain in the religion of my ancestors." The pagan clans of Hashim and al-Muttalib, they say, circled their wagons around Muhammad and protected him and his followers because of kinship solidarity.[37]

How could the Believers have accepted the protection of pagans and continued to socialize with them? For one thing, Muhammad acknowledged the moral autonomy of others; therefore, his followers had no option but to live amicably among the misguided. *The Over-whelming Event* (88:21–22) points out to Muhammad that all he can do is warn people about the bad choices they make in life, after which their course is their responsibility: "Then remind them, for you are only a reminder—you have no sovereignty over them." Further, *Jonah* 10:99 addresses Muhammad, "If your lord had willed, everyone on earth would have believed—all of them, all together. Will you then coerce the people to become believers?" The Qur'an decries coercion of conscience.[38]

MUHAMMAD AS A holy man could tell his contemporaries about the supernal sphere because he visited it in visions. *The Wrapped* 81:19–24 portrays him ascending to the outskirts of paradise: "This is the word of a noble angel, possessing power and an assured place before the Lord of the Throne, obeyed and trusted. Your companion is not deranged; he truly saw him on the clear horizon. He is not grudging with knowledge of the unseen." These spare verses offer no descrip-tion of the throne of the Lord and describe the angel only as pow-erful. The verse uses the horizon symbolically here to demarcate the boundary between the celestial realm and the sublunar domain.[39]

A third vision passage, *The Star* 53:1–18, speaks of the Prophet having an out-of-body experience in which he felt as though he ascended to the "highest horizon," marked by a celestial Lote Tree. A figure descended toward him slightly. *The Star* says that the being came "as close as two bowshots" and then inspired the new prophet with the revelation.[40] The figure descended again, to the boundary between this world below and the one beyond. Then Muhammad "saw the greatest signs of his Lord." In this vision, the Prophet does not actually enter the supernal realm. On the periphery, he can get a good look at the divine figure only because the latter descends toward the gross, material world.[41]

In contrast to some of the apocryphal prophetic ascensions circulating in late antiquity among both Jews and Christians, Muhammad does not pass the boundary marker between this world and the heavenly abode, nor does he become an angel.[42] The Qur'an draws strict lines between the divine and everything else, and the Prophet remains a humble mortal, special only because of the insights conveyed to him by the revelation. These early ascent visions are otherworldly, unlike the historical apocalypses in works like the book of Daniel, with its foretelling of political developments.

As he walked with his companions through the dusty alleyways of Mecca, down on which ominous crenelated jet hills glared, Muhammad urgently preached to them that the world faced calamity as the day of resurrection approached. *The Wrapped* 81:1–11 warns that the sun will darken, the stars will plummet abruptly from the firmament, mountains will be thrust aside, snarling beasts will converge in a predatory horde, oceans will swell beyond their coasts and rush with thalassic rage inland, and the turquoise enamel of the cambered sky will be ripped away. At the same time, it refers to panic among human societies, prophesying that the situation will be so dire that even valuable she-camels near to giving birth will be left untethered and abandoned by their owners and newborn girls will be asked for what sin they were buried alive. The Qur'an is saying that the Arabs of its time, like ancient Athenians and many other peoples, practiced female infanticide as a population-control measure in times of famine and is condemning it as a murder of innocents.[43]

Muhammad recited warnings that on the judgment day, all past humans will be reconstituted from the earth in which they had been buried and will be subjected to the divine verdict. The wicked will be enchained and transported to the torments of hell, roasted and skewered and scalded forever or for as long as God wills. The good will be brought up to the amaranthine garden of delight, where they will perpetually relish its pleasures.[44]

The Qur'an goes on to limn paradise in detail, drawing on imagery used in Near Eastern literary traditions for royal courts and their lush estates. It becomes clear that one reason the descent of angels and of revelation makes the night of power a time of peace is that they bring a little heaven down to earth when they come. The chapter of *The Bee* (16:31–32) describes how "those among the good whom the angels take up" will be greeted by them on arrival: "They say to them 'Peace be upon you: Enter the Garden by virtue of your deeds.'"[45] The blessed will hear the purling of underground streams and will have whatever they want.

The resurrected human beings comprise three distinct groups. The Vanguard and the Companions of the Right Hand will be brought to paradise. The greedy and impious Companions of the Left Hand, who crushed the poor and denied the one God and the afterlife, will be taken to hell, where "scorching fire," "scalding water," and suffocating "black smoke" await them. The devout Vanguard, "a crowd of ancients and a handful of moderns," appear mainly to have lived in earlier ages, though some are contemporaries of the Prophet. Given the predominance of ancients among them, they must be envisaged as being mainly Christian saints, pious Zoroastrians, Neoplatonists, and Jewish mystics of previous generations who stood for the perennial, common monotheistic tradition that the Qur'an calls *islam*. The Qur'an's paradise is, implicitly, a world parliament of religions.[46]

These exemplary persons, both men and women, from past ages will recline on ornamented thrones, facing one another and communing. Immortal young men serve them a cornucopia of fruit platters and succulent fowl and bring them silver goblets and crystal chalices endlessly overflowing with a wine that gladdens without causing a hangover. Almond-eyed, ever-virginal maidens fair as pearls attentively care for them, as a reward for past good deeds and for being charitable to people. Best of all, "Therein they will hear no abusive speech, nor any talk of sin, only the saying, 'Peace, peace.'"[47]

This vision of an empyrean with delicious foodstuffs, good cheer, and "painless" wine resembles other descriptions of the next life elsewhere in the ancient world, not least in the Greek Elysian Fields. In the Bible, Ezekiel proclaims that God's rejuvenation of a devastated landscape will make it "like the garden of Eden" (36:3), and the angel in Ezekiel 47:10–12 reveals to the prophet a future life that involves freshwater fish and always-laden fruit trees. Mark 14:25 has Jesus say to the disciples, "Truly, I say to you, I shall not drink again of the fruit of the vine until that day when I drink it new in the kingdom of God." Later chapters of the Qur'an put less emphasis on the bacchanalia of the afterlife, and the portrayal sounds more like a family reunion. *Thunder* 13:23 refers to "Gardens of Eden which they shall enter, along with the righteous among their fathers, and their wives, and their offspring; and the angels shall enter unto them from every gate."[48]

The Companions of the Right Hand, the second group of good but perhaps not beatific people, are "a crowd of ancients and of moderns." That is, there are more contemporaries of the Prophet in this group. *The Event* (56:90–91) promises, "And if they are among the companions of the right hand, then they will be greeted, 'Peace be to you,' by the companions of the right hand." They will dress up in fine silk and exotic brocade as though Asian royalty. Any lingering rancor or grudges in their hearts for others will be removed, and they will all become siblings.[49] Concord is so central to the Qur'an's view of the afterlife that it names heaven for it, saying, "God summons all to the Abode of Peace." The association of peace with heaven is also made in the New Testament. In Luke 19:38, when Jesus approached the Mount of Olives after entering Jerusalem riding on a donkey, the crowds are said to have shouted, "Blessed is the King who comes in the name of the Lord! Peace in heaven and glory in the highest!"[50]

The chapter of Y.S. 36:53–58 represents paradise as having levels, with enjoyment the most basic, then above that a stage in which you recline on couches facing your spouse, followed by a plane on which you savor luscious fruit. The pinnacle of paradise, however, comes at the fourth stage, when the voice of God addresses you with "Peace!" Many readers will immediately think of the *Paradiso* of Dante Alighieri, which imagines heaven as nine levels. The Qur'an positions peace at the apex of the delights of heaven.[51]

These images have a moral purpose. The Meccan sanctuary on earth dimly reflects the spectral asylum of the next world. The comportment of the Vanguard and the Companions of the Right Hand, the Qur'an implies, exemplifies ideal behavior to be mirrored as well as possible even in this world. Middle Platonism, the "spiritual commonwealth" of late antiquity, held that the spiritual is real and the material earth only participates in the archetypes of the other world. In the classical rhetorical tradition that was all around Muhammad when he journeyed north every year, the aim of a speaker was to use vivid, energetic language that brought the thing described to life before the eyes of the audience, making them feel as though they were witnesses to it. It was not enough, however, simply to describe. The speaker sought to whip up hearers emotionally by appealing to their imagination. The Qur'an uses these literary devices in making paradise present to the Believers.[52]

Likewise, Christian sermonizers urged believers to keep the prospect of joining the concourse of heaven in mind. Cyril of Jerusalem (313–386) preached, "Even now, I beseech you, lift up the eye of your understanding: imagine the angelic choirs, and God, the Lord of all sitting, and his Only-begotten Son sitting with him on his right-hand,

and the Spirit with them present, and thrones and dominions doing service, and each man and woman among you receiving salvation."[53] Cyril employed the techniques of Greek rhetoric here to make heaven real to his listeners by drawing them a powerful word picture that excited their emotions. So too did the Qur'an.

The reason for which harmony is at the center of the divine mystery revealed to Muhammad is, perhaps, made known in the chapter of *The Gathering* (59:23). It discloses that peace is one of the names of God: "He is God, other than whom there is no god, the King, the Holy, the Peace, the Defender, the Guardian, the Mighty, the Omnipotent, the Supreme." God as peace is here associated with other attributes, of providing order and protection by his unchallengeable power.

THE NEW MOVEMENT, according to the Qur'an, was peaceful in character, mirroring below the serenity in the afterlife to which they aspired. Treating the years immediately after Muhammad's public preaching began in 613, later biographers assert that Quraysh pagans sometimes administered beatings to early Believers or that a few especially powerful and angry Believers struck Quraysh notables, but these tales are later embellishments by Muslim storytellers. Muhammad, like other members of the Hashim clan, served as a custodian of the Kaaba, the omphalos of the Meccan sanctuary. As a lay priest, he dedicated himself to preserving its tranquility, mediating among feuding clans. The Qur'an advocates "preferential nonviolence," prioritizing peaceful approaches to conflict resolution where at all possible.[54]

The traditions say that Meccan notable al-Walid ibn al-Mughira and his companions haughtily approached Muhammad at the Kaaba, proposing that he and his followers should honor their religion, in return for which the Meccans would deign to tolerate Muhammad's claim of prophecy. In response, Muhammad is said to have recited to them *Pagans* 109:1–6, rejecting the sought-for syncretism but counseling mutual tolerance or at least a recognition of each other's right to hold a different view: "Say: Pagans! I do not worship what you worship. Nor are you worshipping what I worship. Nor am I worshipping what you have worshipped. Nor are you worshipping what I worship. To you your religion and to me my religion."[55]

Muhammad would not bow down to a plural divine, insisting that there is no god but God. In contrast, the Hejazis and rural Arabs adored a divine pantheon of which God formed only one part. The last verse offers, however, a different kind of compromise, a social one as opposed to a theological one. Let us, the Qur'an is suggesting, agree to disagree as far as daily interactions go. The Qur'an is acknowledging others' right to make their own spiritual choices. In another verse, the scripture praises members of Muhammad's movement for responding to the gibes and harassment of the hostile by expressing a desire for peaceful coexistence: "And when they hear abusive talk, they turn away from it and say, 'to us our deeds and to you yours; peace be upon you—we do not seek out the unruly'" (*Stories* 28:55). "Peace be upon you" or "May the Lord grant you peace" is an ancient ritual blessing and prayer in the Near East, not a simple pleasantry. The Believers replied to these philippics, a medieval commenter pointed out, "with beautiful words." This verse directly ties the sentiment of "to you your religion and to me my religion" to peaceful coexistence.[56]

Muhammad's position on tolerance was not unique in the late-antique era, but it was uncommon during his own lifetime. It resembles that of late third-century Christian thinkers before theirs became an imperial faith. Theologian Arnobius of Sicca (d. 330) protested that the authorities in pagan Rome sometimes compelled Christians to worship the gods by threat of torture. Arnobius wrote that

God does not compel pagans to accept his gift of Christianity since it would be "unjust" to force people to "reverse their inclinations."[57] Arnobius's pupil the rhetorician Lucius Lactantius (ca. 250–320), who taught in Nicomedia, wrote in the early fourth century during the last great pagan persecution of the followers of Jesus, "There is no occasion for violence and injury, for religion cannot be imposed by force; the matter must be carried on by words rather than by blows, that the will may be affected... for nothing is so much a matter of free-will as religion."[58] After Constantine established Christianity as the official religion of the Roman Empire, this sentiment became rarer and rarer among its theologians and state officials, who began actively persecuting pagans.

❧

THE APOCALYPTIC SEVENTH-CENTURY world war, in which Iranian armies swallowed Roman territory and threatened the Holy Land and the Hejaz, set the stage for the jeremiads pronounced by the new prophet in Mecca. Later traditions speak of Muhammad the seeker, looking for inner peace and rejecting the paganism of his contemporaries, of a man who spent a month every year in a desolate lava rock crevice, doing works of charity and meditating. In a bustling if minor Red Sea commercial hub, he pursued the tranquility of a monthlong annual retreat. The Prophet was a man of the world and in the world, but someone who could by virtue of his high moral character offer a self-denying charisma that recalled in some ways the monastic saints to his north. The revelations that seemed to him to come unbidden into his mind nevertheless adopted a middle ground between the ascetic self-denial of the Syrian monastic tradition and the ebullient hedonism of the Hejazi fairs dedicated to the goddesses. His first message was one of inner concord. Not only is Muhammad as seer taken up to the boundary between this world and the next, but on the Night of Power the angels and the Holy Spirit descend to earth and celebrate the peace that is divine self-disclosure.

The Qur'an sees peace as a virtue and a blessing and as one of the benefits of admission to paradise. It depicts the assembly of the raised in heaven as a dynamic community and not just a passive recipient of God's grace. The spiritual Vanguard repose on couch-like thrones facing one another, communing, wishing each other peace. Angels, he preached, will greet those upright persons with blessings of peace on their arrival in the next world. The denizens will wish one another peace. The apex of heaven's delectations is the blessing, bestowed by the voice of God, of peace and well-being. The Qur'an aims to bring hearers to join, in their imaginations, the heavenly host even while on earth and thereby to remain mindful of belonging to both worlds. The Qur'an thus models for Believers in this world the harmonious relationships God expects of them. The scripture implicitly contrasts the peace of paradise with the carnage of the great seventh-century world war and with the building conflict in Mecca between pagans and Muhammad's Believers. Just as a Christian thinker such as Aurelius Augustine of Hippo (354–430 CE) had turned in his imagination to a heavenly "City of God" after the fall of Rome, so the Qur'an initially takes refuge in an otherworldly ideal from a creeping tellurian menace.[59]

◊ 3 ◊

REPEL EVIL WITH GOOD

I N MECCA, ABU LAHAB, ONE OF MUHAMMAD'S PATERNAL UNCLES, broke with the rest of the Banu Hashim and took the lead in tormenting the Prophet. According to later traditions, Abu Lahab stalked Muhammad through Mecca's dusty alleys as the latter preached in public, contradicting him and slandering him, mocking with a vulpine smile. He and his harridan of a wife threw noisome trash and thorny bushes in his path (a treatment late-antique authors also say pagans dealt out to pious Christian leaders).[1] Historians depicted this uncle as "a shrewd, stylish young man with two side curls, sporting an

59

Aden cloak," who earned the nickname Abu Lahab (Fiery) because of his ruddy cheeks, and they spoke of his reputation for blasphemy and loose living.[2] Two of Abu Lahab's sons had married Muhammad's daughters Ruqaya and Umm Kulthum, and the daughters now faced the in-laws from hell. Abu Lahab eventually ordered his sons to divorce the young women.

Some of the dispute was over theology. The Qur'an chastises opponents concerning the one God: "But they have adopted gods other than him, which create nothing—but rather are themselves created." It quotes dedicated traditionalists as complaining that Muhammad would have misguided them away from their numina if they had not insisted on remaining faithful to them.[3] *The Night Journey* 17:42 refutes them, arguing that if there had been a whole pantheon of deities, they would have fought with one another over the top position: "Say: 'If there had been with him other gods, as they say, then they would have sought a path to the master of the throne.'" It is probably referring to the generational war of the Olympians with the Titans in Greek mythology, in which Zeus and his siblings deprived their father, Kronos, of the throne—a myth central to Greek literature, a literature that was cultivated in the Near East. Polytheism, the Qur'an maintains, would lead inevitably to theomachy, a struggle among the gods. Christians refuting Greek religion resorted to this argument as well.[4]

Abu Lahab's real name was 'Abd al-'Uzza, the servant of the goddess Aphrodite. Muhammad at some point began reciting verses that specifically decried the worship of his namesake. *The Star* 53:19–23 says, "Then, have you seen Allat and al-'Uzza and Manat, the third, the other one? Do you have, then, boys and God only girls? That would be an entirely unfair division. They are only names you have given them, you and your ancestors." The Qur'an says that the pagans believed the goddesses were daughters of God, but this belief is unknown in the North Arabian inscriptions. Since many had identified Allat with the Greek Athena, however, and since Athena was held to spring from the brain of Zeus, the motif of the daughters of God may derive from Hellenistic influence.[5]

The goddesses, once worshipped throughout the Arab world from Petra to Palmyra, had been eclipsed by the rise of Christianity in the Roman Near East, though not completely so among rural populations.[6] From Muhammad's point of view, there were no gods, and if the supernatural beings of which the Hejazis spoke had any reality at all, they could only be impotent angels of the one supreme being. This possibility was foreclosed for the goddesses, however. The Qur'an holds, in the biblical tradition, that angels are only gendered male. *Gilded Ornament* 43:19 protests, "And they have made the angels, who are manservants of the Most Merciful, females." Hence, *The Star* 53:23 denies the existence of these goddesses entirely, saying that they are "only names" mouthed by pagans. Ironically, that they branded the Arab deities as category errors and mere figments of the imagination rather than as demons may have contributed to the early Believers' ability to live peaceably with the pagans. In contrast, Christians and Zoroastrians identified idols with Satan or his minions and saw their acolytes as possessed strangelings.[7]

The Star 53:26–27 says, "However many angels subsist in the heavens, their intercession means nothing, except if God permits it, to whomever he wills and pleases. Those who do not believe in the afterlife give female names to the angels."[8] Muhammad urged that the Meccans give up any notion that their gods, even if understood as angels, may be worshipped, possess any share in divinity, or have power to intervene on their own account in the fates of human beings or to sway God. God is the sole decision maker and the only divine being. Augustine had made a similar argument, that traditionalist "gods" might be reconceived as angels if their lack of autonomy were admitted, in his *City of God*.[9]

Relations between the early Believers and the rest of the population worsened dramatically when the Prophet began questioning the existence of their goddesses, according to ʿUrwa: "Some wealthy members of Quraysh came up from Taif who denounced him for that and acted severely toward him and abhorred what he said. They instigated their hangers-on against him, so that the common people turned on him and abandoned him, all save those whom God safeguarded, who were few enough."[10]

The initial pagan backlash hit converted Believers among the slaves and the poor most severely. The Muslim hagiographers tell stories like that about Bilal, an Ethiopian slave belonging to one of the Jumah clan.[11] He embraced the new religion against the wishes of his master.

It is alleged that Umayya ibn Khalaf of the Jumah would bring him out in the heat of the day, make him lie down, and then pin him with a great rock on his chest.

Ibn Hisham asserts that Umayya told the slave, "You will stay here till you die or deny Muhammad and worship Allat and al-ʿUzza."

He refused and continued to whisper with parched lips in the midst of this torture, "One, one."

It is said that Muhammad's friend Abu Bakr remonstrated with Umayya: "Have you no fear of God that you treat this poor fellow like this? How long is this to go on?"

Umayya retorted, "You are the one who corrupted him, so save him from his plight."

Ultimately, Abu Bakr arranged for Bilal to be manumitted, a peaceful way of resolving the conflict.

Muhammad did not put all the pagans on the same level. The negative word the Qur'an used in Arabic for the devotees of the old deities was *kafir*. Since the scripture admits that the Arab pagans believed in the Creator God, the term cannot mean "infidel" or "unbeliever," which is how it has usually been translated. The problem was not that they were atheists but that they made God part of a pantheon. Christian polemicists who wrote against paganism most often contrasted faith not with unbelief but with impiety, and I think Muhammad used the Arabic word in this sense.[12]

Muhammad taught this-worldly magnanimity even toward unreconstructed polytheists. The chapter of *Gilded Ornament* (43:81–89) complains about traditionalists attributing offspring to God, but nevertheless advises, "yet pardon them, and say, 'Peace!' Soon they will know."[13] *The Cattle* 6:108 goes so far as to forbid the Believers from using obscenities for the gods and goddesses: "Do not curse those on whom they call other than God, lest they in their ignorance curse God out of enmity. We have made the deeds of every nation seem beautiful to them." Muhammad, prophet of the compassionate God, understood that Arab traditionalists were taken in by their meretricious betyl stones.

The Arabian prophet's principle of social forbearance toward the pagans differed starkly from religious policy in the eastern Roman Empire of his own day. The Code issued by the emperor Justinian (r. 527–565), under which Muhammad functioned as a merchant when working in Damascus, deprived open pagans of their civil rights and property. It prescribed the death penalty for public idol worship and sacrifice and for deserting Christianity to return to paganism. Muhammad's older contemporary Roman emperor Maurikios had some non-Christians in the pagan-majority city of Harran in eastern Anatolia arrested, tried, and torn limb from limb.[14]

❧

Outside the Hejaz, politics by 612 took a dangerous turn that would inexorably entangle western Arabia. Emperor Herakleios, firmly ensconced in power in Constantinople, sent an embassy to Ctesiphon with peace overtures. There is every reason to believe that an astute long-distance merchant like Muhammad would have had good intelligence on such negotiations, the outcome of which affected the conditions of commerce. We can picture the scene. The Roman envoys arrived at the Sasanian capital. The two prostrated themselves in the throne room of the fabled White Palace, which was adorned with a great seat of power for the king of kings and sported three miniature thrones, symbolizing his alleged vassals, the rulers of China, the Turks, and Rome. Behind a diaphanous curtain sat the shah. At a certain point attendants abruptly drew the curtain, revealing his majesty, adorned in colorful, perfumed robes, his beard glinting with flecks of gold. A magnificent bejeweled crown, too heavy for a mortal neck to sustain, was suspended above his head from the ceiling. The ambassadors, holding handkerchiefs before their mouths, communicated directly only with the Keeper of the Curtain, who would convey their message to the king. One of the ambassadors read out the letter of Herakleios in which he pointed out that he had avenged the assassination of Maurikios by overthrowing and executing the usurper Phokas, whose coup had been the pretext for Iran's invasion a decade before. The Iranian emperor haughtily rejected this approach and had the emissaries summarily executed. In 615 the Roman senate attempted to parley again, claiming a republican authority that Herakleios lacked and dispatched new ambassadors. Khosrow II, lip curled in cruel disdain, had these remarkably brave diplomats clapped in chains and sent to his dungeon.[15]

In his summer trade missions north, the Prophet would have heard anxiety in the voices of the monks who offered his cameleers hospitality in cities such as Bostra and Damascus. The Sasanian army continued its invasion, taking Antioch in 612, thus splitting the Roman Empire in two and preventing Niketas the Patrician in Syria from coordinating with the emperor in Asia Minor. A biographer then alive wrote that the monk Theodoros of Sykeon said of the Iranians, "We were all, both those in the monastery and all the residents in our area, in great fear, apprehensive that they would launch a raid against us."[16]

In 613 Khosrow II made a breathtakingly audacious play for the entire Near East. The king of kings dispatched General Shahr Varaz Ardashir-Zadag of the House of Mehran. He led troops as numerous as stars in the Milky Way into the Levant, likely headed up by a fearsome elephant cavalry blaring war cries. Cities surrendered one after another on terms. Damascus fell. Terror spread in Roman Arabia, the three provinces of Palestine, and the Hejaz. Sasanian geographical manuals claim the Tihama as Iranian territory, and the Iranians had made Medina a vassal city-state in Muhammad's youth.[17] The question of whether Mecca could retain its independence in the face of Sasanian advances would have weighed heavily on Muhammad and his followers.

Despite Mecca's need to import summer wheat, it must have been impossible for Muhammad to think of mounting a caravan into the Near East in the warm season of 613, as the Sasanians routed Niketas the Patrician.[18] He and the rest of the Quraysh would have been dependent on what grain devotees brought to the Kaaba from around the region in the way of votive offerings. As war came to their doorstep, Meccans risked starvation.

❧

MUHAMMAD, OUTRAGED AT Iranian predations, boldly prophesied that the usurpation would not stand. The Qur'an (*Rome* 30:1–6) says, "Rome lies vanquished in the nearest province. But in the wake of their defeat, they will triumph after a few years. Before and after, it is

God who is in command. On that day, the believers will rejoice in the victory of God; he causes to triumph whomever he will, and he is the Mighty, the Merciful. It is the promise of God; God does not break his promises, but most people do not know it."[19] The verses clearly identify the prophesied victory of Constantinople over the Sasanids as God's (Allah's) victory, which will be a cause of rejoicing for Muhammad's Believers.

By 616 the strapped Herakleios no longer had enough bullion on hand to mint gold currency, and he instead issued a six-gram silver coin that bore the war-cry inscription "May God help the Romans!"[20] This passage of the Qur'an seems to share in that sentiment. The feeling was not unusual for Roman subjects of the era. The historian Theophylaktos Simokates predicted twenty-one years of Sasanian rule and then seven years of Roman restoration, after which the expected end-time would arrive and the epoch of destruction would give way to a better life. Likewise, the seventh-century Christian literary novel *Jacob the Newly Baptized* has its protagonist say of the Roman Empire, "Though it may be somewhat diminished, we expect that it will rise again," since that was a precondition for Christ's return, according to the novelist's reading of the book of Daniel.[21]

One of the earlier commenters on the Qur'an wrote of *Rome* 30:1–6, "Rome and the Iranians fought, and Rome was vanquished, and this news reached the prophet and his companions in Mecca and was grievous for them. The pagans rejoiced and gloated and confronted the companions of the prophet, saying, 'You are people of the Book and the Romans are people of the Book, but our brethren the people of Iran have triumphed over your siblings from the Roman Empire.'" Very early Muslim political identity was somehow wrought up with the fortunes of Constantinople. Muhammad seems to have envisioned the Believers as being members of the eastern Roman Commonwealth, the areas where Constantinople ruled or was diplomatically welcome and influential.[22]

It has been suggested that some Quraysh saw the decline of other Arab power centers such as the Nasrids at Hira and of the Jafnid alliance around Damascus as an opportunity. They may well have thought they could volunteer, once Iran had been repelled, to replace the Jafnids by buttressing the Roman Empire's security along the Arabian Line and so contribute to the Pax Romana. As allies of the empire, they would share directly in the emperor's well-being. Unlike Jewish authors of that time, the Qur'an never engages in a critique of Constantinople's power.[23]

Later in the chapter of *Rome*, the Qur'an (30:22) celebrates multiculturalism: "And among his signs is the creation of the heavens and earth and the variety of your languages and complexions. Surely in that are signs for all living beings." The Qur'an likely brings up this theme, of the virtues of a polyglot and multiracial society, in this chapter precisely because it began by announcing hopes for the restoration of the Roman Commonwealth. It is God's commonwealth. This verse may be compared to the New Testament proclamation in Colossians 3:11, "Here there cannot be Greek and Jew, circumcised and uncircumcised, barbarian, Scythian, slave, free, but Christ is all, and in all," which, it has been argued, resonated with Roman conceptions of universal peace and order emanating from the imperial center.[24]

If Muhammad praised Herakleios, did he censure Khosrow II? The figure of Pharaoh in the later chapters of the Meccan period may well serve as a veiled reference to the Iranian monarch. Early passages of the Qur'an mention the ruins of Pharaoh's civilization as a warning against polytheism and decadence. Later in the book, as Iran advanced, the Egyptian monarch takes on the attributes of a tyrant. In *Stories* 28:4, the Qur'an says, "Now Pharaoh exalted himself in the land and divided its inhabitants into factions, abasing one party of them, slaughtering their sons, and sparing their women; for he was a worker of corruption." These are precisely the allegations Christians were circulating about the Iranian king of kings in 614 and after. If the Qur'an did use such Aesopian techniques, it would be entirely understandable. Muhammad was still going on caravan journeys down to Sasanian Yemen and up to Iranian-held Palestine and Syria, and it would have been dangerous to denounce Ctesiphon openly and repeatedly.

❧

THERE IS REASON to think that in the 610s, the Prophet led Khadija's caravans down to Yemen on urgent missions to purchase winter wheat. He would have found the Iranian garrison commanders in Sana'a and Aden supercilious and exulting about their army's victories in the North. They offered up magnificent sacrifices at the barracks' fire temple, an unadorned square building with a Persian arch on either side and a ritual flame in the center, honoring Ohrmazd and his angels. Muhammad may have seen similarities between the biblical traditions and Iranian religion. Zoroastrians held that the great God of good, Ohrmazd, was engaged in a cosmic war with the evil principle, Ahriman. Ohrmazd sent his messenger Zarathustra (called Zoroaster in Greek) to teach human beings that every time they lied or sinned, they strengthened the god of evil against the God of good. In the end, a savior, Saoshyant, would arise to transfigure the world, and Ohrmazd would defeat his nemesis.[25]

Muhammad and the other Hejazi traders may have suffered some humiliation at the hands of the Iranian military. Zoroastrians in the Sasanian period firmly distinguished between Iran and non-Iran, looking down on external barbarians, and the warrior caste entertained a poor opinion of merchants. Nevertheless, Muhammad discussed things with and likely preached to Zoroastrian audiences.

The Qur'an uses a Persian word for the notion of "religion." It calls Muhammad a messenger, like Zarathustra.[26]

Muhammad would also have associated with Yemenis of various faith traditions, pagan, Jewish, and Christian. Indigenous Yemeni inscriptions call the one God "the All-Merciful" and contain the name "Muhammad." Since both terms are used in the Qur'an, it seems likely that Islam has a Yemeni context to some extent. Yemen's startling religious history in late antiquity is mainly known from somewhat cryptic inscriptions, but it seems clear that from about 380 CE, the ruling elite of the kingdom of Himyar adopted some form of monolatry (the worship of only one divinity), centered on a figure they called "the All-Merciful." Its state-sponsored temples to the many gods abruptly fell into desuetude, though commoners continued pagan worship. Jewish and Christian inscriptions also call God "the All-Merciful" in Yemen, but it seems most likely that the royal family followed a homegrown cult. Some of their inscriptions call on both the Himyarite All-Merciful and the lord of the Jews, which does not sound exactly like monotheism but certainly is not Judaism. By the early 500s, some princes and commoners had converted to Judaism and others to Christianity, and those two biblical communities fell to warring with one another. In this struggle the Christians, backed by Ethiopia and the Roman Empire, prevailed in the 520s through about 570. Then Iran invaded and dethroned the Ethiopian Christian elite, depending politically instead on local pagans, pagan monotheists, and Jews among the Yemenis.[27]

Muhammad celebrated the children of Israel, displaying clear pro-Jewish sentiments. The Qur'an sees Jews as God's chosen people and objects of divine grace. *The Hobbling* 45:16 says, "We bestowed scripture, judgment and prophethood on the children of Israel and nourished them with good things and preferred them above the nations." Muhammad clearly knew the Palestinian Talmud, and it has been argued that the middle chapters of the Qur'an show knowledge of rabbinical forms of argumentation, suggesting dialogue and discussion with learned Jews.[28]

In his downtime in the highlands of Sana'a amid its gingerbread multistoried stone buildings or in the steamy Arabian Sea port of Aden with its nacreous coral stone homes, Muhammad wrote out some passages of the Qur'an (literally, "book of recitations") and shared them with Arab Jewish friends among the rabbis, who were likely serving merchants from Medina. *The Poets* 26:192–199 says of the Qur'an, "It is in a clear Arabic, written in the script of the ancients. Is it not a sign to them that the scholars of the children of Israel recognize it? If we had revealed it to someone who did not speak Arabic as a mother tongue, and he had recited it to them, they would not have believed in it." The script (*zubur*) to which the Qur'an refers here was used for the southern Sabaic language, but apparently expatriate Arabic-speakers in Yemen in this period also adopted it. Muhammad held out Arab Jews' ability to read the new scripture in it and their affirmation of its similarity to the Bible as proofs of its validity.[29] The Qur'an configures Jews of the Tihama as a symbol of Arab cultural authenticity and sees their positive response as confirmatory of Muhammad's own Arabic-language revelation, implicitly contrasting them to Christian missionaries from Syria, with their heavy Aramaic accents.

MUHAMMAD AND HIS new community would have listened with horror to the reports of travelers in spring of 614 that the troops of General Shahr Varaz had surrounded the holy city of Jerusalem. As Godfearers or monotheistic Gentiles who observed some Jewish law and customs, the Believers initially prayed toward Jerusalem, some nine hundred miles to the north, and honored the Holy Land, which they sometimes visited on trade journeys.[30]

Seventh-century chroniclers alleged that fighting broke out in First Palestine between Christians and local Jewish communities because the latter supported the advancing Sasanians. *Jacob the Newly Baptized*, about a Jew forcibly converted to Christianity, has Jacob recall the year 614: "When Christians at Ptolemais departed because of the Persian invasion, the Jews found an occasion to burn Christian churches and pillage their houses, harassing and killing many Christians."[31]

The Iranians besieged Jerusalem for some three weeks. Strategos, an eyewitness, wrote that monks held that each of the towers and battlements of the holy city was initially guarded by "an angel holding a flaming lance," but late in the siege they abruptly departed. Then, the monks lamented, "We knew that our sins had stood in the way of God's mercy."[32] The forces of General Shahr Varaz successfully breached its stone ramparts with a missile-throwing ballista and flooded angrily into it, "snarling like dogs." They "killed everyone they encountered, showing no mercy," and mowed them down like grass, Strategos alleged. Some Christian residents were shut up in the reservoir at Mamilla, and hundreds suffocated or starved to death there. "The heavenly Jerusalem wept for the one down below."[33]

Rumors may have reached the Hejaz that the holy city was virtually in flames and razed to the ground, distressing Muhammad and the Believers, who reverenced the prophets who had taught there, from Solomon to Jesus. The Christian clergymen who described this invasion, however, vastly exaggerated its brutality. Archaeologists do not find evidence that the whole city was torched, substantial damage was done to most churches, or large numbers of residents were killed. Even Strategos admitted that "from among the people of Jerusalem a multitude remained who had not been killed."[34]

The victorious General Shahr Varaz, clad in a glittering suit of scale armor made up of overlapping plates of iron, his face covered by a mail aventail suspended from his round helmet so that only his intense eyes could be seen, strode with his elite guard into the nave of the Church of the Holy Sepulchre and marched up to the altar. He took Patriarch Zachariah and the keeper of the relic of the true cross captive and had them tortured until they revealed its hiding place (some say it was buried in a vegetable garden in the atrium before the church). The Iranians rounded up skilled artisans such as stoneworkers and carpenters and sent thousands of them, along with the patriarch and the reliquary of the Holy Rood, as trophies to Ctesiphon. Then the Iranian military trooped over to a garrison at Caesarea Maritima on the Mediterranean and left Jews in charge of Jerusalem for five years.[35]

Roman authors portrayed these actions of Khosrow II as signs of his enmity to Christianity, and they unfairly excoriated Zoroastrians as idolaters. It has been argued, however, that in this period, he was seeking support from Christians in his realm and making a bid to be their king as well. The religious policy of Sasanian Iran was to support firmly the dominant faith of Zarathustra but to offer relative practical tolerance to eastern Syrian Christians and Jews. By the sixth century, the Sasanian monarch came to recognize a Christian bishop in Ctesiphon and generally to tolerate that religion as long as its adherents remained loyal. The 561–562 peace treaty between Justinian and Khosrow I insisted that Sasanian Christians be allowed freely to worship, though they could not proselytize, and apostasy from Zoroastrianism was punishable by death.[36]

One strand in Jewish and Christian thinking identified Jerusalem with the Garden of Eden, and Christians there surely felt they had suffered another fall from grace. In the view of Muhammad, the consequence of the loss of paradise was above all violent conflict. *The Heights* 7:19–25 tells the story of the expulsion of Adam and Eve after Satan succeeded in tempting them. It reports (7:24) that God commanded, "Descend, being enemies to one another." The scripture then says that human beings entered a world of division and violence, cautioning humankind, "Children of Adam, if messengers come to you from among you, relating our verses, whoever fears God and makes peace will have no fear, nor will they sorrow" (7:35).[37] The Qur'an goes so far as to present peace activism and beneficence as the vehicle of redemption from the fall, rather than, as in Christian theology, the sacrifice of Christ on the cross.

Muhammad confronted these clashes by preaching ecumenical harmony. *The Cow* 2:113 castigates Jews and Christians for each denying the truth of the other's religion, even though they both believe in the Bible: "The Jews say, 'The Christians have nothing to stand on'; and the Christians say, 'The Jews have nothing to stand on'—even though they both recite the Bible." It goes on to scold them for violently attacking one another's religious edifices: "Who is more of a despot than one who forbids the mention of God's name in the houses of God, and strives to tear them down? They should not have entered them save in fearful reverence. Their lot in this world is disgrace, and in the next they face severe torment" (2:114).[38]

Christian-Jewish relations were roiled long before the Sasanian invasion. The aristocratic Bishop Ambrose of Milan (340–397) had justified the burning of a synagogue at Callinicum in Syria by a Christian mob and convinced Emperor Theodosius I (who had been inclined to uphold the Jewish right to worship) not to rebuild it or punish the perpetrators, on the grounds that it had been "a home of unbelief, a house of impiety, a receptacle of folly, which God himself has condemned."[39] This episode was not typical of the late Christian Roman Empire, under which synagogues proliferated and became central to Jewish life, despite what the laws may have said. But by the middle of the 500s, at least de jure, Judaism had been demoted in Roman discourse from a religion to a superstition (like paganism).

Jews were forbidden to testify against Christians in court, formal Roman law prohibited Jews from building new places of worship, and sixth-century Emperor Justinian ordered that the synagogues in Africa be turned into churches (likely only a few were).[40] In contrast, Muhammad urged that Christians and Jews recognize their common biblical roots and respect the sanctity of churches and synagogues, safeguarding them and entering them in reverence.

In Palestine speculation about the end-times ran rampant, given that both Jews and Christians viewed Jerusalem as a symbol of eschatological hope and peace. Many Christians, faced with the loss of the holy city, came to believe that Christ's Second Coming was imminent. Some Jews expected the Messiah, and claimants seeking to fulfill such hopes launched movements throughout the region. In Sasanian Balughta (today's Fallujah), a Jew claimed to be the Messiah, probably in the 620s, gathering the support of artisans. Some four hundred of his followers staged an uprising and were said to have burned three churches and killed the governor before Iranian troops crushed them.[41]

❧

MUHAMMAD FACED INCREASING opposition in Mecca. It was alleged that the florid-faced Abu Lahab or others used to toss a bloody sheep's uterus through the open window of Khadija and Muhammad's villa. A biographer said that "when they threw this objectionable thing at him the prophet took it out on a stick, and standing at the door of his house, he would say, 'My tribe, `Abd Manaf, what sort of protection is this?' Then he would throw it in the street."[42]

Women were especially vulnerable to bullying. The tall, athletic Omar ibn al-Khattab, depicted as initially a militant pagan, converted in an especially dramatic way.[43] Someone revealed to Omar that his sister Fatima had embraced the new religion, enraging him. She was alleged to scratch out Qur'an verses on camel bone, and she had given up eating carrion.

He rushed to Fatima's place. "What is this shoulder blade that I hear you have in your possession?"

"I don't have a shoulder blade," she replied.

He struck her and went about her room, looking for the piece of bone. When he found it, he hit her with it, drawing blood. Some versions of the story have him regretting his actions at that point. Others say he took the shoulder blade with him while still in a lather, and, being illiterate, found someone to read it to him. He became entranced with the verses and then went to Muhammad and converted.

An imposing man with a quick temper, he became a support for the persecuted Believers. The details vary in the many later tellings of Omar's story, but they have in common that his sister converted before he did and that he was upset about it before he found his own path to the faith. The later storyteller who depicted him as striking her with the Qur'an itself, drawing blood, was mining a rich vein of symbolism. The gender dynamics of this narrative are also suggestive, with a large, angry pagan male abusing a devout woman Believer who stands her ground. Belief is here feminized and made nonviolent, but nevertheless victorious.

Even Meccan notables began coming under pressure. At some point, 'Urwa said, the Quraysh elite made a collective decision to shut down the new religion. "Then their leaders conspired to coerce the consciences of his followers, among their sons, brothers and tribesmen, to make them recant the religion of God. It was coercion on the scale of an earthquake for the people of Islam who adhered to the messenger of God. Some of them succumbed to the pressure to apostatize, while God protected whomever he willed."[44]

Muhammad responded to the pressures put on his flock by urging on them nonviolence. The Qur'an (*Distinguished* 41:34) says, "Good and evil are not equal. Repel the latter with the highest good, and behold, your enemy will become a devoted patron."[45] The scripture celebrates the moral alembic wherein returning good for evil transforms base antagonism into the gold of benefaction. The chapter of *The Criterion* (25:63) praises Muhammad's followers for their self-restraint in the face of provocations, speaking of "the servants of the All-Merciful who walk humbly upon the earth—and when the unruly taunt them, they reply, 'Peace!'" The "unruly" here are those lacking in self-control, and literally the word means "ignorant." The Qur'an makes wishing your enemies peace and well-being one of the signs of piety. The later commentator Muhammad ibn Jarir Tabari (d. 923) said of the Believers mentioned in *The Criterion* 25:63, "When those ignorant of God addressed them with words they were loathe to hear, they replied with kind words and upright speech."[46] It is difficult to avoid a comparison of such Qur'an verses with Matthew 5:43–44, where Jesus says, "You have heard that it was said, 'You shall love your neighbor and hate your enemy.' But I say to you, Love your enemies and pray for those who persecute you."[47]

The Qur'an was counseling peaceful behavior, but nevertheless insisted that the Believers confront the pagans about their theological errors. *The Criterion* 25:52 instructs Muhammad, "So do not obey the pagans; rather struggle thereby steadfastly against them." For *struggle* in Arabic, the Qur'an uses the verb from which the noun *jihad* derives. It bears no connotation of fighting or war here and does not explicitly do so anywhere in the scripture. Instead, the Qur'an is ordering Muhammad to engage in oral argument with the opponent. An early interpreter, `Abd al-Rahman ibn Zayd, termed this nonviolent contest with the hostile pagans "the greatest struggle." The Arabic notion of jihad, or exertion for the sake of virtue, was paralleled in Aristotle, Plotinus, and the New Testament.[48]

Muhammad prioritized nonviolence in the face of harassment, but he did allow retribution for a crime of violence such as injury or murder. In the absence of a state, clan justice prevailed. Even there, however, the Qur'an counsels compassion instead. Meccan chapters restate the "eye for an eye" rule of Deuteronomy 19:21. *Consultation* 42:40 says, "The retribution for a wrong is a wrong the like of it." But like the New Testament, the rest of this Qur'an verse points to a higher law, of forgiveness: "But God will recompense whoever pardons and makes peace; surely he does not love wrongdoers."[49] Believers are not to injure the guiltless, and it is God who will punish the iniquitous (*Consultation* 42:42): "The way is only open against those who do wrong to people and transgress in the land without any right; there awaits them a painful chastisement." Yet even with regard to such offenders, it is better, *Consultation* 42:43 says, to avoid extracting vengeance: "Still, truly the one who is patient and forgives displays steadfastness." It has been argued that counseling "patience" is one of the Qur'an's ways of recommending peaceful courses of action.[50]

Unfortunately, the outraged traditionalists began tossing aside the genteel conventions of the Meccan sanctuary, just as some had done during the Sacrilegious Wars in Muhammad's youth. Quraysh bullies began launching violent threats at the Prophet in hopes that he would leave the city. *The Night Journey* 17:76 says to Muhammad, "In truth they wished to frighten you from the land, to expel you from it, but then they would have remained in it after you only a little."

❧

ONCE THE POLITICAL situation had settled somewhat in the Near East, from 615 forward, there is reason to believe that Muhammad resumed leading trading missions up to Syria and Palestine. At one point, the scripture complains about pagan Arab tribes setting aside some of their crops and cattle as sacrifices not only for God but for the divine pantheon. Muhammad must have been in Sasanian Transjordan or Syria, where there were more likely to be crops and cattle than in arid Mecca.[51]

At another point, the Prophet recited the Qur'an to an audience in Palestine, discoursing on the biblical stories of Noah, Moses, Elijah, Abraham, and Lot and then reminding them of how God destroyed Sodom for its wickedness. The passage says these hearers passed by its derelict ruins "every morning" (*Serried Ranks* 37:136–137). The Piacenza Pilgrim had written four decades before, "Leaving Jericho, we traveled towards Jerusalem...proceeding from the east towards the west, we had on our left hand the ashes of Sodom and Gomorrah, over which country there always hangs a dark cloud with a sulphurous odour." The Prophet would have likely been preaching to Christian Arabs of the Banu Judham on that occasion, whether pastoralists or villagers, in the vicinity of Jericho.[52]

That Muhammad attracted Arab Christian admirers up north, and that he thought well of their values, is demonstrated by *Stories* 28:52–54. These verses contrast the hostile pagans to Christians who had received a revelation before the Qur'an and who therefore could recognize its truth: "Those to whom we gave a Book before this one have believed in it. When it is recited to them they say, 'we have believed in it, it is the truth from our lord. Even before this, we were monotheists.' They will be given their reward twice over inasmuch as they patiently endure and repel evil with good deeds and share the provisions we gave them."[53]

The Qur'an reaffirms Jesus's teachings in the Sermon on the Mount and holds them up as an example for all. The passage suggests that Muhammad was already making Christian converts in places like the Transjordan, though it is possible that they simply acknowledged the virtues of the Qur'an. Muhammad's Believers movement was socially ecumenical, though he steadfastly insisted on his Unitarian theology.[54]

The phrase "we were monotheists" in *Stories* 28:53 is in the Arabic "we were *muslims*." The root of the Arabic here has to do with surrendering, that is, to God, but it is likely underlain by Aramaic and Greek words that have to do not only with submission but also with passing on or accepting a tradition.[55] All those who submit to the one God and accept the Word or tradition of Abraham about his unicity are thus *muslims* with a small *m*, from Solomon to the disciples of Jesus. The Qur'an does not employ the terms *muslim* and *islam* to refer to the religion of Muhammad in specific (it instead uses terminology also found in the letters of Paul, calling his followers "those who have believed").[56]

I read the Qur'an to suggest that Muhammad and his caravan, traveling at night to avoid the torrid sun, stopped off in Jerusalem on their way up to Damascus, perhaps in summer of 617. Let us imagine what such a visit would have looked like. The Piacenza Pilgrim explained the route he would have taken the next morning once they had stabled their steeds with an ostler at a monastery.[57] The Prophet and his companions would have crossed the Mount of Olives, where Christians believe Jesus had urged the turning of the other cheek, had wept for Jerusalem, and had ascended to heaven. They would have tread a swept earth pathway rimmed with hardy cock's-foot grass, passing through coppices of gnarled, portly olive trees. The city stretched below, the Church of the Holy Sepulchre peeking up behind the largely abandoned temple mount. They wended their way down the steep, serpentine path to the Valley of Gethsemane, given shade by stately cypress trees veiled by hanging Spanish moss. Perhaps they paid their respects to the basilica of Mary in the same valley, noting with regret the blackened wall where a fire had broken out and been extinguished during the Iranian conquest. The Qur'an's account of

Mary (chapter 19) is longer than that of the New Testament, and she is praised for her faith so warmly that some later Muslim theologians maintained that she was a prophet.

Then they might have hiked up numerous steps to the Gate of Jerusalem. It abutted the remnants of the gate of the old Jewish temple, the stone threshold and plinths of which pilgrims thought they could still discern. And there on the plateau of the temple mount, some sources suggest, would have stood a makeshift altar for revived Jewish worship, permitted by the Iranians. Did Muhammad and his companions kneel to prostrate and pray at close range toward what had long been their cynosure? As Godfearers, Gentile monotheists who admired and associated with Jews, Muhammad's early Believers prayed toward Jerusalem until about 624, though some traditions maintained that they stood south of the Kaaba and so could pray toward it and the holy city to the north simultaneously.[58]

The Night Journey 17:1 relates that the Prophet experienced a fourth apocalyptic vision: "Exalted is he who took his servant by night from the sacred temple to the farthest temple, whose surroundings we have blessed, to show him of our signs. Indeed, he is the hearing, the seeing." Like Muhammad's earlier ascensions, the site taught him the "signs" of God's mystery, suggesting that the Farthest Temple, like the Lote Tree on the horizon, functioned to demarcate the boundary between earth and heaven. Later Muslims turned this passage into a miracle story, seeing it as being about a supernatural bodily journey from Mecca to Jerusalem in the space of a single night, venerating the footprint they held the Prophet left in the surface rock of the mount.[59]

I am suggesting instead that he journeyed overland to Jerusalem. If he did visit then, Muhammad would have found the holy city no longer an emblem of Christian sovereignty but the trophy of a distant Zoroastrian emperor. His old Christian merchant contacts were gone or circumspect, the monks he knew from previous visits so tearful that their vespers could barely be distinguished from funerary rites. A contemporary, the prominent monk Sophronios (d. 638), exemplified Christian anguish at the loss of the holy city, writing, "Children of the blessed Christians, come lament for Jerusalem on its high hills!"[60] He said, "The perfidious Mede advanced from calamitous Persia, making war on the cities and villages, battling against the Emperor of Rome." He described a great massacre of civilians and alleged that local Jews allied with "their friends," the Iranians.

The Christians of the holy city began wishing that their savior were less meek, in his telling: "Then, all together, they raised their pure hands toward the heavens, calling on Christ the king to engage in combat for the sake of his own." Growing angrier and forgetting the Sermon on the Mount entirely, the outraged monk cried out, "Christ, grant to us that we may soon see Persia consumed by flames, in reprisal for the holy places!" The idea of holy war arose in late antiquity in part as a Christian Roman response to the Sasanian conquest of Jerusalem, as is visible in this passage by Sophronios, which reconfigures Christ as an Ares-like god of war.[61]

Some of Muhammad's Jewish contacts, in contrast, would have been jubilant at their good fortune. General Shahr Varaz is alleged to have formally allowed substantial numbers of Jews to live in Jerusalem for the first time in five hundred years and to have put Jewish leaders in charge of it, from 614 to 619. One lead seal from Sasanian Palestine suggests that Jews were allowed to hold civil office in this period, unlike under late Roman law, or at the very least that Jewish communities were recognized as self-governing. A contemporaneous Jewish work speaks of a leader in Jerusalem named Nehemiah leading Israel in making an offering to the lord and registering Jewish families. It appears that the community established a provisional votive site on the temple mount where the devout performed sacrifices, hoping for permission to rebuild the temple. Jewish religious poetry of the 610s spoke of how "the monarch of the east will fight a deadly war with the monarch of the west."[62] Israel would be purified of its sins and no longer be excluded from the house of prayer. This poetry contains some of the same themes as the Qur'an.

The Night Journey 17:1–8 responds to the Iranian capture of Jerusalem.[63] Meccans appear to have nicknamed the Roman provinces by proximity, so that Roman Arabia (northern Transjordan and southern Syria) was the "nearest land" to Mecca, while First Palestine, the last province before the Mediterranean as caravans headed north to the port at Gaza, was the "farthest land." The sacred temple mentioned here is the Kaaba. The Farthest Temple is the makeshift altar set up by Jews under Sasanian rule on the hitherto long-abandoned temple mount in Jerusalem.[64]

Muhammad almost certainly saw the fall of Jerusalem in 614 as a sign of the end-times and a herald of his own prophetic advent. Later Jewish tradition held that the temple was constructed on the site of Mount Moriah, where Abraham had been spared from offering up his son, thus identifying it with the temple mount (Gen. 22:2). In 2 Chronicles 3:1 it says, "Solomon began to build the house of the Lord in Jerusalem on Mount Moriah." The early Believers appear to have seen the line between Mecca and Jerusalem as an Abrahamic world axis.

It has been suggested that the rest of the chapter of *The Night Journey* may be seen as a sermon exploring the significance of and commenting on the first verse.[65] It says (17:4), "We decreed for the children of Israel in the Bible that: 'You will commit abuses in the land twice, and will rise exceedingly high.'" This verse is referring to the history of how the Israelites built their temple twice, only to see it destroyed both times. The Bible describes how they constructed it the first time under Solomon but then scoffed at his prophets and angered God until he "brought against them the king of the Babylonians."[66]

The Qur'an (17:5) says in the voice of God addressing the Jews, "Then when the appointed time came with regard to the first of those two, we dispatched against you our servants, possessors of great might, and they penetrated into your edifices, and thus was the warning fulfilled." It is referring to the destruction of the first temple by the Babylonian ruler Nebuchadrezzar II in 586 BCE. The Jews rebuilt the temple under the Achaemenid Empire, when Cyrus the Great (d. 529 BCE) of Iran, having conquered Mesopotamia and the Near East, allowed them to return from their Babylonian exile to Palestine. For another period, the Qur'an says, they prospered and grew powerful. Then Judea came under direct Roman rule in 6 BCE. Through the first two-thirds of the first century, the Zealot movement mounted a series of revolts against Roman rule. *The Night Journey* (17:7) observes, "And when the second appointed time arrived we sent against you our servants to sadden your countenances and to enter the Temple as they entered it the first time, and to raze it to the ground once they ascended to it." This verse is recounting how the Romans burned the second temple in 70 CE in the wake of the Great Revolt.

Many Christian thinkers believed that the destruction of the second Jewish temple marked the permanent debasement of Jews, who had been supplanted as God's chosen people by the Christians. The Qur'an (17:8) disagrees: "It may be that your Lord will have mercy on you. If you return to your ways, we will return to ours. But we created Gehenna as a prison for pagans."[67] It may be implying that supporting or embracing the new prophet would lead to the eschatological restoration of the temple.

The Qur'an (17:4) says that the Bible contains a prophecy that the temple would be destroyed twice, coinciding with two moments of Jewish faithlessness. The most likely reference is to Daniel 9:25–26, which mentions the rebuilding of Jerusalem for "seven weeks," and then after sixty-two weeks "an anointed one shall be cut off and shall have nothing, and the troops of the prince who is to come shall destroy the city and the sanctuary." Like the Qur'an, Christians held that Daniel here prophesied Jesus's advent (the "anointed one") and the Roman repression of the Great Revolt of 66–70 CE, eventuating in the destruction of the second temple by "the troops of the prince" in 70 CE (they interpreted Daniel's "weeks" as years). John Chrysostom, for example, wrote that Daniel was predicting the razing of the temple under Pompey, Emperor Vespasian, and his son ("the prince") General Titus.[68]

A Jewish contemporary of Muhammad also imagined a third temple in his apocalyptic *Book of Elijah*.[69] This author said that the Sasanian invasion signaled the nearness of the Judgment Day, when a celestial Jerusalem would descend from heaven "wherein it had been built." Its houses, gates, and thresholds would be constructed of precious stones, and within its restored temple would be treasures, including the Pentateuch and "peace." I am not arguing for the influence of this Jewish apocalyptic work on the Qur'an, simply pointing to a shared vocabulary of thinking about history and the last days that is common across different cultural traditions.[70]

The difference between the Qur'an's understanding of sacred history and that of the Roman Christians can be seen vividly if we look at a contemporary account of the same themes. Theodoros Synkellos, a church official in Constantinople, delivered a homily in the capital during the 626 siege by the Avar tribes and their Iranian allies in which he depicted the capital as the New Jerusalem, Emperor Herakleios as superior to the ancient kings of Judah, and the protection proffered by Mary, Mother of God, as unparalleled. He offered an allegorical reading of Bible prophesies such as Ezekiel 38–39, concerning the future victory of the kingdom of Israel over the hosts of Gog as a promise to the Roman Christians that the Iranian hordes would be defeated. He asserts that any reasonable observer would agree that "the Jews live today entirely dispersed [*diaspora*] among all the peoples, and Israel, according to the flesh, does not possess its own territory." The verses, therefore, must be interpreted figuratively as referring to the New Jerusalem of Constantinople. It has been argued that Theodoros implies that the Jews have permanently been deprived of God's grace, as their scattered and stateless condition proved.[71] Unlike Theodoros and other theologians in Constantinople, the Qur'an (17:8) does not contrast Jews and Christians, instead affirming that God continues to proffer his forgiveness to the Jewish community.

After their string of victories in the wake of Constantine's conversion, Christians, having lost Jerusalem, now for the first time confronted the possibility that God was punishing them for their collective sin. One anonymous eastern Christian historian of the day, the "Khuzistan Chronicler," observed that God allowed the holy city to fall "to teach the Romans a lesson, for they pridefully believed that the Iranians could not take Jerusalem."[72] What the Qur'an says about the third chance God was willing to give the Jews if they returned to righteousness may have been intended to have implications for Christian Rome as well.

MUHAMMAD EDUCATED THE Believers to utter a prayer and blessing of peace on their persecutors, as he became more like a bishop with a congregation than like a solitary holy man. He asked them not to attempt to coerce anyone's faith, however fervent their preaching. Muhammad's social lenience toward paganism yet theological denunciation of it was not novel. Early Christians such as Tertullian had likewise argued that they could wish their fellow Roman citizens and the emperor and his armies well in this life, even while they viewed them as doomed to eternal torment for their idolatry.[73]

Muhammad's message of tolerance and peace building concerned not only the disputes in the Hejaz but also those in the wider region. He regretted the outbreak of fierce hostility between Jews and Christians in the wake of the 614 Iranian capture of Jerusalem, to the point where they assaulted each other's houses of worship and denied the validity of each other's faith. He urged instead ecumenism in light of their common biblical heritage and devotion to the one God. Muhammad recited verses from the Qur'an forbidding belligerence and imposing the duty to accept peace overtures from the enemy. When Ctesiphon twice rejected such overtures, he thundered that the Iranian aggression would fail. The Qur'an's implicit critique of Iranian imperialism and its vatic pronouncement on the restoration of sovereignty over the Near East for a righteous Abrahamic king falls into the genre of apocalypse. The opening verses of *Rome* describe the eventual success of a Christian monarch as a triumph for the God preached by Muhammad, revealing the Deity as universal rather than tribal or sectarian, as working in secular history. The eighth-century exegete Muqatil ibn Sulayman maintained that whereas Muhammad and the Believers were pro-Roman, their pagan foes exulted in the victories of Khosrow II. *Rome* 30:1–6 sees participation in a Christian-ruled polity as perfectly natural for Muslims, a conclusion that has enormous implications for the question of Islam and peace. As for whether the stridently orthodox Roman Empire could have accepted the offer, it should be remembered that it deployed German Arians and Arab Miaphysites and pagans as federate cavalry to protect its frontiers.

Later Muslim writers maintained that the Qur'an spoke of a parallel victory for the Muslims that would coincide with the triumph of Herakleios.[74] The verses, however, identify the predicted victory of the Christian emperor as the victory of God himself. The chapter of *Rome* might best be characterized as "civil millenarianism," an upset of the contemporary order that leads not to the rule of angels but to the incorporation of the Believers into the world's most powerful commonwealth. This willingness to become part of the Roman ecumene helps explain why the Qur'an, unlike the historical apocalypses of the previous religious traditions, has no political theology. Political peace would come with the restoration of the Pax Romana.

Later in the Meccan period, the Qur'an shows increasing pessimism about the possibility of the conversion of the pagans.[75] Abu Talib died in 619 or 620, and the militant Abu Lahab became the leader of the Hashim clan, a dangerous turn of events for Muhammad and the Believers. In the same year, Khadija died, and the biographers' reports of his suddenly straitened circumstances make it likely that Muhammad inherited only a small portion of her vast estate. As a result, in the following years, the condition of the small Meccan community of a few hundred mostly lower-class Believers, which he and Khadija had earlier protected from the effects of pagan opprobrium, worsened alarmingly.

§ 4 §

CITY OF THE PROPHET

ECCA, IMPUDENTLY RENOUNCING THE CONVENTIONS OF SANCTU-
ary, grew alien and menacing to Muhammad and his community in the early 620s. *The Spoils* 8:30 addresses him: "Recall when
the pagans were intriguing against you, to kidnap you, or murder you,
or to expel you; and they were plotting, and God was plotting; and
God is the best conspirator." The precarious condition in which the
Believers and their leader found themselves may have reflected in part
geopolitical developments. Khosrow II had by 619 taken the entire
Near East, including Egypt, from Herakleios, dramatically worsening

the strategic situation for Muhammad and his pro-Roman community. Iranian power flowed all around Mecca, save across the Red Sea in Ethiopia. If the Hejaz pagans allied with Iran, they may have been emboldened by this foreign support in their struggle against Muhammad and his Believers.

In the late spring of 622, later sources allege, a group of Medinans met furtively with Muhammad at Aqaba outside Mecca, pledging their fealty to him. They vowed that they would stick with Muhammad in good times and bad and "that we would not wrong anyone; that we would speak the truth at all times; and that in God's service we would fear the censure of none."[1] It probably cannot be called a conversion in the modern individual and psychological sense, but many among the Banu Khazraj back in Medina are said to have joined Muhammad's Believers after this pledge, under the influence of their clan chiefs. This movement may have been spearheaded by the Banu Najjar of the Khazraj tribe, Muhammad's relatives through his great-grandmother, who inducted him as a ceremonial official of their clan. Such crowd "conversions," however sincere, were not an informed choice of individual conscience. People often migrated en masse into a new religious identity in late antiquity, and we have stories of throngs of pagans collectively joining Christian churches because, for instance, a bishop managed to summon rain to end a drought.[2] Actually growing into the faith and internalizing its values took time thereafter.

The Khazraj who invited Muhammad had ties with the Banu Ghassan, who had been federates of Constantinople. It has been suggested that they may have been searching for pro-Roman allies in the darkest days of the Iranian occupation and just as Herakleios began his major 622 counterthrust in Asia Minor. They may have been especially desperate during this period of Sasanian triumph, when, it appears, even many Christian Arabs had defected to Iran, angered by

Chalcedonian intolerance of their Miaphysite creed and tempted by the relative tolerance of the Iranians. Pro-Sasanian Arab auxiliaries ("a battalion of long-haired Saracens") came up from Syria to attack the army of Herakleios in that year.[3]

Muhammad began encouraging his small Meccan community to slip away to Medina. Ibn Hisham says that when they found out about the migration, some Meccan pagans tried to stop Believers from leaving by kidnapping them and would especially insist that the women in the household stay.

According to a letter of `Urwa ibn al-Zubayr, after most of Muhammad's followers emigrated to Medina, Abu Bakr asked the Prophet for permission to leave with his associates.[4]

Muhammad replied, "Give me some time. I do not know, perhaps I will be permitted to depart."

Abu Bakr in the meantime prepared two steeds for a quick escape if the time came. `Urwa said Aisha told him that one day Muhammad came to the house of her father, Abu Bakr, at noon when she and her sister Asma' were there rather than—according to his habit—in the morning or evening. On that day in 622, Abu Bakr knew something was afoot.

The Prophet said, "God has given me permission to emigrate to Medina." Abu Bakr asked, "Messenger of God, in the company of someone?"

"Yes," the Prophet replied.

"Take one of the riding camels," Abu Bakr said.

The two went secretly to a place nearby called Thawr and hid in one of the area's inky caves overhung by jagged slabs of pink karst limestone. In the evenings a freedman of Abu Bakr, `Amer ibn Fuhayra, under the guise of shepherding, brought them simple provisions.

They hired a pagan, Abdullah ibn Arqad, as a guide over the back ways to Medina. Once again, the late Muslim sources say that the Messenger trusted and owed his life to a devotee of the old gods. Muhammad received reassurances and a gift of spiritual peace at this perilous moment.

Repentance 9:40 recalled these events: "The pagans drove him away, the second of two, when both were in the cave. He said to his companion, 'Do not sorrow; surely God is with us.' Then God sent down on him his Peace (*Sakina*), and confirmed him with invisible hosts; and he made the word of the unbelievers the most abject; and God's word is most exalted; God is Almighty, All-Wise."

The Arabic *Sakina* derives from the Hebrew "Shechinah," indicating God's presence in the world and the calm of the soul that it bestows. The term came into Arabic and English from rabbinic literature (it does not occur in the Bible).[5] Both in Hebrew and in Arabic its root has to do with "dwelling," though it also bears the connotation of stillness. In the Qur'an it connotes self-control and inner peace in the face of aggression and a commitment to establishing peace as the end state.

The Bible tells the story of how Solomon brought the Ark of the Covenant (the ornate gold-plated chest containing the tablets inscribed with the Ten Commandments) to the temple in Jerusalem. He had it deposited there before the city's masses, when the glory of the lord filled the temple. Later commentators identified this "glory" with the Shechinah (1 Kings 8).[6] After the Romans burned the second temple in 70 CE, the sage Rabbi Ishmael ben Elisha (90–135 CE) said, "Whithersoever Israel was exiled, the Shechinah, as it were, went into exile with them."[7] In deploying the Arabic equivalent, *Sakina*, in connection with the Emigration, the Qur'an may make an analogy between Muhammad's exile from Mecca to Medina and the diaspora of the children of Israel. Just as the Romans had barred the Jews from the temple mount in Jerusalem and forced some of them abroad, so

Abu Jahl and Abu Sufyan had banished Muhammad and the Believers from the shrine of the lord in Mecca.

One version of 'Urwa's narrative says that the irate Meccan leadership, not satisfied to have expelled the Prophet, placed a bounty of one hundred camels on Muhammad's head, turning him into a fugitive, wanted dead or alive.[8]

When the frenzy caused in Mecca by their disappearance had died down, Muhammad and Abu Bakr called their pagan camel driver, who brought their steeds.[9] They set off on the darkling path. Riding camels can travel about 80 miles a day, so this journey of 280 miles would have taken four days or so. They followed a circuitous nocturnal route like a salamander's tail down to the humid Red Sea coast and back up toward Medina to their northeast, guided by hilltop marker cairns silhouetted against the buck moon. They would have ridden uncertainly through the desert gloom, fed their dromedaries from the spiny leaves of hardy tamarisk trees, and avoided palm-hut villages where the barking of shepherd dogs might have alerted people to their passage. Their guide, Abdullah ibn Arqad, knew where the out-of-the-way wells lay, essential despite the brackishness of their stale water, and which ones were not infested with snakes. They would have tried to catch some sleep in the shade of serrated flint-stone outcroppings in the sizzling Hejaz mornings. All the while, they had to assume that Meccan search parties were close on their heels, attempting to discover and summarily execute them.

❧

REDDISH-BLACK LAVA HILLSIDES brooded over Medina, an emerald oasis of date orchards and farms dotted with tribal hamlets among which stood imposing tower houses and defensive redoubts. Muhammad, on arriving, stayed with supporters in Upper Medina, while he had his own mansion built, as well as a place of prayer, in the more central Lower Medina. The Prophet created a sanctuary in his adopted city, where hunting, cutting down trees, and carrying weapons were forbidden, suggesting that he intended to turn it into a site of sacred peace and, likely, of expanded trade. Later traditionists attributed to him the saying "Mecca was Abraham's sanctuary and Medina is mine."[10]

Later Muslims saw the Emigration (*hijra*) as a pivotal event in the history of Muhammad's religion and began their calendar with the year 622, so that subsequent dates are given according to the lunar year as After Hijra (AH). The earliest surviving document with such a date, a bilingual papyrus in Greek and Arabic, comes from AH 22. The idea of emigrating for the cause of God became central to the faith.[11]

A historian of the city wrote some two hundred years later,

> When the prophet, may the peace and blessings of God be upon him, came to Medina, it had a mixed population. Some were Muslims who had been gathered together by the Messenger's preaching, and some were polytheists who worshipped idols, and some were Jews, who possessed weaponry and fortresses. The latter were allies of the Aws and the Khazraj. The Messenger of God, on his arrival, wanted to reconcile them and make peace among them. At that time, one man might be a Muslim and his father or his brother a polytheist. When Muhammad came to Medina, the polytheists and Jews used to severely persecute him and his companions.[12]

Medina had had a turbulent political history. Later Arab legends say many of its Jews were expelled in the sixth century but that the minority who remained retained ownership and control of some important towers, blockhouses, and weapons stockpiles. In the middle of the 500s, the Christian ruler of Himyar in Yemen, Abraha, claimed in an inscription to have subjected Yathrib and much of Arabia, and another inscription suggests he made a follow-up foray around 567, in the Year of the Elephant, when Muhammad was born. Then in the 570s a wave of Sasanian rule and influence washed over Arabia, as Yemen fell to an Iranian admiral. The dominant Khazraj in Yathrib became indirect vassals of Sasanian Iran. By the early 600s, in turn, Iran's influence waned north of Yemen, leaving Medinans to make their own political arrangements.[13]

The Medinans had proved not to be very good at self-rule. In the first two decades of the seventh century, the two major tribes, the Aws and the Khazraj, pursued violent feuding in the city over scarce cultivable land and over springs and aquifers for irrigation. They fought several major urban battles with one another, including, around 617, "the Battle of Bu'ath." This conflict pitted the Aws and two small Jewish clans against the Khazraj (who were supported by a third Jewish group). The Khazraj had come out on top in previous such struggles, but this time they suffered defeat. This rout may have made some Khazraj more open to the message of Muhammad. In addition, they may have been primed to hear the message of Muhammad in part by their greater familiarity with biblical themes through local Jews and Christians and by the literacy of some of them in Aramaic or its eastern dialect, Syriac.[14]

In the new city, Muhammad sought harmony within his blossoming religious community. *The Cow* 2:208 instructs the Believers in this era, "You who have believed, enter into Peace all together. Do not follow in the footsteps of Satan, for he is an open enemy."[15]

The Qur'an later praised the partnership of Muhammad's followers among both displaced Meccans and local Medinans (the latter became known as "Helpers"): "The initial vanguard among the Emigrants and the Helpers, and those who followed them in doing good—God will be well-pleased with them and they are well-pleased with him. He has prepared for them gardens underneath which rivers flow, therein to dwell forever and ever; that is a magnificent victory" (*Repentance* 9:100).

Later writers maintained that Muhammad gained converts from among pagans and Jews in his new city. For instance, Ibn Hisham alleges that Rabbi Abdullah ibn Salam said,

> When I heard about the messenger I knew by his description, name, and the time at which he appeared that he was the one we were waiting for, and I rejoiced greatly, though I kept silent about it until the messenger came to Medina. When he stayed in Quba` among the Banu `Amr ibn Awf, a man came with the news while I was working at the top of a palm-tree.

He asserted that his aunt Khalida, sitting below, heard him crying out to God. She exclaimed, "Good gracious, if you had heard that Moses Ben Amram had come back you could not have made more fuss!"

"Indeed, my aunt," he said, "he is the brother of Moses and follows his religion, being sent with the same mission."[16]

These hagiographical stories of conversions have to be taken with a grain of salt. We know, however, that Jewish millenarian movements arose in this era, in Jerusalem and Balughta, and that some in that community saw Muhammad as the Messiah seems plausible. Subsequent Muslim biographers insisted that the Medinan Believers comprised many groups, including a Jewish convert faction, such as the wealthy and formidable Rabbi Mukhayriq, who distinguished themselves on the battlefield against belligerent Meccan pagans.[17]

❧

WHAT THE LATER Muslim historical tradition says of Medina makes it sound very much like a late fourth-century Roman city, as though it were twenty decades behind the times. Its pagans maintained a Tycheion (temple to the goddess of fate), its Jews served as prominent civic leaders, and its Christians were in the minority. Likely many non-Jews joined in the fall commemorations of the High Holy Days, including the Jewish New Year and the Day of Atonement, marked by the blowing of the ram's horn (or shofar), extra recitations of the Psalms, and fasting. Some Medinan Christians and Jews, according to the Qur'an, also joined in pagan festivals and worship: "Have you not seen those given a portion of the scripture believing in Jibt and Taghut, who say to the pagans that they are better guided to the path than the believers?" (*The Women* 4:51).[18]

The Qur'an's description of Medinan society, which originates in the 620s, differs significantly from that of the Prophet's later biographers who lived in the era of the Abbasid Caliphate (750–1258). The scripture speaks of six communities there—Jews, Christians, pagans, those called Sabians, the Believers, and the Hypocrites, or inconstant followers of Muhammad. The Prophet did not become the ruler of Medina but rather functioned as a holy man or senator among the diverse clan chiefs who ruled by consensus, aiming to mediate conflicts both inside his own community and outside. Since Christians bulk so large in the Medinan chapters, and are depicted as engaging in polemics with Jews, the Qur'an is telling us of a Christian neighborhood in the city. We now know there were also Hejazi Christian monasteries far north of Medina.[19] The later biographers, living in societies where Muslim rulers heavily depended on Christian allies, largely erased these Medinan Christians, so clearly limned by the Qur'an, from history, possibly because Medinan Christians were not always favorable to the Messenger. (Miaphysite Arab tribes, no less than Jewish burghers, often declared for Sasanian Iran in this era.) Muhammad, in addition, perhaps led some caravans up to Bostra or Damascus in the early 620s, so that some of these debates occurred at his summer mansion there.

Theologians have identified the possible stances on the salvation of members of other traditions as exclusivism, inclusivism, and pluralism.[20] Exclusivists hold that only members of their own religion are saved. Inclusivists say that their tradition has the whole truth, but others may have a portion of it. Pluralism is the position that various faiths offer equally valid paths to paradise. The declining population of pagans of late antiquity sometimes espoused this latter view, arguing (with no success) to Christians that no one spiritual path could hope to encompass God, given his ineffability.[21] Muhammad taught a form of salvific pluralism that included all the monotheist traditions but excluded the hostile North Arabian pagans, and he deployed this ecumenism in a bid to unite much of the city behind him. Ecumenism does not imply a surrender on matters of doctrine but rather implies a willingness to dialogue and coexist. Indeed, on matters of doctrine the Qur'an takes instead an inclusivist position, that it has the full truth but that members of the previous rites had forgotten or distorted some of what had been revealed to them.

Later authors wrote that not everyone in Medina, still a diverse city, rushed to embrace Muhammad's new faith: "Now some of the shaykhs still kept to their old paganism, among whom was `Amr ibn al-Jamuh.... `Amr was one of the tribal nobles and leaders and had set up in his house a wooden idol called Manat as the nobles used to do, reverencing it as a god and keeping it clean."[22]

`Amr was not alone. Nabtal al-Harith, "a sturdy black man with long flowing hair, inflamed eyes and ruddy black cheeks...used to come and talk to the prophet and listen to him and then carry what he had said to the Hypocrites." He observed, "Muhammad will listen to anyone, and gullibly falls for their stories."[23]

Muhammad yielded nothing to the polytheists theologically, even as he sought cordial social relations with them. *The Family of Amram*

3:85 remonstrates with them, "Whoever follows a religion other than the monotheistic tradition (*islam*), it shall not be accepted, and that one will be among the losers in the hereafter" (again, in the Qur'an *islam* denotes general monotheism of the Abrahamic sort, not the specific religion of Muhammad). Nevertheless, the Prophet showed willingness to seek political arrangements with friendly traditionalists.

Some of the Khazraj tribe also remained pagans, worshipping local cult gods, and for others their "conversion" was superficial or they came to regret it. Abdullah ibn Ubayy led a faction of Khazraj in Medina. A local notable, he had been on the verge of being recognized as the leader of his tribe when the rest of the city made its arrangement with Muhammad, forestalling his ambitions and creating some hard feelings.[24] He is alleged to have led a faction of lukewarm Believers known as Hypocrites, who felt it was legitimate to have differences of opinion with Muhammad.

The Prophet also faced difficulties from another group. The clans that had been known earlier in Medinan history as Aws Manat did not convert until 627, five years later. A medieval historian wrote of Abu Qays ibn al-Aslat, a poet and leader of this section of the Aws, "He did not accept Islam until after the Battle of the Trench. Likewise delayed in their belief were the Khatma clan of Banu Jusham ibn Malik bin Aws, and the assemblage of the Waqif clan... and the Aws Allah, drawn from those clans, from the children of Murra ibn Malik ibn al-Aws."[25]

Before Muhammad's Emigration, the Aws Manat clans changed their name and became known as Aws Allah, trading the goddess of fate for the All-High God. The sources say Abu Qays ibn al-Aslat had investigated Judaism but declined to adopt it. Then he spent some time in Damascus and discussed Christianity with monks, but did not embrace it. He returned and declared himself an Abrahamian, declining to worship any deity but God or to eat any flesh that had been sacrificed to other gods. He purportedly acted as a peacemaker after the Battle of Buʿath between Aws and Khazraj. Later authors blame him for the refusal of Aws Allah to join Muhammad's movement. Another Aws Allah figure, Abu ʿAmer of the clan of Dubayʿa, had also been an important leader in Medina before the Prophet's advent. A Hanif, or pagan monotheist, he experimented briefly with asceticism, which may explain his sobriquet, "the Monk." Some say he came into conflict with Muhammad soon after the Emigration of 622 concerning Gentile monotheism and the legacy of Abraham, accusing him of not practicing it correctly.[26]

Abu ʿAmer the Monk is said to have come to Muhammad to inquire about his beliefs.

Muhammad replied, "The Hanifiya, the religion of Abraham."

Abu ʿAmer said, "That is what I follow."

"You do not."

"But I do! You, Muhammad, have introduced into the Hanifiya things that do not belong to it."

"I have not. I have brought it pure and white."

Abu ʿAmer exploded, "May God let the liar die a lonely, homeless, fugitive!"

"Well and good. May God so reward him."

We can conclude that some Aws had moved toward a form of pagan monotheism since tradition remembered that both of the Hanif figures in Medina hailed from Aws and that one of them led the clans making up Aws Allah. Both leaders allegedly spent time in Damascus, where a Godfearer cult may have survived and attracted Arab converts. In the Medina period of the 620s, the Qur'an abruptly begins speaking of a major monotheistic religious group, the Sabians. The later Muslim chroniclers forgot who they were. Some scholars, however, have recently derived *Sabian* from the Greek root for

Godfearers, that is, pagan monotheists.[27] If the Aws had already conducted a monotheistic reform of their cult, Muhammad's new faith
might have been less appealing to them. Since Godfearers typically
were influenced by the Bible, and they may have had a lectionary
from Damascus of Greek and Aramaic hymns, the Qur'an possibly
includes them when it speaks of "the scriptural communities," or,
literally, "the people of the Book." There is evidence that associates
of Abu `Amer the Monk who were less hotheaded than he and who
remained in Medina established a Sabian temple in the city, which
the Qur'an later denounced for its hostility to the Prophet and urged
the Believers to avoid.[28]

Abu `Amer and some of his Aws clansmen fell out so vehemently
with Muhammad that at some point, the biographers say, they engaged
in a reverse Emigration. This band headed off to Mecca, where they
allied with the Quraysh pagans against him and, ominously, prepared
to launch an invasion of Medina.

*

IN THE EARLY 620s, Muhammad engaged in treaty negotiations with
clan heads to forge a social contract among the Quraysh Emigrants,
eight clans of the Helpers, Jewish clients of the latter, and what was
likely a Christian tribe. The talks resulted in a renowned document,
the "Constitution of Medina," the surviving text of which scholars
widely view as authentic.[29]

Both full Believers and mere submitters are parties to the Constitution. All the signatories would stand together, Muhammad hoped,
against the onslaughts of the militant Quraysh: "The contracting parties undertake to help one another against any attack on Yathrib."
The text prohibits polytheist signatories from friendly relations with
the traditionalists in Mecca.[30] Some members of the contracting clans

were therefore still pagans, while others may have been Christians, so that this Constitution involved at least some members of all the major groups in the city, save the Aws Allah. Any internal controversy that arose had to be referred for resolution to Muhammad, the arbiter of disputes.

The Constitution provided for a kind of clan federalism in the city of Medina. It made the Khazraj and Aws responsible for paying blood money at the clan level when a member committed a tort. The Quraysh Emigrants remained liable for paying the wergild if one of their number injured or killed someone, as well as for ransoming any who were taken captive. This clause suggests that the Medinans did not want to become responsible for the ransom when the militant Meccans kidnapped Emigrants, as they strove to do. The document also forbids Quraysh Emigrants from siding with an outside clan against other Believers.

The Jewish signatories would not be wronged, would be treated with equality, and would be given help. The Believers would not ally with their enemies. Jews who fought alongside the Believers were to contribute to defraying the cost of war. The Jews allied with the Khazraj and Aws clans, and any clients of these Jews "are one nation with the Believers (the Jews have their religion and the Believers have theirs)." This phrase demonstrates that Muhammad was continuing with his project of an ecumenical Believers movement, in which other monotheists could retain their own rituals, beliefs, and practices. These provisions "granted the named Jewish clans protection of the law and religious tolerance."[31] Jewish parties to the compact pledged, "Each must help the other against anyone who makes war on the people of this document."

Later histories say many Jews retained their own faith, as the Constitution allowed. Ibn Hisham reports that Abu Saluba al-Fityuni said to him, "Muhammad, you have not brought us anything we recognize, and God has not sent down to you any sign that we should follow you."

Zayd ibn al-Lusayt, from the Jewish Qaynuqa' clan, observed when the Prophet's steed wandered off at one point, "Muhammad alleges that revelations come to him from heaven, but he doesn't know where his camel is!"

Muhammad replied, "I only know what God lets me know."[32]

Muhammad's Constitution appears to recognize at least one Christian group as a signatory, the Jafna clan of Banu Tha'laba. The Tha'laba also had Jewish members who signed on to this treaty. Up until the rupture of the 580s, the Jafnids had provided the phylarch of the Christian Arabs for the Romans in central and eastern Syria.[33]

The treaty proclaimed that these diverse groups had become one nation by virtue of their defensive alliance with Muhammad against militant Mecca. In late antiquity, words for *nation* and *ethnicity* were also commonly applied to religious groupings, including to Christians, who were sometimes called a "third race" between pagans and Jews. Muhammad was building two nations, a narrow one comprising full-fledged Believers and "submitters" and a broad, ecumenical one that grouped the latter with friendly allies from among the other monotheists. Muhammad likely conceived of the second as a nation of Abrahamians. Like Paul, the Qur'an views Abraham as a universal forebear and not the patriarch of Judaism alone (in Galatians 3:17 Paul observed that Abraham lived 430 years before Moses brought down the law; see also Rom. 4:9–11).[34]

The Qur'an (*The Table* 5:5) underlined their common Abrahamic ethnicity by allowing Believers to intermarry with Jews and Christians and to share meals with them. Modern sociologists often demarcate ethnic groups on the basis that they practice endogamy, preferring to marry other members of the same group. In contrast, Christian Roman law forbade Jews from marrying Christians on pain of death, and Christian authorities criticized eating Jewish food as "shameful and sacrilegious." (Most rabbis were not enthusiastic about such social and marital mixing, either.) Christian law helped create the endogamous Christian "race" or "nation," whereas the law of the Qur'an creates a rainbow race of Abrahamians.[35]

The Constitution of Medina differs entirely from the norms of the seventh-century Christian Roman Empire. It offers a vision of a nondoctrinal, religiously multicultural society ("nation") based on social loyalty, granting of security, and tribal mechanisms for settling torts. It established obligations of nonbelligerence in the city of the Prophet. These policies clearly aimed at finding a basis for solidarity in the face of a building Meccan assault.

❧

EVEN AS MUHAMMAD was cobbling together a legal framework for multicultural politics in Medina, he had the continuing task of keeping his own growing community together. The Qur'an speaks of social tensions among the Believers in Medina. The tradition remembered one of these conflicts as being between Khazraj and Aws converts, or Helpers, who had pursued over decades a long-standing tribal feud. The Aws purportedly refused to worship behind a Khazraj prayer leader and vice versa, so an Emigrant took up that duty.[36]

Ibn Hisham tells an anecdote about the fervent pagan Shas ibn Qays, who worried that Muhammad's growing community would place him and his ilk at a disadvantage in Medina.[37] The biographer invites us to imagine the scene. Shas mischievously sent emissaries to a gathering of Believers that included Aws and Khazraj, with instructions to recite the poetry of Bu'ath battle days.

"Thereupon the people began to talk and to quarrel and to boast until two men of the two clans leapt up."

Aws ibn Qays and Jabbar ibn Sakhr, noses flaring, "began to taunt one another until one of them said, 'If you want a fight, we can go again!'"

At that point, the men of the other tribe replied, "'We will! Look for us outside'—that being the volcanic tract." In their febrile agitation, they prepared to brawl.

Word reached Muhammad of the impending fracas, and he rushed urgently to the billowing guesthouse pavilion beside the basalt lava bed where they had gathered. Standing before the scowling tribesmen, face gray as lead, the Prophet delivered an impassioned homily calling for unity. Perhaps it resembled a passage in *The Family of Amram* (3:103), which instructs the Believers, "Hold fast, all of you, to the cord of God, and do not divide into factions. Remember God's favor to you, inasmuch as you were enemies, but he united your hearts—so that by his blessing you became siblings. You were on the brink of a pit of fire, and he delivered you from it. In this way does God make clear his signs to you, so that you might be guided." Brought up short by what he said, they wept, "and the men of the Aws and Khazraj embraced one another."

Regardless of this story's veracity, the Qur'an certainly indicates that the Medinan community suffered fissures that the Prophet strove to repair. Later Muslims made the phrase "united your hearts" a cornerstone of their political theology.

As their composition became more diverse, maintaining the unity of the Believers became more difficult, and Muhammad was increasingly preoccupied with this task. The Qur'an warns the Believers against falling into sectarianism in the way that Jews and Christians had: "Do not be like those who divided into sects and disputed, after clear verses came to them, for severe torment awaits them."[38] It appears that at one point, some Believers strayed but then wanted to make amends and to pray with Muhammad's congregants in good standing. *The Cattle* 6:52 says of them, "Do not drive out those who call on their lord morning and evening, seeking his countenance. It is not for you to bring them to account, nor can they bring you to account. Were you to expel them, you would be acting unjustly." Remarkably, the Qur'an forbids the Messenger from excommunicating them or even from judging them as long as they prove repentant and mend their ways. *The Cattle* 6:54 instructed Muhammad with regard to these contrite Believers, "When those who believe in our verses come to you, say 'Peace be upon you.' God has prescribed for himself compassion. Whoever among you commits a sin out of ignorance, and then repents and makes restitution—God is forgiving, merciful."

Precisely because so many in Medina had joined the new movement by acclamation, there were many levels of knowledge about and commitment to the faith among its adherents. To speak of the "Believers" (or, more anachronistically, "Muslims") in a monolithic way would go against everything we know about late antiquity.[39] *The Chambers* 49:14 distinguishes between full Believers and those, still in the apprentice stage, who have merely "submitted" or become monotheists (*muslims*). The latter, lacking intimate knowledge of the Prophet and the Qur'an, are analogous to the catechumens of Christianity awaiting baptism while they study its teachings, and it appears that bedouin followers in particular fell into this category.

Moreover, levels of commitment differed from person to person. One of the wages of the mixing of spirituality with political power is hypocrisy, which emerged as a problem in Medina just as it had in newly Christian-ruled Rome under Constantine three centuries before. The first Christian emperor's panegyrist, Eusebius, had complained of "the scandalous hypocrisy of those who crept into the church, and assumed the name and character of Christians" once it became lucrative to do so.[40] The Qur'an (*The Women* 4:142) likewise complained of some in Medina: "The hypocrites would deceive God, but he is the one who deceives them. They perform the prayer lazily, just to show off before the people. In truth they seldom remember God."

The existence within the community of an unreliable faction at a time when Mecca was preparing open warfare profoundly endangered the Prophet's mission. In October 623, a Meccan brave named Kurz ibn Jabr al-Fihri is alleged to have come up to the pastures around Medina with his men. At dawn they would have drunk off their morning draft of frothy wine, summoning their battle lust. They rode their chargers, fierce as leopards, down on Medina's unsuspecting flocks, rustling them. Muhammad and his men mounted up and pursued them to the vicinity of the wells of Badr, which lay between Medina and Mecca. Kurz and his cheeky band, however, eluded them. The Believers' need for unity in the face of Meccan enmity remained urgent.[41]

The Qur'an suggests that the Meccan pagans, in addition to raiding Medina's herds, ranged up toward the city in hopes of coming across individuals or small bands of the Believers whom they could kidnap and return to Mecca, forcing them back into paganism. In August 623, after he had been in Medina for about a year, Muhammad, his future son-in-law Ali, and some of the Emigrants went out of the city along an uneven hill path known to the Prophet's relatives, the Banu al-Najjar of the Khazraj tribe. They would have made their way through granite ridges down into glassy ebony ravines lined with dark volcanic sand and then descended into the sere fawn Khabar desert. They made camp beneath a lonely acacia tree, propping their cooking pots up on a circle of rocks, and brought water from the nearby Mushayrab spring. They prayed at dawn, still turning toward Iranian-occupied Jerusalem, though soon they would be instructed to pray instead toward Mecca, as Muhammad's religion declared its independence. At length they reached a place called al-'Abwa. There, Muhammad came across the pagan tribe Banu Damra ibn Bakr and succeeded in making a peace treaty with them. The Believers returned to Medina, having avoided any violence with the surrounding pastoralists.[42] Later Muslim historians insisted on calling these exploratory journeys of the Prophet into the Medinan hinterland raids, but the first six they mention never involved fighting and seem instead to have been a search for rural allies.

The Qur'an confirms that pagan tribes concluded political agreements with Muhammad. Some of them, it complained, later broke that treaty and went over to Mecca politically: "The vilest of creatures in the sight of God are the pagans who do not believe, those with whom you made a compact, and who then on every occasion broke that covenant, and who are not god-fearing" (The Spoils 8:55–56).[43] Here, this group achieves the distinction of the worst among creatures not because they embraced paganism but because they committed treason, reneging on the alliance.

During this same expedition, the Prophet is said to have dispatched another emigrant Believer, one 'Ubayda ibn al-Harith, with a few dozen men to a watering hole known as Ahya'. There they came upon a band of the Quraysh led by a son of the militant pagan and city notable Abu Jahl of Banu Makhzum, though they avoided a fight. Two Believers who were with the pagans managed to escape and come over to 'Ubayda. The medieval historian Tabari says that these two had been sent by the Prophet to Mecca in an attempt to effect a reconciliation with its pagans, but they had been detained and now escaped to the side of the Believers.

The community faced the constant problem of how to deal with Believers who had been abducted and then eluded their pagan captors. *The Bee* 16:110 instructs forgiveness, assuming the lapsed individuals make personal sacrifices and come to Medina: "Your lord—for those who emigrated after having been coerced out of their religion, and then struggled and were patient, your lord in truth is, after all that, forgiving and compassionate."

~

IF THE CONSTITUTION of Medina embodied Muhammad's political charter for peace and unity, the notion of the community of the saved, which encompasses upright members of all the monotheistic traditions, expressed his theological framework for municipal concord. Just as the Qur'an presents the next world as a society of peace and as a model for life on earth, likewise, in the Medina era, the Qur'an pledged joint entry into heaven to those communities—Believers, Jews, Christians, and pagan monotheists—which served to knit them together politically. The Qur'an sees religious diversity as permitted by God's will: "If your lord had desired, he would have made the people one nation; but they continue to differ" (*Hud* 11:118).[44]

The Qur'an says that followers of the monotheistic religions all fall into the category of the potentially saved. *The Cow* 2:62 proclaims,

> Those who believed, and the Jews, and the Christians, and the Sabians, and whoever has believed in God and the Last Day and performed good works, they shall have their reward with their Lord.

These verses are clearly talking about Jews, Christians, and Sabians who remained in their faiths and did not convert, as some early Muslim

exegetes recognized. The followers of Muhammad are mentioned separately as "those who believed." The requirements for salvation that it
specifies—including acceptance of the resurrection of the dead and
the Judgment Day, were the same basic doctrines that Emperor Justinian had laid out as an obligation upon the Jews of the Roman Empire.[45]

The Qur'an could speak of various true spiritual traditions in part
because Arabic had borrowed from Persian a term for "a religion,"
which could be used to refer to one valid faith among others. Greek-
speaking Christians in that era did have ways of talking about the
religions, but these terms were either vague (*piety* or *worship*) or invid-
ious (*heresy* and *impiety*). By referring to a set of equally valid spiritual
paths with this term, the Qur'an was one of the first texts explicitly to
imagine the category of multiple peer "world religions."[46]

The tradition remembered Muhammad treating equitably groups
such as Christians who declined to convert. Ibn Hisham speaks of
Arab Christians who came to Muhammad sometime in the 620s and
engaged him in debate.[47] We can imagine dozens of these followers
of Christ, bedizened in fine caftans after the way of Banu al-Harith
of the Kalb tribe, coming in a procession to the Messenger's mosque
as he prayed the afternoon prayer, the silver crosses about their necks
coruscating in the fiery sun. They would have entered the sturdy coral
stone building and been shown to the cool interior courtyard that
sheltered worshippers from Arabia's searing gales.

`Abd al-Masih, a deacon, and al-Ayham, a priest, sat and discussed
religion with Muhammad. Ibn Hisham wrote,

> When the two divines spoke to him the apostle said to them,
>   "Submit yourselves."
> They said, "We have submitted."
> He rejected this assertion, saying that they maintained that
>   God has a son.

They said, "But who is his father, Muhammad?"

The messenger was silent and did not answer them.

The priests put the Prophet in a difficult situation with their clever question. The Qur'an denies the fatherhood of God but affirms the virgin birth of Jesus. They are reported to have played on this potential contradiction. The answer, of course, is that the Qur'an views God not as anyone's father but as everyone's creator, including Jesus. He says, "Be!" and it is (Qur'an 3:47).

The Christians consulted among one another. Did they argue and gesticulate as they sat on the mosque's soft imported carpets, jerking the loose sleeves of their umber robes? In the end, they decided to reject Muhammad's claim to prophethood.

He allegedly offered to resolve the conflict by engaging in a ceremony of mutual imprecations, where the two parties sit and ask God to strike down the false one.[48]

The deacon, `Abd al-Masih, cautioned the Christians against this proceeding, with Ibn Hisham implying he feared they would lose the contest. He addressed his flock, "But if you decide to adhere to your religion and maintain your doctrine about your master, then take your leave of the man and go home."

The Spider 29:46 says, "Debate the scriptural communities only in the best of ways, except for those who do wrong. Say 'We believe in the revelation sent down to us, and the revelation sent down to you; our God and your God is one, and to him we have submitted.'" The verse suggests that Muhammad often engaged in polite exchanges with members of other communities.

The Qur'an views a rejection of the new message as regrettable but continues to insist on Christians' eligibility for salvation. The scripture depicts God as promising Jesus about future Christians in *The Family of Amram* 3:55: "I...will render those who follow you superior to the pagans until the Judgment Day." There will always be, the Qur'an vowed, a difference between followers of Jesus and the damned.

The early seventh century was not known for religious tolerance. Most religious groups held that outsiders were doomed to hell. Zoroastrians, for instance, called their rite the Good Religion and referred to followers of other traditions as people of "bad religion." A late Sasanian text tells the story of the Zoroastrian seeker Danag. He asks, bewildered, "Since it is known that the Divine Religion is true...why are there so many doctrines, beliefs and cosmic principles among the people?"[49]

As for Christianity, one seventh-century Roman text aimed at converting Jews warns that on Jesus's Second Coming, those who had declined to believe in him will be delivered into eternal condemnation. From the third century, influential Christian theologians such as Origen had begun putting forward the exclusivist precept that "outside the Church there is no salvation," and Christians widely adopted it.[50] Some Christians did advocate forms of inclusivism, holding that they had the whole truth but that others might have possessed part of it. The early Christian thinker Justin Martyr took a somewhat inclusivist position in replying to pagans who berated Christians as cruel for condemning to hell all human beings born before Jesus of Nazareth. Justin Martyr wrote that Christ is the Word or Logos, the principle of universal reason, "of whom every race of men were partakers; and those who lived reasonably are Christians." They included ancient Greek philosophers such as Socrates as well as the patriarch Abraham. When Jesus was sent, he held, those who rejected him could no longer be saved by the general principle of universal reason.[51]

The exclusivist doctrines of salvation asserted by the Jews and Christians he knew distressed Muhammad. *The Cow* (2:111–112) says, "They maintain that no one will enter heaven but Jews or Christians. Such are their vain notions. Say: produce your proof, if you speak truly.

Rather, all those who submit to God and do good works will receive their recompense with their Lord, and no fear will be upon them, nor will they sorrow." It denounces exclusivism as a "vain notion" and makes universal criteria such as acceptance of the one God and good deeds the grounds for deliverance.

Later in *The Cow* (2:135), the Qur'an complains, "They say: 'Become Jews and Christians and be guided.' No, the philosophy of Abraham, the pious gentile. He was no polytheist." Muhammad insisted on a pluralism centered on Abraham. The Qur'an, like the Epistle of James in the New Testament, sees salvation as dependent on both faith and works and, like James, sees Abraham as the paragon of both (James 2:14–26).[52]

The scripture (*The Cow* 2:138) goes on to compare following this philosophy of Abraham with being dyed by God in divine colors: "Take on the dye of God, and what dye is better than that of God?" This metaphor also occurs in Greek philosophy. Plato in *The Republic* compares the training of youth in virtues to dying wool with fast colors.[53]

Justin Martyr held that living in accordance with the preexistent Word of Jesus saved ancient Greek philosophers and patriarchs such as Abraham. The Jewish thinker Philo of Alexandria (d. ca. 50 CE), however, portrayed Abraham as bearing such a Word or reasoned discourse, bestowed by God, inasmuch as he exemplified piety and monotheism, the two paramount virtues.[54] The Qur'an concurs and goes on to say that living in accord with the monotheistic philosophy of Abraham suffices for salvation. It has been pointed out that Abraham is here a universal figure, not only the founder of the Kaaba, and his philosophy or Word is an interpretive process, not a finished product. Another scholar observes that the "philosophy of Abraham" is in the singular, showing that the Qur'an views it as one encompassing tradition. Judaism, Christianity, and the faith of Muhammad (and any other monotheistic belief) are all Platonic forms of this transcendent Word. Unlike the Gospel of John (8:31–59) and Christian writers such as Justin Martyr, the Qur'an includes Jews in Abrahamic universalism rather than using it to exclude them.[55]

Muhammad taught that each faith community takes on two covenantal obligations. One relates to its own messenger. The Qur'an sees faithfulness to that specific dispensation as sufficient for salvation. *The Table* 5:44 depicts God as saying, "We, in truth, revealed the Torah, in which is guidance and light." It is important that the Qur'an uses the present tense. The Hebrew Bible, the work of the same God as spoke to Muhammad, still contains guidance and light. The Qur'an laments, as does the Bible, that some Jews were not always faithful to the Mosaic commandments, as when they turned to worshipping the golden calf or when they grew weary of eating manna as they wandered in the wilderness and violated the Sabbath to bring home other food.[56] The exemplary character of the chosen people was not, however, lost as a result of these momentary lapses. *The Heights* 7:159 insists, "Among the people of Moses is a nation that guides others by the truth and establishes justice."

Then *The Table* 5:46 talks of the dispensation after the Jews: "And we sent, following in their footsteps, Jesus the son of Mary, in confirmation of what was in the Torah, and we bestowed upon him the Gospel, in which is guidance and light, in verification of the Torah and as direction and admonition for the God-fearing."

In addition to the specific historical covenant of each religious community, *The Family of Amram* 3:81 describes a moment when preexistent souls concluded a general pact with the divine. In the Hebrew Bible, scholars have pointed out, the covenant is made in historical time and binds descendants of the patriarchs. New Testament authors viewed the covenant as universal, contracted with all humankind. The Qur'an describes God as calling all future humans together and asking them if they would accept each new messenger that God sent. These unborn generations agreed, saying, "We affirm it."[57]

To renege on the universal pledge made before time to recognize all new messengers as they arrive is a moral shortcoming (3:82). This doctrine of the Covenant of the Prophets is not pluralist but inclusivist. When Jews declined to accept Jesus or Christians refused to acknowledge Muhammad, they contravened this commitment. The scripture implies that while this violation puts them in the wrong, and even involves a minor form of paganizing, it is not a mortal sin of the sort that might exclude them from salvation, assuming they live a righteous life in the framework of their own tradition.

The Family of Amram 3:113 declares that each of the religions contains persons of higher and lower ethical values. It says, "They are not all the same: Some among the scriptural communities are an upstanding nation, who recite God's verses in the watches of the night while bowing in prayer." These Jews and Christians demonstrate their goodness not only by extra nighttime prayers but also by charity toward others and by believing in God and the Resurrection Day. The passage concludes (3:115), "Whatever philanthropy they do, God will not blot it out."[58] It has been shown that the earliest known author of a commentary on the Qur'an, Mujahid ibn Jabr (642–722), explains that the meaning of the "upstanding community" here is any "just" community, by which he clearly meant to indicate that the Qur'an is speaking in general terms rather than specifying Muhammad's Believers.[59]

The Family of Amram 3:64 calls for unity among the Hejazi monotheists: "Say: 'People of the Book, come to a common Word between you and us, that we will only worship God and not associate anything with him, and that we will not take some of us as lords for others apart from God.' If they turn away, say: 'Bear witness that we are monotheists.'" The later commentator Tabari interpreted the passage as advocating a tolerant universalism, reading the last phrase as saying that if Jews and Christians did not wish to embrace Muhammad's new religion, it was enough for them to acknowledge that the Believers were monotheists.[60]

The Qur'an's broad vision of salvation was not unprecedented in late antiquity, though few groups went as far as it did. The rabbis who authored the Babylonian Talmud adopted the inclusivist position that non-Jews can have a portion in paradise if they abide by the 7 laws of Noah intended for all humankind, while Jews have an obligation of adhering to 613 laws or good deeds.[61]

This Jewish stance of salvational inclusivism overlaps with but differs in some details from the Qur'anic doctrine. Both forbid adultery, murder, theft, and consuming blood. The Qur'an insists on a positive belief in the one God and in the Resurrection Day as basic requirements even for other religious communities. Still, Muhammad's moral laws are more complex than the seven Noahide laws. It has been argued that there are passages of the Qur'an where something close to the Ten Commandments given to Moses are required of the Believers.[62]

THE EPIC EMIGRATION, despite the severe dangers attending it, is identified with the peace (*Sakina*) that derives from the calming presence of God. On establishing the Medinan community of Believers, the Qur'an (2:208) instructs them, "You who have believed, enter into Peace all together." In transforming Medina into a sanctuary city, Muhammad was creating a penumbra of tranquility there, mirroring the one that had governed Mecca and attempting to forestall any further civil wars such as the Battle of Bu'ath.

The Qur'an (3:103) says that Muhammad adopted the role in Medina of peace builder, "uniting the hearts" of former foes among the feuding clans of that city. The Qur'an embraces pluralism on the level of salvation but inclusivism at the level of theology. It allows that members of other faith communities can reach heaven. At the same time, it sees the older religions as somewhat corrupted by ideas and practices introduced over time that departed from the pure, exemplary faith of Abraham, and it does not hesitate to reproach them for these lapses. Still, God will forgive everything but outright polytheism.

Religions have to be looked at both with regard to their insistence on right doctrine and with regard to the breadth of their notion of salvation.[63] Each dimension can be categorized as pluralist, inclusivist, or exclusivist. Roman Christianity of this period was exclusivist in both columns, insisting on the Chalcedonian Creed as the only true doctrine and on members of the church as the only group saved from damnation. In contrast, the Qur'an is inclusivist with regard to doctrine (it maintains that its monotheistic canons are superior to those of contemporary Jews and Christians, who nevertheless have a large portion of the truth) and pluralist with regard to salvation (it asserts that monotheists will enter the Garden after death regardless of lapses of dogma).

In its version of pluralism, the Qur'an makes the Logos of Abraham do the work done for broad-minded rabbis by the seven laws of Noah. The Qur'an implies that members of other faiths might be granted a doctrinally less strict path to redemption, dependent on divine mercy, than is required of Muhammad's Believers. Neither the Talmudic scholars who upheld the Noahide theory of salvation for Gentiles nor the Qur'an approved of Christian Trinitarianism, but neither one gave any signs of excluding Christians from having "a portion" of heaven.[64]

The Qur'an sought to play down creedal formulas in favor of a political community of vaguely defined monotheists who could confront external attacks together. Attaining a state of ecumenical harmony inside the city would prove a nearly insuperable task. But the even more portentous challenge would come from the militant pagans of Mecca, who were plotting to conquer Medina, to extinguish the threat they saw in Muhammad and his embryonic faith, and perhaps to align the Hejaz unanimously with the ambitions of the Iranian king of kings.

§ 5 §

JUST WAR

IN LATE DECEMBER 623, MUHAMMAD IS SAID BY THE EARLY MUSLIM Muhammad al-San`ani to have dispatched a band of men with Abdullah ibn Jahsh, with the mission of keeping an eye on Quraysh movements. The pagans were combing the areas around Medina for vulnerable Believers in order to kidnap them or watching for unattended flocks to rustle, and it was clearly advisable to monitor them. The Prophet gave him a letter, but instructed him not to read it until he reached a certain place. They would have set out at the incarnadine dusk through the parched copper Hejaz countryside, hugged by sedges and by outcroppings from which spiny-tailed lizards and the occasional sand cat eyed them warily.

When they halted at the designated site, perhaps a well where they could water their camels, Abdullah discovered that the instruction was, "Do not force any of your friends to go with you."

He murmured, "I hear and obey," and gathered his companions to tell them the contents of the missive. Two men returned, but the others continued.

As they proceeded, the scouting party espied a Meccan band led by one `Amr ibn al-Hadrami, and somehow he discovered them. A fight broke out, and later authors assert that al-Hadrami ended up being killed. The Believers had lost track of time and had not known whether that day was the last day of Jumada II or the first day of Rajab (a sacred month for the Arabs). If the latter, it was January 1, 624. Presumably, a Rajab date would have required them to avoid the Meccan party entirely or to fade away on discovering it or being discovered, to be on the safe side.

Then the pagans of Mecca screamed bloody murder about Muhammad's followers fighting in the holy month.[1] Both sides were appealing for support to the clans and tribes of the Hejaz outside the two warring cities, and Abu Jahl wanted to cast the Believers as blasphemers against the laws of tribal concord.

This complaint put the Prophet in a difficult position. As a member of Banu Hashim, he shared responsibility for upholding the sacred conventions of peace, such as the prohibition on warfare during the four months of Muharram, Rajab, Dhu al-Qa`da, and Dhu al-Hijja. Could the behavior of the Believers be justified? The Qur'an weighed in.

"They ask you," *The Cow* 2:217 says, "about fighting in the sacred month. Say: Battling in it is a grave infraction." The scripture concedes the Meccans' point, as far as it goes. Morality, however, is not black and white, and these matters are located on a spectrum. The passage continues: "Barring the path of God, however, rejecting it in favor of paganism, and blockading the sacred shrine and expelling its people from it are more serious sins yet in the eyes of God." The Meccan elite had exiled the Believers and then refused them the right of pilgrimage to God's tabernacle and access to its blessings, even though by the conventions of the Hejaz, they were required to suspend feuds in the precincts of the shrine. The verse implies that the pagans also owed the Emigrants restitution for their lost property. A contemporary translation of the Qur'an here might be "You have a lot of nerve!"

The verse now surges to its crescendo: "Coercion of conscience is worse than warfare, for they will not stop fighting you until they turn you away from your religion, if they can." The medieval commentator Tabari glossed "coercion of conscience" as "torturing believers because of their religion until they recant it and become polytheists again after having accepted Islam."[2] In the Qur'an's hierarchy of values, the most important of all is the liberty of individual faith since the fate of the immortal soul lies in the balance for eternity. The Qur'an 2:217 concludes by warning the captured Believers who might be broken by pagan pressure, "Those of you who give up your religion and die in a state of paganism, your works will count for nothing in this world and the next. They will be consigned to hellfire and subsist in it forever."

This passage weighs the single breach of tribal law committed by the Believers in this Rajab encounter (which it characterizes only as "fighting," mentioning no combat death, unlike the later Muslim writers) against the multitude of evils committed by the Quraysh. For all Muhammad's option for peace and forbearance, the Qur'an preaches that the innocent must never acquiesce in an involuntary distortion of their own innermost selves. *The Cow* 2:256 says, "There can be no compulsion at all in religion."

Reconnoitering the movements of militant Meccan bands entailed danger. If the Quraysh spotted the Medinan scouts, they might attempt to take them captive so as to reimpose paganism on them. If the anecdote from al-San'ani told above has any truth to it, this menace to the integrity of the self may have accounted for Muhammad's request to Abdullah ibn Jahsh that he not compel any of his companions to risk the cloak-and-dagger assignment.[3] The verse implies that such an abduction was at the root of the clash with al-Hadrami's party. Christian thinkers of this era also recognized the importance of defending their rights of conscience by any means necessary. Church father Gregory of Nazianzos (d. 390) had maintained that a praiseworthy war is superior to a peace that separates one from God.[4]

This verse offered only an ad hoc justification for the actions of Abdullah ibn Jahsh and his companions rather than announcing a change in basic norms. At some point in the early Medina period, however, the Qur'an formally mandated fighting in defense of the community as a duty. *The Cow* 2:190 says, "Fight in the path of God those who enter into combat against you, but do not commit aggression. God does not love aggressors." The Qur'an allows warfare only in self-defense.[5] Authorizing a battle with the aggressive Quraysh at Mecca itself, 2:191 thunders, "Fight them with deadly force wherever you encounter them and expel them from those places from which they exiled you. For coercion of conscience is more grievous than fighting." Still, to the extent possible, the verse urges that the peace of the Kaaba be observed even during warfare: "Do not deploy lethal force against them near the sacred tabernacle, unless they fight you in it. If they do kill you there, kill them there. That is the recompense of the pagans."[6] While the Qur'an in this early Medinan passage permits the Believers to raid into Mecca, it does not go on to mention them ever doing so. Later verses do speak of some raids, but the major encounters the Qur'an describes are clearly defensive in character. The Qur'an uses the phrase "fighting in the path of God," but the word for "fighting" (*qital*) is a secular one, and similar phrases were deployed by contemporary Christians and Zoroastrians. The passages about fighting do not use the Arabic term *jihad*, which in the Qur'an refers to ethical struggle and carries no implication of holy war.[7]

The Cow 2:192 offers an armistice to any pagans who lay down their arms, saying, "If they desist, God is forgiving and merciful."[8] The next verse tells the Believers, "Fight them until there is no longer any coercion of conscience and until the religion is God's. If they cease, there is no enmity save toward wrongdoers." The phrase "the religion is God's" in context here seems to mean "until freedom to worship God is established." The Believers are not fighting to impose Muhammad's religion on anyone since the Qur'an objects to coercion of private conscience.

Muhammad and the Emigrants grew up in the sanctuary city of Mecca, where many of them, as Banu Hashim, specialized in conflict resolution, and this change in policy provoked controversy in the community. *The Cow* 2:216 pushed back against any such utopian pacifism: "Fighting is prescribed for you, even if it is hateful to you. It may be that you hate a thing that is better for you; and it may be that you love a thing that is worse for you; God knows and you do not know." The Qur'an complains more than once of this reluctance for battle among Muhammad's followers.[9]

Other late-antique authors expressed similar sentiments. Christian monk Athanasios of Alexandria (d. 373) too had written that "one is not supposed to kill but killing in battle is both lawful and praiseworthy." Augustine insisted that where a leader with legitimate authority decides that it is necessary to go to war to right an injustice, his soldiers have a responsibility to obey this command, and they do not thereby violate the commandment not to kill.[10] Whatever happened at the beginning of January 624 was a small affair, but the conflict to which it pointed was clearly building, and a much larger confrontation loomed.

❧

THE MUSLIM TRADITION reports that in mid-March 624, hundreds of men fought a battle at Badr, traditionally thought to be referred to in the eighth chapter of the scripture, *The Spoils*. Let us attempt to reconstruct this encounter as the Qur'an describes it. Muhammad was instructed by the revelation to go out of Medina to make a defensive stand but met stiff resistance from many of his own followers. He must have gathered his loyal men, in helmets and simple chain mail, with swords and lances and leather shields, along with a unit of archers on horseback. Some in the date oasis angrily refused to saddle up and join him: "A faction of the believers disliked it." These reluctant Medinans could not discern that inaction itself posed extreme danger to them. "They dispute with you over the truth after it became clear," the verse says, "as though they were being driven toward death with their eyes wide open" (8:5–6). This passage reverses ordinary expectations. Those Believers ready to go out to the field of battle were preserving themselves, while those who remained timidly in Medina were rushing toward their physical demise. The passage strongly implies that Muhammad was leading a preemptive raid in the face of enemy plans for a lethal assault on Medina, of which he had gotten wind. The Prophet warned that if the Believers did not take up arms to defend their dignity, they would be reduced again to being kidnapped and made to recant their faith. *The Spoils* 8:26 says, "Remember when you were few and weak in the land and you feared that the people would abduct you. Then he gave you a refuge and aided you with his succor."

The Believers were ordered to attend to psychological warfare as well as to material preparations in this defensive campaign. "Prepare against them whatever you can in the way of force and lines of horse, so as to strike fear into the enemy of God" (*The Spoils* 8:60).[11]

Muhammad's more loyal followers headed south, between the squat hills of glistening lava rock that stood sentinel some ways outside the oasis. His trackers must have discerned two distinct bands of Meccans heading toward the market town of Badr, some one hundred miles southeast of Medina, one only lightly armed and the other a formidable war party armored in corselets and greaves. Understandably, the Believers were hoping to come upon the former and evade the latter.[12] It may be that they aimed to take hostages from among the civilian Quraysh party and to make abandonment of the Meccan offensive a prerequisite for their release. The men involved in this anticipatory expedition were so disorganized that they did not leave at once; the Prophet headed up the lead units, but others straggled after. The Constitution of Medina would lead us to expect his small contingent to be made up of not only Emigrants and Khazraji Helpers but also their pagan clients, along with an Orthodox Jewish battalion (who probably equipped the entire army) and perhaps a Christian platoon of Banu Jafna. They would have ridden hard all day, passing over prairie tufted with short white-tipped grasses and occasional flat-topped acacia trees, then eased their camels down russet escarpments through loose scree. They made camp at twilight and set out again the next morning after dawn prayers.

Muhammad's men were brought up short when they came upon both Quraysh parties at the same time and in the same place. His small vanguard of Believers would have been in some danger from the armed Meccan battalion. As it happened, however, all the Medinan forces found one another around the same time, even though they had not agreed on an hour when they would meet up, and, given their internal disputes over tactics and even the wisdom of the entire mission, they probably could have settled on no such exact plans.

Medina's defenders took up a position on high ground above the mounted enemy at some distance below, perhaps watering at the Badr wells, while more Meccans positioned themselves on a facing hillside. *The Spoils* 8:42 paints the scene: "Remember when you were on the near side of the hill and they were on the far side, and the camel cavalry was beneath you."[13]

It also celebrates the serendipity whereby all the Medinans found one another: "If you had made a rendezvous, you would have disagreed on the appointment, but God determines a matter so that it is accomplished—so that some might be winked out of existence and others might live. God is All-Hearing, All-Knowing." This passage demonstrates that Muhammad was anything but a theocrat and was unable to impose on his supposed acolytes so much as a time for a rendezvous.

Having unexpectedly come face-to-face with the best Quraysh warriors in full battle gear, their eyes blazing with bloodlust and their blades coruscating in the Arabian sun, the Believers began saying their prayers. To shore up morale, the Qur'an tells them (*The Spoils* 8:9), "Recall when you implored your lord, and he answered you, 'I will support you with a thousand angels in serried ranks.'"

Muhammad ordered his Believers to charge even though they were outnumbered. A handful proved faint of heart in the face of a much bigger military force. Even as the bulk of his company advanced, some turned on their heels, endangering their comrades by abandoning them to their fate. Muhammad, furious, threatened them with eternal damnation. "Those who turn their backs to them on that day, save if it is a war tactic or to rejoin their unit, have drawn down on themselves the wrath of God, and their dwelling will be hell, and an abject fate" (*The Spoils* 8:15–16). In the end, the line of the Medinans held firm, and they engaged the fierce Meccans with renewed determination. The Qur'an (8:17) reassures the Believers that this campaign was divinely ordained: "You did not kill them but rather God killed them, and you did not cast your weapon, but rather God cast it, to test the believers thereby with an exquisite trial."

After hard fighting, amid the clang of iron blades and the guttural bellow of war camels, the Believers routed the Quraysh, despite taking dozens of casualties. The *Family of Amram* 3:169 observed, "Do not consider those who were killed in the path of God to be dead. Rather, they are alive, with their lord, who is feasting them."

The early Christian idea of the martyr evoked hapless civilian witnesses to the faith who were struck down by puissant persecutors rather than soldiers fallen on the battlefield. As a result of continual wars with Iran, however, a different conception of martyrdom was emerging in late antiquity. Theophylaktos Simokates, a late sixth-century historian and contemporary of Muhammad, reported the speech of a Christian Roman general encouraging his men to march against the Zoroastrian army, saying, "Today angels are recruiting you and are recording the souls of the dead, providing for them not a corresponding recompense, but one that infinitely exceeds the weight of the gifts."[14] It has been suggested that this author was innovating by invoking Christian martyrdom but placing it for the first time on the battlefield. Herakleios officially adopted the doctrine of the Roman soldier-martyr in 624 during his riposte against Iranian incursions into western Anatolia.[15]

Although the taking of booty on the battlefield at Badr created discontents with regard to its distribution, *The Spoils* 8:1 urges the Believers to trust God and the Prophet on this issue and "make peace among yourselves." Likewise, captives were taken, and the Qur'an specifies how prisoners of war are to be treated. *Muhammad* 47:4 instructs, "Tie fast the bonds; then set them free, either by grace or ransom, till the war lays down its burden." The Qur'an insists that prisoners of war be released, one way or another, and not harmed. Since the Meccans had been kidnapping Believers, taking a pagan captive was a way of arranging to ransom one of Muhammad's flock.

The Believers, delirious with joy at having triumphed over their more numerous and experienced foe, would have exulted on the ride back to Medina. *The Spoils* 8:62–63 celebrates the increased ties of affection and the internal peace achieved among the Believers of Medina in the wake of the victory, telling Muhammad, "He is the one who supported you with his succor and with the believers, and united their hearts. Even if you had spent everything on the whole earth you could not have brought their hearts together, but God unified them. He is mighty and wise."

The Qur'an (*The Spoils* 8:19) offers the Meccans a way out, after their defeat, if they will climb down and make peace: "If you sought a victory, a victory was visited on you. But if you desist, it is better for you. If you turn back, we will turn back. Your warrior host will do you no good at all, even if you could expand it. God is truly with the believers." Later 8:38 reaffirms, "Say to the pagans that if they desist they will be forgiven for what went before. But if they backslide, the way of the ancients has already passed." Moreover, any reconsideration by the Meccans of their belligerence would lay an obligation on Muhammad and the Believers. *The Spoils* 8:61 says, "If they incline toward peace, you must incline toward it. Trust in God—he is all-hearing and omniscient."

The early biographer 'Urwa ibn al-Zubayr's account of the battle written decades afterward differed in significant ways from what the Qur'an said, and later authors diverged even more. He alleged that the battle began as an attempted Medinan raid on a caravan of the pagan Meccan notable Abu Sufyan, but the scripture mentions no such attack on a trading mission. Indeed, *The Spoils* strongly implies that the Quraysh were planning to invade Medina. `Urwa has the Believers take up their position at the wells of Badr, whereas the Qur'an portrays them as occupying high ground above the enemy cavalry (which would have been, in any case, better military strategy). Later authors imposed on the Prophet's biography the secular "battle days" traditions of Arabic poetry, including chases during attempts at plunder, cheeky challenges, and single combat before the main engagement.[16]

The Qur'an implicitly compares Muhammad's victory over the much larger and more formidable Quraysh army to King David's defeat of the Philistines. The chapter of *The Cow* retells the biblical story concerning the controversies over the establishment of Saul (ca. 1021–1000 BCE) as king of Israel despite the opposition of the anarchic Israelites. At the time of these arguments, the Philistines had carried off the Ark of the Covenant. The Qur'an portrays the prophet Samuel prophesying to the Jews about King Saul, "The sign of his sovereignty is that the Ark will come to you, within which is the *Sakina* from your lord" (*The Cow* 2:248). It then tells the story of the Philistine attack on Jerusalem and David's defeat of their giant champion, Goliath (*The Cow* 2:249–251).[17] The Qur'an is comparing Muhammad to David here, who is forced to battle a much bigger foe for the sake of preserving his people and safeguarding their access to the latter-day Ark, that is, the Kaaba, within which dwells the Peace of God.

Christians in late antiquity appealed to similar biblical imagery. Court writers configured Emperor Herakleios as a new David. Ambrose of Milan had, two centuries earlier, extolled David as a ruler who never waged a war unless driven to it by the enemy and who always consulted God about such campaigns. Augustine pointed to David when he wanted to justify imperial warfare against Donatist heretics.[18]

In one of the great ironies of history, Muhammad, who had preached returning evil with good and praying for peace for one's foes, had violent conflict thrust upon him in the last third of his prophetic career. The Qur'an maintains that he waged even that struggle, however, in self-defense and in the interests ultimately of restoring tranquility, the late-antique definition of the just war. Just war theorists of this era allowed for war as an exception to the general rule of peace, but only if it aimed at preventing an injustice more heinous than the war itself. The ancient thinker of pagan Rome Cicero (106–43 BCE) had written that a war is just only if prosecuted as an obligation of an alliance, in self-defense against aggression, or in search for compensation after a wrong and if it aims at establishing a lasting peace as its ultimate goal. Some early Christian thinkers such as Tertullian and Origen, in contrast, seemed uncomfortable with war, though they may not have represented the majority of their inchoate community. Once Christianity became the religion of empire, its major thinkers reconsidered the rights and wrongs of warfare. The Qur'an's move from pacifism to a mandate for just war recapitulated in a decade the course that high Christian theology took over the century spanning 300 to 400 CE.[19]

It has been pointed out that people tend to call their own struggles a *just war* and reserve the term *holy war* for others. The Christian tradition largely recognizes the legitimacy of "just war." In the course of the fourth century, Christian Roman emperors began turning Christianity into a martial faith whose adherents were willing to deploy Roman armies for conquest as well as for the suppression of other religions and of what they saw as heresies. Christians had long served in the imperial military, but now they joined in even greater numbers.[20]

Augustine had faced critiques of war from absolute pacifists among his Manichaean acquaintances. In Augustine's view, a just war can issue only from a just cause. That is, a state must have been injured by the actions of another state or of its subjects. "It is the wrongdoing of the opposing party which compels the wise man to wage just wars," Augustine observes.[21] The implication of his position is that a just war need not be waged in direct self-defense in the face of an attack but may be fought to gain compensation for a tort. "And on this principle, if the commonwealth observe the precepts of the Christian religion, even its wars themselves will not be carried on without the benevolent design that, after the resisting nations have been conquered, provision may be more easily made for enjoying in peace the mutual bond of piety and justice." Once a battle is joined, Augustine favored using all the tools of war and praised the emperor, in his military campaign against heretics, for deploying "fear and compulsion." He thus agreed with the Qur'an about the necessity of striking fear into the hearts of the opposing army.[22] Christian theorists had already encountered the moral paradox now bedeviling the Medinans, that sometimes the only path to peace wends through a battlefield.

LATER MUSLIM AUTHORS held that about a year after the battle of Badr, on or about March 23, 625, the Meccans again marched on Medina and met them at a ravine near the twin-peaked Mount Uhud. They alleged that the Meccan general Khalid ibn al-Walid of the militantly pagan Mahzum clan led their army and that the saga of the Believers' defense is referred to in the Qur'an (3:121–168). There is no dispute in the Qur'an or later sources about this campaign's having been an act of aggression on the part of Mecca.

The Qur'an suggests that Muhammad, acting as a sort of senator or community organizer, led the city's notables in a debate over how best to deal with the approaching army. A majority of the Believers, who were personally much more loyal to the Prophet than the Jews, pagans, Christians, and Sabians, appears to have favored going out to meet it. *The Family of Amram* (3:121) reminds Muhammad of the time "when you set forth from your family at dawn, to post the believers at their battle stations; and God is All-Hearing, All-Knowing."

A turning point in the battle of Uhud near Medina came when some men disobeyed an order of the Prophet, apparently halting their advance to loot the fallen enemy and giving the Quraysh time to regroup (3:155): "God was true to his promise to you when you were laying them low by his leave. Then, behold, you lost heart, and disputed over the order, and rebelled, after you had been shown what you loved. Some of you want this world and some of you want the next. Then he turned you away from them in order to test you. But he has pardoned you, for God is gracious to the Believers." Whereas the old Arabic poetry of battle days would have celebrated the plunder of the enemy and pledged revenge for the defeat, the Qur'an upbraids the Believers for falling victim to greed and indiscipline but also offers them forgiveness.

The cupidity of some of the Believers cost them victory. Muhammad appears to have almost died during this encounter (*The Family of Amram* 3:144): "Muhammad is only a messenger. Messengers have passed away before him. Why, if he should die or be killed, will you turn your backs? If you do so, you are not harming God in any way. God will recompense the thankful." The early historian 'Urwa alleged, "One of the prophet's teeth was broken and his face bruised."

Some of the Believers lost heart and ran from the Quraysh (3:155): "Those among you who turned around on the day when the two groups encountered one another were caused to stumble by Satan because of some of their deeds. But God forgave them. God is forgiving, merciful." Although Muhammad's forces suffered defeat, they appear to have been able to sustain an orderly retreat, so that the reversal did not turn into a rout and was more of a draw.

It is said that "victory has a thousand fathers but defeat is an orphan." On the beaten battalion's return to Medina, the Battle of Uhud was decidedly fatherless. The Qur'an replied to the disgruntled among the trounced Believers in *The Family of Amram* (3:164), reminding them of the blessing God sent among them in the form of a prophet from among themselves who rescued them when they had gone astray. It continues (3:165), "Or when a single disaster befalls you, even after you had visited one twice as great on them, do you say 'Where did this come from?' Say: 'It is from yourselves, for God is powerful over all things. What befell you on the day two armies met took place by God's permission, so that the believers should know.'"

Some factions in Medina on whom Muhammad had thought he could count had declined to join the battle, including some of his own followers. The Qur'an (3:167) complains bitterly, "They were told, 'Come, fight in the path of God, or at least take a defensive position.' They replied, 'If we knew how to fight, we would have followed you.' That day, they were closer to paganism than to faith, inasmuch as they said with their lips what was not in their hearts. God knows best what they are concealing." Later historians say that some Medinans contended that they should have defended their city from its precincts and that their side's battlefield deaths came from bad strategy in going out to meet the enemy.[23] This controversy may lie behind 3:168, which quotes these critics as saying, "If only they had listened to us, they would not have been slain."

Despite Muhammad's dismay at having been left in the lurch by these Hypocrites (led according to later historians by the Medinan notable Abdullah ibn Ubayy), he decided that reacting with harshness risked splitting the city. *The Family of Amram* 3:159 has God address the Prophet, "By what mercy of God were you able to be so lenient with them? Had you been harsh and hard of heart, they would have surely dispersed from around you. Pardon them and beseech for them to be forgiven, and consult them in the affair." The Qur'an, in its search for social peace, advises Muhammad to treat with gentleness those Medinans who had differed with him on war strategy. He is even instructed to continue to consult with urban notables, including apparently non-Believers, on important decisions, as he is said to have done before Uhud.

It has been argued that the late Roman Empire under Herakleios still had republican features and that the senate functioned as a significant consultative body.[24] This model, very different from the absolute monarchy of Khosrow II of Iran, may have been important for the pro-Roman Muhammad. Such sentiments would have been reinforced by the Arab preference for consultation among clan chiefs over centralized power. (Obviously, he expected the Believers to obey the directives of the scripture, but other Medinans had no such obligation, and at least the later tradition routinely depicts Believers as differing with him on nonscriptural issues.)

Had they lost the contest more decisively, the Qur'an implies, all the Believers might have been captured and returned to paganism, and the new religion would have been smothered in its crib. The legitimacy of a war of defense was not in question for most late-antique thinkers. Church father Ambrose wrote that a "courage, which... defends the weak, or comrades from robbers, is full of justice" and "He who does not keep harm off a friend, if he can, is as much in fault as he who causes it."[25]

Increasingly, in the 620s, war came to be justified on the grounds of religion. Constantinopolitan court poet Georgios of Pisidia began by writing poetry about the secular warfare between Romans and Iranians, a very old theme. After General Shahr Varaz's sack of Jerusalem and capture of the relic of the true cross, however, Georgios began exploring religious themes. In the early 620s, as Constantinople battled Balkan pagans and their Zoroastrian Iranian allies, he wrote that it was fitting that the God-created Christian Romans took to the field against "enemies who bow to created things; who defile the altars that were undefiled by blood." He contrasted the saintly Herakleios, who listened to sacred hymns sung by virginal nuns, to the "erring" General Shahr Varaz, who spent his evenings with "the sound of instruments and cymbals and the contorting dance of women who ended their frenzy by disrobing." The poet now turned an imperial struggle into a crusade of monotheists against those he saw as polluted Iranian polytheists, and he called the Christian God the commanding "General of heaven and earth." These themes of struggle for the true faith are apparent in the Qur'an in the same era, in response to similar challenges.[26]

THE LATER BIOGRAPHERS say that two years passed before Mecca again assaulted Medina frontally, at the Siege of the Trench—the third great military encounter between the two.[27] After the draw at Uhud, the Prophet and his followers had allegedly dug a deep and broad Persian-style trench between steep outcroppings and swampland to stop the enemy cavalry from charging in so fast it could evade the vigilant Medinan archers. The technique may have been suggested by Salman Ruzbeh, a spiritual seeker of Iranian Zoroastrian heritage from Isfahan who had first converted to Christianity and then came to Medina and embraced the new faith of Muhammad.

Geopolitics once again may be part of the story. In 626 Constantinople had fought off a siege by the Balkan Avars and Iranian troops. The following year, the Roman emperor Herakleios launched a counterstrike against the forces of the king of kings in Asia Minor. Khosrow II's officials may have encouraged pagan allies against the pro-Roman Medinans. The Ghatafan tribe, based in Najd near

Sasanian territory, was said by later sources to have been among the belligerents marching on Medina. Given its geographical position, it was likely an Iranian client. Pagan leader Abu Sufyan and the Quraysh in Mecca aligned with them.

The Qur'an, the later sources hold, reflected on the monthlong contest at the Siege of the Trench of March–April 627 in *The Confederates* (33). The Quraysh and their Ghatafan allies launched a sneak attack. Verse 33:10 describes the Believers as abruptly surrounded and terrified: "Behold, they came at you from above and from below, while your eyes bulged and your hearts came into your throats, and you began to wonder about God." At least in later times, Arab tribes made a distinction between the routine raiding of one clan by another and a formal state of war. When a tribe pursued such warfare with a major battle, it aimed at completely overwhelming the enemy—expelling them and taking over their territory.[28] Abu Sufyan and his pastoralist confederates had plotted the total conquest of Medina.

Being thus blockaded severely tested the faith of the Believers, and it inspired even more uncertainty in those Hypocrites, who already had their doubts about Muhammad. Some residents, in a panic, urged that everyone flee to the countryside and take refuge with friendly bedouins, saying, "People of Yathrib, there is nowhere here for you to make a stand, retreat!" The idea of adopting the better part of valor had broad appeal, even in Muhammad's own community: "And some of them asked leave of the prophet, declaring, 'Our houses are exposed'" (*The Confederates* 33:13).

The Messenger firmly rebuffed them, confident in the city's defenses and needing volunteers to man the barricades. He took a dim view of their intestinal fortitude. "But they were not exposed—those people just wanted to flee. And if the enemy had entered in upon them from their surroundings and demanded they recant their faith, after only a brief hesitation they would have acquiesced" (33:13–14). Here, as in the other war passages, the chief preoccupation of the Qur'an is with the ever-present danger that the Quraysh might succeed in coercing the Believers' consciences and returning them forcibly to paganism. The scripture reminds them that they had taken a formal vow not to bolt and points out that running away from death would buy them only a little time, given their anyway fleeting lives (33:15–16).

In the end, *The Confederates* 33:25 exults, "God repelled the pagans by means of their own rage. They obtained nothing of value and God spared the believers from the fight. God is powerful and august."[29]

The later Abbasid-era historians told stories of a monthlong siege in which the enemy attempted on several occasions to find a way around the trench and into the assemblage of villages, farms, and date orchards that made up Medina. They spoke of internal divisions among the attackers, darkly intimating that Jews had been behind the whole campaign but then had second thoughts and intrigued between the Quraysh and Ghatafan tribes. The Qur'an's account also points to an increasingly disunited set of besiegers, but it does not mention Jews as a player here, speaking only of a pagan onslaught.

The attack on Medina appears to have faltered in part because of a khamsin wind. These spring mistrals barrel down from the north at a hundred miles an hour like a racing yellow fog, launching volleys of pricking sand grains, sucking all the moisture out of everything in their path, and spewing suffocating, searing air like the effluent of a giant forge bellows. *The Confederates* 33:9 says, "You who have believed, call to mind the bounty of God upon you, when troops marched on you and we dispatched against them a gale and invisible hosts. God sees your actions." Later accounts spoke of campfires extinguished, utensils caroming like tumbleweed, steeds spooked, and tents going airborne. The disheartened parties led by Abu Sufyan of Quraysh and Uyayna of Ghatafan, they said, abruptly decamped.

The Qur'an's attribution of success in resisting the siege to unseen, angelic hosts was paralleled in eastern Roman writings in this period concerning the life-and-death struggle between Constantinople and Ctesiphon. In 626, when the capital was caught "like a fish in a net" during the joint Avar and Iranian siege, Theodoros Synkellos portrayed Mary, the protector of Constantinople, as an Athena figure. He called the Turkic Avar tribesmen who penetrated the walls of Constantinople "godless" (*atheos*), which is probably a stronger condemnation than the Qur'an's *kafir*. Theodoros said that Mary, Mother of God, "drew a large number of the Khagan's soldiers to a position before one of her churches which stood just outside the city walls." He continued, "The Virgin, by massacring the barbarians at the hands of Christian soldiers, cast upon the ground the arrogance of the Khagan and weakened his entire army."[30] The minions of the Mother of God slew (literally, "cut the sinews" of) the enemy wherever they encountered them. Theodoros's account uses a diction similar to the Qur'an's narrative of God's hosts fending off the Ghatafan and Quraysh pagans. Some Christians within the besieged capital even spoke of Mary descending to fight with her own hands.[31]

The Qur'an describes the 627 Siege of the Trench around Medina by the Quraysh as a contest of wills. Would the Believers and the Hypocrites find the courage to stand up to the militant pagans? It is in no doubt that some proportion of the city would, if its defenses were breached, be perfectly willing to return to paganism at the point of a spear. The nascent faith could still be extinguished.

❧

AFTER THE ENGAGEMENT ended, the Qur'an says that God dealt harshly with an errant scriptural community that had, despite its belief in the Bible and God's prophets, allied with pagan Mecca during the Siege of the Trench. *The Confederates* 33:26 remarks, "He brought down their supporters from among the people of the Book from their strongholds, and cast fear into their hearts, so that you slew some of them and took others captive. And he made you heirs to their farms and dwellings and possessions, and land on which you had never set foot." The Believers launched a punitive raid against the Bible-believing community that had conspired to see them conquered and killed or enslaved and deprived of their liberty of conscience. The Qur'an, in describing the ensuing clash, spoke of deaths on the battlefield and then the taking of prisoners of war, after which, it says, the Believers expropriated the property of this enemy population in punishment for their treason. We have already seen that *Muhammad* 47:4 gives instructions on the treatment of men captured in war: "Tie fast the bonds; then set them free, either by grace or ransom, till the war lays down its burden."

In the Medina period, a new category emerges for some disloyal factions. *The Cow* 2:105 says, "Neither those who paganized from among the people of the Book, nor the pagans themselves, desire that good from your lord descend upon you." Parties with a biblical heritage had allied with the pagans and by such a pact with the devil had forfeited their claims to be monotheists (*muslims*) submissive to the Abrahamic prophetic tradition. The Qur'an did not condemn all the scriptural communities, which it repeatedly praised and to whom it pledged entry into paradise if they lived a righteous life. The *people of the Book* is an overarching term, analogous to *bird*. You could put under that latter rubric individual species such as the noble hawk or the carrion-eating vulture. The phrase "those who paganized from among the people of the Book" is like "vulture" in being a more specific member of the category.[32]

Elsewhere, a different chapter of the Qur'an, *The Gathering* 59:2, refers to yet another clash provoked by a monotheistic village's throwing in with pagan Mecca. The Qur'an addresses the Medinans and says of God, "He it was who expelled from their homes the scriptural community that paganized, at the first gathering." This expedition was by no means guaranteed success since, just as Medina had withstood a siege, this fortified, walled settlement might have been able to hunker down for a long resistance. "You did not believe that they would leave, and they thought that their fortresses would protect them from God." Moreover, they were expecting succor from the Hypocrite faction in Medina, which appears to have differed with its own prophet about the need to penalize the turncoats. The Qur'an recalls that the Hypocrites said to their friends, those who paganized from among the people of the Book, "If you are expelled, we will leave with you... and if you are fought, we will come to your aid" (*The Gathering* 59:11).

In conducting a reprisal raid on the perfidious followers of the Bible who had allied with the bellicose Meccan pagans in an attempt to murder the Believers, the adherents of the Qur'an made no attempt to breach the town fortifications or engage in a long siege. They instead cut down the date palms that lay outside the walls, which provided the livelihood of its inhabitants (*The Gathering* 59:5). With the palm grove gone, the villagers had no means of support and lacked any incentive to attempt to wait out the siege. They sought to avoid any further military riposte by signaling their surrender and by tearing down their own homes, with the Believers enthusiastically lending a helping hand. Then they departed for the North.[33]

In *The Gathering* 59:3, the Qur'an shows remarkable solicitude for this double-crossing monotheistic enemy that is said to have colluded with Abu Sufyan to destroy the Believers: "If God had not prescribed for them exile, he would have tortured them in this world and they would have undergone the torments of fire in the next." Now that they were removed from the fray, it says, these believers in the Bible were no longer succumbing to the blandishments of paganism, theologically or politically. They had regained their status as a saved community and were out of the way of this-worldly harm, having left their exposed settlement. This discourse of stern action against the recalcitrant for their own spiritual good recalls what Augustine of Hippo said about opponents of the church: "If these enemies are loved, they exercise her benevolence, or even her beneficence, whether she deals with them by persuasive doctrine or by terrible discipline." The difference is that Muhammad does not urge "terrible discipline" or violence merely for doctrinal sins but only for military attacks, or abetting attacks, on the Believers.[34]

The Qur'an does not identify the monotheists who fought alongside the pagans of Mecca. They may have been diverse. The general phrase "from among the people of the Book" suggests that both some Christians and some Jews joined Mecca against the Muslims (and perhaps Sabians as well)—otherwise, why is it not "those who paganized from among the Jews"?

The early biographer Ibn Shihab al-Zuhri said that the passage (33:26) about deadly combat and taking captives after the Siege of the Trench concerned the Qurayza tribe in the largely Jewish town of Khaybar, which was alleged to have allied with Mecca against Muhammad.[35] Although accounts written during the later Abbasid caliphate after 750 speak of an execution of male Jewish prisoners of war seen as guilty of treason, the Qur'an does not mention anything about a mass slaying of the men of Khaybar and rather suggests that deaths occurred during a battle but that the Believers offered the enemy quarter and took prisoners. In *Stories* 28:4, the Qur'an condemned tyranny, saying, "Now Pharaoh exalted himself in the land and divided its inhabitants into factions, abasing one party of them, slaughtering their sons, and sparing their women; for he was a worker of corruption." It is impossible that Muhammad at Khaybar gave the same order as Pharaoh.

As for the separate anecdote in The Gathering, ʿUrwa ibn al-Zubayr identified those expelled as the Jewish Banu Nadir, who lived in a town outside Medina on the way to Mecca and so became a severe security concern when they switched allegiance to the Quraysh. He says that they were sent away to Syria. Since later generations lost contact with the situation in the 620s, we cannot be sure that these verses concerned the Banu Nadir as opposed to an Arab Christian settlement or a Sabian Aws outpost (Abu ʿAmer the Monk and some of his men are also said to have gone into exile in Damascus). It is not clear exactly when the offending community was exiled, though recent scholarship suggests it was after the Siege of the Trench.[36]

The few details in the Qur'an do not support, and indeed starkly contradict, the tales of Abbasid-era biographers. It is possible that later Muslim conflicts with Jewish communities in Damascus and Baghdad have been projected back onto the early seventh-century Hejaz and that Jews sometimes have been substituted for a Christian minority or for Sabian tribes who actually allied with Mecca. It is suspicious that the gradual exclusion of Jews from Medina and its environs alleged by the biographers follows the pattern of occasional Christian expulsions of Jews in late antiquity from cities such as Alexandria, Constantinople proper, and Jerusalem, a progression later Muslim converts from Christianity would have thought natural.[37] In contrast, the very late Qur'anic chapter of The Table, dated by most scholars to 631–632, speaks of the Believers having common meals with and intermarrying with nonconvert Jews in Medina.

In any case, even if The Gathering 59:2 and The Confederates 33:26 referred, respectively, to Jewish tribes of the Banu Nadir and to the Banu Qurayza, these events were a matter of everyday politics and do not affect Qur'anic ideals. Jews in general did not cease being God's chosen people, stop having true scripture, or stop being candidates for paradise just because some local clans allied with Mecca. While the Qur'an laments that most Jews deserted the cause, it says in *The Women* 4:46 that "a few" remained in Muhammad's coalition and issues no blanket condemnation.

Both the Qur'an and subsequent biographers remembered Muhammad's response to the naked act of Meccan aggression in 627, which allegedly aimed at snuffing out the new faith of Muhammad in its cradle, as depending on techniques of minimalist warfare. According to the Qur'an, internal divisions led to the Meccan failure. This approach pointed the way forward to a negotiated settlement with Mecca rather than a bloody Armageddon.

🙝

THE STATE OF raiding and counterraiding that persisted after the Siege of the Trench put some Quraysh pagans who considered themselves neutral, and some bedouins, in a difficult situation. The Believers, having been so often on the receiving end of aggression, viewed outsiders with intense suspicion. The Qur'an urges them instead to give those professing neutrality the benefit of the doubt. *The Women* 4:86 says, "If you receive a greeting, reply with a better one, or with a salutation at least as good. God keeps account of all things."

Still, neutrality could not simply be claimed. It had to be demonstrated. The Qur'an describes a group in Mecca who secretly got word to Medina that they actually viewed themselves as allies of the Prophet. The Abbasid sources identified the Khuza'a clan as among these covert adherents of the Believers movement. Some of these groups, however, were easily enlisted back into the ranks of the pagans with a little pressure, and so the Qur'an feared that they would abruptly ambush the

Believers, having lulled them with promises of fealty. It says, "You will find others who wish to be secure both from you and their own people. But whenever they fall victim to the coercion of conscience they yield to it. If they decline to withdraw from you and to greet you with 'Peace!' or to restrain their hands, then capture them, and fight them with deadly force, wherever you encounter them. We have given you clear authority over them" (*The Women* 4:91).

The Qur'an did not demand that neutrals or pro-Muhammad Quraysh clans come all the way to Medina. Departing Mecca for a nonaligned area would also show good faith among these non-Believers reluctant to fight the Prophet. *The Women* 4:90 speaks of Meccan pagans who "seek refuge with a people who have a compact with you, or come to you with no desire to fight you or their own people. Had God wished, he could have ensconced them in power over you, such that they would have fought you. So if they withdraw and decline to engage you in combat, and offer you peace, God has not ordained for you any way to go against them."

The Qur'an forbids the raiding of such nonaligned pagans. *The Women* 4:94 says, "Believers, when you fight in the way of God, be discriminating. Do not say to one who greets you with 'Peace!' 'You are not a believer!' You aspire to the goods of this world, but with God are many riches. You were like them in the past, but God conferred his favor on you. So scrutinize carefully. God is aware of what you do." The Qur'an urges them to have the social intelligence necessary to tell the difference between a friendly pagan and a belligerent one.[38]

THE QUR'AN PORTRAYS the turn of Muhammad and his Believers to warfare with militant pagan Mecca as a search for restitution for serious wrongs and as self-defense. It is difficult to see in what way the

Qur'an's doctrine of just war differs from the Ciceronian Roman tradition of thought on the subject, which was incorporated by clerics such as Augustine and Ambrose into Christianity. Muhammad did not aim in these Medinan wars at imperial aggrandizement but sought the restoration of a previous balance. The fighting would cease if the Meccans made restitution for their torts against the Believers.

It is clear from the Qur'an that a few small battles took place in the Medina period. Later biographers multiplied these military encounters and structured the last decade of the Prophet's life around dozens of "raids." They list numerous small expeditions that inexplicably involved no real battle or significant outcome. One suspects later generations of inventing exploits for the glory of an ancestor. Even some events described as major battles appear to be fiction, such as a supposed campaign at Mu'ta in the Sasanian Transjordan sometime in the period 627–629. Moreover, commentators misunderstood the Qur'an verses to progress from allowing defensive war to mandating offensive operations. This medieval stance on the evolution of the Qur'an's position has been shown to be problematic.[39]

The Qur'an largely concurs with Augustine and Ambrose on the subject of just war, seeing battle as a legitimate response to aggression. Unlike them, it does not speak of fighting paganism per se or seeking the forcible extermination of the opponent's religious ideas. Augustine argued that a Christian war on a pagan foe exemplified the principle that "even wars might be waged by the good, in order that, by bringing under the yoke the unbridled lusts of men, those vices might be abolished which ought, under a just government, to be either extirpated or suppressed."[40] In contrast, the Qur'an gives Lockean grounds for warfare, reacting against civil and property wrongs as well as against pressuring individuals over their internal beliefs.

One of the grounds given by contemporary apologists for Herakleios's campaign against Zoroastrian Iran was the occupation of the holy city of Jerusalem by those they saw as fire-worshipping infidels. Some have argued that the contest took on the aspect of a holy war. Some have even asserted that this seventh-century world war pre-figured the Crusades.[41] In contrast, the Qur'an uses a secular word for fighting, though it urges that this endeavor sometimes be pursued in the path of God. *Jihad* took on a connotation of holy war (and it remained only one of its meanings) only later in Muslim history, in competition with the Byzantine Empire that continued Eastern Roman traditions.

§ 6 ̧

THE HEART OF MECCA

I N THE FIRST HALF OF 627, THE PROSPECTS, IN WHICH MUHAMMAD
had placed his hopes, for the triumph of Christian Rome over the
belligerent Sasanian armies looked grim. Despite the failure of Iran
and its Avar allies to take Constantinople the year before, the Sasanians kept the upper hand, controlling much of Asia Minor and all of
the Near East. One chronicler wrote that Khosrow II sent the beleaguered Herakleios an insulting letter, inviting him to surrender and
offering him the sinecure of a feudal estate in a lush region of Iran.

The Augustus gathered the nobles of the Roman Empire together in the great cathedral, the Hagia Sophia. He had the slighting missive read out before the sacred altar. Then they all fell to the stone floor in front of it, weeping, to show Christ how abject they had become.[1]

Still, Muhammad eagerly awaited the triumph of Constantinople, as we saw in the opening verses of the chapter of *Rome*: "Rome lies vanquished in the nearest province. But in the wake of their defeat, they will triumph after a few years. Before and after, it is God who is in command. On that day, the believers will rejoice in the victory of God." In addition, the Prophet appears to have seen the defensive battles he commanded in and around Medina as beneficial to the Roman war effort. *Pilgrimage* 22:39–40 observes, "He endorsed those who fought because they had been wronged, and in truth God is able to aid them—those who were expelled from their homes unjustly, solely for saying our lord is God. Had God not checked one people with another, then monasteries, churches, oratories and places of worship wherein God is much mentioned would have been razed to the ground."[2]

Muhammad saw the establishment of the nation of the Believers just to the south of the Roman provinces of Palestine and Arabia, and the wars they fought against militant pagans, as an attempt to push back creeping Iranian occupation and so protecting the abbeys and basilicas to the north. It had been one of the functions of the Arab phylarchs in the Roman Near East to warn cloisters of the approach of hostile pro-Iranian tribes when they feared they would not be able to stop the invasion, and the Believers may have been taking on that role.[3] *The Pilgrimage* 22:40 also gives us insight into the Qur'an's theory of social peace. Given the anarchy that prevailed in the seventh century, the best one can hope for is checks and balances. When one people launches aggression, it says, others must restrain them, in an effort at establishing collective security.

❧

THE MEDINAN BELIEVERS' hopes in the Roman emperor were not, in the end, misplaced. Through 627 Herakleios composed himself and launched a campaign deep into Iran-held Anatolia. Then, allying with pagan inner Asian Turkic forces, the emperor led an audacious surprise strike into northern Mesopotamia late in that year.[4]

Herakleios and his army succeeded in defeating the Sasanian army at Nineveh on December 12, 627. Three hundred miles to the south, Khosrow II heard the news as he wintered at his favorite palace, the domed Dastagerd, with its glittering mosaics, fabulous gardens, and hunting grounds. He hastily withdrew from the exposed palace across the Tigris River, nicknamed "the Arrow" for the swiftness of its flow, to his nearby fortified capital of Ctesiphon. The Romans marched down south and sacked the abandoned royal residence in January 628.

The invaders were stymied, however, on finding that Iranian sappers had destroyed the bridge over to the citadel. Some sources say that Khosrow II's eldest son, Shiroyeh, managed to sneak out a message promising a coup and a peace treaty, convincing the attackers to leave. The Romans then began a retreat without having taken the capital, having made their point. Khosrow's humiliating flight before the enemy had ended him politically. After years of defeat, Herakleios abruptly achieved success, in one of the more remarkable reversals of military fortunes in history. Muhammad and his Believers would have, indeed, exulted on hearing the news, if the prospect of Sasanian humiliation also discouraged their pagan foes, who were Iranian allies.

The shah's chamberlain, Farrukhzad, a powerful notable in his own right, maintained a military force loyal to him. He conspired long distance with General Shahr Varaz in the Near East as well as with some Armenian notables to depose Khosrow II and put Shiroyeh on the throne. They released the prince, who had been imprisoned by his father. The conspirators cast the former ruler of the Iranian world empire into a dungeon in chains. On February 28, 628, the new shah had his father executed. The old Zoroastrian myths said that a shah fell when he adopted false speech and untrue thought, and the halo of divine approval flew away from his head like a falcon, hiding in the cosmic Lake Vouroukasha.[5]

Shiroyeh took the throne name Kavad II and concluded the promised armistice with Herakleios. He offered to return the wood of the Holy Rood and withdraw Iranian armies from the Near East. In Constantinople the author of the *Easter Chronicle* could barely contain his joy. He urged all to raise a cry of gladness and praise God since "Christ is Lord." Haughty Khosrow who insulted Jesus Christ and his pure mother, he said, had fallen and his memory been expunged. Georgios of Pisidia addressed the victorious Herakleios concerning the fallen monarch: "He worshiped fire; you, mighty sovereign, adore the sublime wood of the Cross; when this wood rose high into the heavens, the fire of Persia could not touch it."[6]

General Shahr Varaz in Alexandria, however, resisted the neophyte shah's initiative to bring troops home from the Near East. He still held Egypt and Syria securely, having governed them for many years, and he had not been defeated in the way that the imperial army at Nineveh had. In Iran the new king of kings, Kavad II, ruled only for six or seven months and then died along with thousands of his subjects in a plague outbreak in late summer 628.[7]

With the rise of Muhammad's religion in the West, Ctesiphon faced a further challenge. The ruling caste of Sasanid Yemen, who were the children of Iranian officers and local women, faced both rebellion and the blandishments of the new religion in Medina.[8] Many of them likely retained the Zoroastrianism of their fathers and grandfathers, who had come in the expedition of the 570s. Some of them must have met Muhammad during his years as a merchant trading down to Sana'a and Aden, and the Prophet appears to have dispatched missionaries there from Medina in the 620s. According to the Muslim tradition, this mixed, cosmopolitan elite found the message of the new scripture compelling.

The Qur'an began reaching out to the Zoroastrians, adding them to the ranks of the saved monotheistic communities. *The Pilgrimage* 22:17 says, "The believers, the Jews, the Sabians, the Christians, the Zoroastrians, and the pagans—God will decide among them on the Resurrection Day. God sees all things." Unlike previous such statements, this verse catalogs all the major groups in the Tihama and includes, after the monotheistic religions, the traditionalists who recognized a pantheon of divinities (those who "join partners to God"). Since pagans are mentioned as a final and distinct category, this verse shows that ordinary Jews, Sabians, Christians, and Zoroastrians are not placed in their ranks.[9] Rather, the first five communities are the monotheists. As a catalog, this verse has a different purpose than other similar passages, which list the communities of the saved. Given the inclusion of the pagans, the Qur'an does not promise salvation to all those groups mentioned. The verse implies that these six religious communities should coexist peacefully since it is God who will make the final determination as to their truth or falsehood.

The addition for the first time of the Zoroastrians to the list of the saved indicates that Muhammad accepted this religion as part of the commonwealth of monotheists and now looked forward to incorporating this largely Iranian community into his coalition or even converting them to Islam. His antipathy had been directed toward Khosrow II as an aggressor, not toward Iran or its religion. Zoroastrians after all had a prophet (Zarathustra), a set of scriptures, a form of monotheism (inasmuch as the good deity Ohrmazd ultimately prevails over the evil principle of Ahriman), and a belief in the Resurrection

Day. Some among the Iranian elite in Yemen may have begun seeing Muhammad as the Saoshyant, the Zoroastrian messiah. Tabari asserts that the Sasanian viceroy of Yemen, Badhan Sasan-Zadag, embraced the faith of the Prophet along with his chief generals among the Iranians. Muhammad affirmed him in his post until his death, after which he sent a group of his companions as governors. This account alleges that the Prophet succeeded in incorporating Yemen by gaining influential converts rather than by force of arms. These narratives about elite Iranian conversion in Yemen cannot be corroborated from the Qur'an, but they are consistent with passages of that work about peaceful mass conversion in this era. The Qur'an's soft power began to win the day.[10]

❧

MUHAMMAD ABRUPTLY SET out with a band of Emigrants and Helpers from Medina in March 628, determined to perform a lesser pilgrimage to the Kaaba in Mecca, according to the early biographer `Urwa ibn al-Zubayr.[11] As `Urwa told the story, this 628 attempt at peacefully visiting the sacred shrine in the teeth of potential armed opposition from the bellicose traditionalists resembles a brave act of civil disobedience. The Meccan pagan elite, led by Abu Sufyan and Khalid ibn al-Walid, were still in control of the Kaaba and still hostile to Muhammad, so severe danger attended this procession. Everyone involved likely understood that by then, Iran was too absorbed in internal politics to marshal Arab clients in support of Mecca. When he and his party stopped at a place called Dhu al-Hulayfah, the Prophet garlanded his sacrificial camel and made an incision on its hump to indicate it would be offered up. He and his companions then put on the white robes of peaceful pilgrims to Mecca to announce that they were no war party.

Muhammad had repeatedly railed against the way the militant pagans of Mecca had cut the Believers off from their primary shrine and source of blessings. *Pilgrimage* 22:25 says, "We will visit a painful torment on the pagans who have barred the path of God and the sacred shrine—which we have made for those who dwell in its precincts and for nomads alike—and on those who intend to violate it with injustice." The verse appeals for support not only to urban worshippers but also to hinterland bedouins in rolling back this unfair practice, which contravened the peace of the sanctuary.

In the late 620s, their scripture had begun preparing the Medinans for the possibility of reconciliation with the traditionalists: "Perhaps God will create love between you and those among whom were your enemies" (*The Woman Tested* 60:7). After all, not all pagans had committed war crimes, and many were, practically speaking, neutral even if they lived among the militants. Verse 60:8 continues, "God does not forbid you, with regard to those who have not fought you over religion nor expelled you from your homes, from being righteous and just toward them, for God loves those who are just." The verse insists that the Believers must treat nonhostile pagans fairly, a principle of civil government unknown in neighboring Christian Rome or Zoroastrian Iran and one largely suppressed by the later Muslim commentary tradition.[12]

According to `Urwa, when Muhammad and his parched band reached a spring near Usfan, he was met by a friendly from Mecca, Bishr al-Ka`bi, who informed him that scouts had warned the Quraysh of his approach. He reported that warriors had come out of the city apace. In some versions they were wearing leopard skins and bringing their milch camels and camped at Dhu Tawa. The Quraysh warrior Khalid ibn al-Walid led an advance party of their cavalry out to al-Ghamim, about eight miles from the Prophet's position. They were swearing that he "would never enter Mecca in defiance of them."

Muhammad consulted with his companions, according to the report attributed to ʿUrwa, about the best course of action, and they said, "Prophet of God! We have only come as pilgrims and not to engage in combat with anyone."[13]

At the pass of al-Murar, near the springs of Hudaibiya, Muhammad's camel knelt and refused to get up. The Believers are said to have taken it as a sign of the divine will. Tabari relays a tradition that news of the Sasanid emperor's death reached Muhammad there at Hudaibiya where the Believers made camp.[14]

Then the Meccan Budayl al-Khuzaʿi rode out with some of his fellow Khuzaʿa tribesmen to parlay with Muhammad. This clan in Mecca contained some covert Believers, and even the pagan Khuzaʿa were said to favor the Prophet politically. ʿUrwa tells a story here that is consistent with the existence of pagan allies of Muhammad inside Mecca at which *The Women* 4:94 hinted, and he says they provided him with intelligence on the situation there.

Muhammad told Budayl, "We have not come to engage anyone in combat. Instead, it is as pilgrims that we have come."

Budayl reported what Muhammad said back to Mecca, but its notables reacted wrathfully, saying Muhammad may not have wanted a battle but they were ready to give him one and vowing that he would not enter the city against their will. Nor, they pledged, would the surrounding bedouins detect any such weakness in them.

A series of negotiations ensued, with envoys sent back and forth between Hudaibiya and Mecca. At one point, Abu Bakr is said testily to have told one haughty pagan negotiator what he could do with his goddess, Allat.

Finally, a man of Kinana, seeing that the camels had been garlanded and marked for sacrifice, concluded that by the norms of the Kaaba sanctuary, the Believers should not be sent away. He persuaded the Quraysh to compromise.

The pagans then sent Suhayl ibn ʿAmr to dicker with Muhammad, suggesting that he could come back the following year and perform the pilgrimage then but would have to withdraw at that time so that the Quraysh did not lose face with the surrounding bedouins. ʿUrwa implies that the Meccan leadership engaged in political competition with Muhammad for the allegiance of these rural clans, and they feared that if it appeared the Believers had forced their way into the city, it would set in motion a new wave of alliances between Medina and the hinterland. On the other hand, if they violently attacked white-garbed pilgrims in a holy month, they could also have lost the allegiance of their pastoralist allies as unholy tyrants.

In ʿUrwa's telling, the Prophet's companions did not like the proposal one little bit.

The quick-tempered, brawny Omar leaped up and went to the elderly Abu Bakr: "Is he not God's apostle, and are we not Muslims, and are they not polytheists?"

The rawboned old Abu Bakr agreed.

"Then why should we agree to what is demeaning to our religion?"

Abu Bakr demurred. "Stick with what he says, for I bear witness that he is God's Messenger."

That remark deflated the volatile Omar. "And so do I."

According to a narrative of al-Zuhri, Muhammad asked for a scribe to write out a treaty. He began, "In the name of God, the merciful, the compassionate."

Suhayl, like many Meccans, found the diction about divine mercy (influenced by the Bible and Yemeni traditions) to be alien and insisted it be changed to just "In your name, God."

Despite the objections of the Believers, Muhammad found this acceptable and had the scribe write it down. He continued, "This is what Muhammad the messenger of God has agreed."

Suhayl objected. "By God, if we knew that you were God's messenger, we would not have barred you from the shrine or fought you. Write 'Muhammad ibn Abdullah.'"

Muhammad, with the possibility of the restoration of peace hanging in the balance, again swallowed his pride and agreed: "Write: 'This is what Muhammad ibn Abdullah has agreed with Suhayl ibn `Amr.'"

In this document, which became known as the Treaty of Hudaibiya, they agreed that the Believers would have to postpone their pilgrimage for a year so that the Quraysh could save face but could then come for three days lightly armed and with blades sheathed. They would refrain from hostilities for ten years, during which both Medinans and Meccans would be safe from attack. Those who wished to ally with either party were free to do so. The agreement contained a significant inequity. Those who wished to desert Muhammad's camp and go to the Quraysh would be free to do so. Quraysh converts to the new faith who wished to relocate to Medina and join Muhammad, however, would be returned.

The later Muslim writers imply that the Prophet's agreement to return to Mecca any Believers who managed to get to Medina was viewed by some as shameful. Likely, these later inhabitants of great Muslim empires could not imagine that pagans should ever be treated as equals for contractual purposes. In contrast, the Qur'an is clear in insisting on fair dealing with all human beings on the grounds of what can only be called a sort of late-antique humanism.[15] The objections are anyway anachronistic or contradictory. Since the scripture taught freedom of conscience, Muhammad would not have wanted to have an apostate who fled to pagan Mecca returned to him. Since the treaty allowed Quraysh clans to declare for Muhammad and remain in Mecca, they had no reason any longer to emigrate to Medina.

`Urwa says that Muhammad asked the Believers, stymied for that year, to sacrifice their camels at Hudaibiya instead. They declined, since they were not technically in the sacred precincts of the Kaaba. Then Muhammad performed his sacrifice and had his head shaved, shaming the rest of his party into doing so.

The narrative of Hudaibiya attributed to `Urwa ibn al-Zubayr by several later authors cannot be corroborated from the Qur'an. The `Urwa version shows signs of being reworked by the folk process (storytellers like to triple some elements, and there is a miracle story about Muhammad providing his band with water). Some of the provisions mentioned resemble those in the 561–562 peace treaty between the Roman Empire and the House of Sasan, including the agreement to decline to receive defectors, the binding of tribal Arab allies to the peace, and the provision for freedom of religion of adherents living under alien rule.[16] We would now call the episode an instance of nonviolent collective action, aiming at the restoration of social calm in the Hejaz. The sentiments about compromising with the traditionalists and making peace if they inclined to it are also present in the Qur'an.

❧

IN THE WAKE of Iran's agony and defeat, Constantinople's propagandists portrayed Herakleios as a second Alexander, destined to defeat his Iranian nemesis, just as the Macedonian had brought down the Achaemenid dynasty in ancient times. Alexander (356–323 BCE) had swept out of Europe with a Greek army that gathered up local volunteers, conquering Asia Minor, Syria, Egypt, Mesopotamia, and Iran. After Khosrow II's fall, the Syriac-speaking Roman scribes, eager to regain the loyalty of Near Eastern Christians who had lived under Sasanid rule for a decade and a half, reworked these preexisting epic materials, known as "The Alexander Romance." They inserted into the story the biblical theme that the world conqueror had built an iron wall to keep out the menacing eastern hordes of Gog and Magog, which seventh-century Romans identified as Iran.[17] The Qur'an's chapter of *The Cave* (18:83–99) gives a capsule summary of this epic, with details found only in the version intended to bolster support among Near Eastern populations for Constantinople's recovery of all its territory. Believers in the late 620s would have, like Syrians and others, read the story as a rallying cry for Herakleios against the Sasanian war of aggression.

Because the Macedonian conqueror had destroyed the magnificent Achaemenid capital of Persepolis in 330 BCE, generations of Iranian writers detested him. One Middle Persian romance portrayed him as an abject, sinful, baleful dupe of Ahriman, the Persian Satan. It excoriated him for having burned the scriptures, the Avesta and Zand, which pious priests had "written with gold ink on prepared parchment":

> Thus they say that the righteous Zarathustra promulgated in the world the well-accepted religion. Until three hundred years had passed, the religion remained pure and the people were free of doubts. Then the accursed, lying Evil Spirit, in order to inspire people with doubts about this religion, misled the damned Alexander the Greek who dwelled in Egypt, and dispatched him to the realm of Iran with great tyranny and bellicosity and misery. He killed the Iranian emperor and left the court and its sovereignty in ruins and devastation.[18]

"The Alexander Romance" produced under Herakleios predicts that at the end of time, the Macedonian's barricade against the barbarians would crumble, allowing them to flood into cultured realms. The author intended this imagery to imply that in the face of Iranian advances, only Herakleios, the second Alexander, could rebuild the wall and save civilization.

The Cave (18:83–99) says that in the course of his wide-ranging conquests, "the Two-Horned" (an apocalyptic sobriquet for Alexander) discovered a people barely able to understand speech. His troops point out to him their wickedness (18:94). "They said: behold, you of the two horns, Gog and Magog are wreaking corruption in the land." Alexander replies (18:95), "I will set up a rampart between you and them." Exactly as in the Syriac romance, he and his army build an iron wall to keep the hordes out. The ancient general then warns (18:98), "But when the pledge of my Lord comes to pass, he will pulverize it; and my Lord's promise is ever true." Likely, given *Rome* 30:1, the Qur'an concurred that Herakleios as a second Alexander was civilization's only hope of reversing the onslaught from the Iranian East, while at the same time indicating that these world-shaking events announced a new prophetic mission.

Daniel 7, by speaking of Greek rule as the last before the advent of the reign of the Holy Ones, had allowed Roman Christians to connect Alexander (the initiator of Greek rule) with the apocalyptic figure known as "the last Roman emperor." Daniel 7:7–8 says, "After this I saw in the night visions, and behold, a fourth beast, terrible and dreadful and exceedingly strong; and it had great iron teeth; it devoured and broke in pieces, and stamped the residue with its feet. It was different from all the beasts that were before it; and it had ten horns. I considered the horns, and behold, there came up among them another horn, a little one, before which three of the first horns were plucked up by the roots; and behold, in this horn were eyes like the eyes of a man, and a mouth speaking great things." Later in the chapter (7:24), an interpreting angel explains that the fourth beast, with ten horns, is the Greek empire with ten kings (Alexander and nine successors), who would be succeeded by yet another Greek king, the "little horn," who would defeat three royal rivals.[19]

Later Roman writers of apocalypses described this figure in a positive way. They saw the "little horn" as the "last Roman Emperor" of the eastern Greek-speaking empire before the apocalyptic reign of the Holy Ones begins. This interpretation of the Greek rulers as a beast with a "horn" in Daniel 7 may be one origin of the Qur'an's sobriquet for Alexander "the Two-Horned." In his own establishment of a world empire, he was the first horn, and his distant apocalyptic successor is the "little horn."[20]

⁀

THE CHAPTER OF *The Cave* (18), which has recently been redated to 629 or 630, also contains the late-antique version of the Rip van Winkle tale, the story of the seven sleepers of Ephesos.[21] These young Christian converts fell asleep in a cave at a time when Roman pagans persecuted persons of their persuasion, but awoke two centuries later to discover that they were living in a Christian empire. The Qur'an comments on this celebrated legend in the same chapter as it retells "The Alexander Romance" and likely is also using it to refer to current events. I wonder whether the Qur'an viewed the Christians of Syria and Egypt to have been in suspended animation politically under the rule of the Zoroastrian Shahr Varaz, but now to have awoken to find themselves again in the realm of a pious Christian monarch.

Given that the chapter begins by scolding Christians for (literally) attributing to God a son, Muhammad may also have hoped that these political upheavals would cause them to rethink the doctrinal morass into which their theologians had argued themselves and turn to a form of Unitarianism. The Prophet might have been encouraged in these hopes by Herakleios's own attempts to find a compromise between Chalcedonians and Miaphysites, as he searched for a new overarching formula depicting Christ as having a single energy or will and leaving aside the question of whether he had one or two natures.[22]

⁂

As LATER MUSLIMS remembered it, the Treaty of Hudaibiya of 628 did not last ten years but only until January 630. `Urwa explained in a letter that the agreement had specified that clans were free to ally with the Meccan elite or with Muhammad in Medina and forbade attacks by one coalition on the other. The Banu Ka`b in Mecca, a mix of traditionalists and Believers, declared for the Prophet politically. Their rivals, the militantly pagan Banu Bakr, allied with the Quraysh. It so happened that very late in 629, the Banu Bakr and the Ka`b fought. The Quraysh came in on the side of their clients, the Bakr clan, giving the latter weapons. A fracas between Banu Bakr and Banu Ka`b in and of itself might not have disturbed the peace of the Hejaz, but the Quraysh violated the armistice with the Prophet's followers by actively arming Bakr. Muhammad and the Believers thus considered the treaty to have been violated, allowing them to set out for the Kaaba without asking anyone's permission.[23]

According to the Qur'an, at this juncture Muhammad had a vision of going to Mecca and entering the Kaaba: "You will enter the sacred shrine if God so wills, in security, your heads shaved and your locks shorn, without fear" (48:27).[24]

Thus, he gathered his followers and set out: "He is the one who sent down divine peace (Sakina) into the hearts of the believers, to increase their faith" (Success 48:4).

In a state of divinely bestowed calm, they would have traveled through the chilly winter desert, perhaps crossing occasional thin runnels of icy water biting into the broad, deep wadis, which were fed by an abrupt, ephemeral squall or two. Did they pass by unwontedly green grasses and ruderals amid clusters of yellow yarrow as they headed steadfastly into what could well be the jaws of death at pugnacious Mecca?

The chapter remonstrates with those erratic pagan bedouin allies who had declined to accompany the Medinans:

"Our property and our families preoccupied us, so forgive us," they said archly (Qur'an 48:11).

"Rather, you thought that the messenger and the believers would never return to their families, and the thought was made to seem pleasing to your hearts. You conceived an evil notion, and were a doomed people," *Success* 48:12 scolded these nomadic tribes.

These verses suggest that the Medinans were left in the lurch by some putative bedouin confederates during their approach to the sanctuary city in early January 630 and that, moreover, the bedouins had a low estimation of the chances the Believers would avoid being massacred.

"Those who stayed behind will assert, 'When you plan to take booty, then let us follow you'" (*Success* 48:15).

"They wish to alter the very words of God! Say: 'You will never follow us, for God has predicted it aforetime,'" the verse concludes.

This exchange demonstrates that Muhammad had decided beforehand that the procession would be peaceful, and that the Prophet had therefore let his followers know that no plunder would be taken from the sanctuary city. His avaricious sometime allies among the bedouins, probably still pagans, along with some Hypocrites, could not see why they should put themselves to such trouble under those circumstances. It would have been advantageous to the Believers, however, if they had added to the number of the marchers, making them appear all the more formidable, so as to dissuade any hotheaded Meccan offensive.

The scripture warns the reluctant bedouins (48:16) that although the Meccan procession would be peaceful, there are still some hard fights ahead, and God will judge them on their constancy. Lest some who stayed behind out of necessity feel badly, *Success* 48:17 underlines that the blind and lame were excused and would nevertheless attain paradise.

As the Qur'an tells the story, the Believers would have peacefully entered Mecca, wending in their multitudes between humble dwellings of palm fronds and adobe through cramped passageways toward the Kaaba, and the pagans, watching exasperatedly from within, did not dare attack them.

"If the pagans had fought you, they would have ended up turning tail, nor would they have found any patron or helper" (*Success* 48:22).

The scripture is quite clear that there was no battle or bloodshed as the Believers entered the holy city. The Quraysh had for years been violating the norms of the sanctuary but appear to have perceived that the political tide in the Hejaz had turned against them, and they did not dare attempt to massacre the peaceful Medinans who had already signaled to surrounding bedouins that they intended to avoid battle and plunder.

"This is the tradition of God, as ever before, and you will find no change in the tradition of God. He it is who withheld their hands from you and your hands from them in the heart of Mecca after he made you ascendant over them" (*Success* 48:23–24). These two verses refer to the divine wont of reconciling former enemies and establishing peace and make it clear that the Prophet's entry into the square around the Kaaba was nonviolent.

Later Muslim commentators called the move on Mecca a "conquest," but it appears to have signally lacked a military dimension. In his account, the early biographer ʿUrwa ibn al-Zubayr said that his father, al-Zubayr ibn al-ʿAwwam (594–656), carried a battle standard and said that the Prophet designated safe houses for the cowering Meccans as the armed Believers entered the city and that there was a minor skirmish—all details not only absent from but contradicted by the Qur'anic account. It has been argued that the word the Qur'an uses to describe the entry into Mecca means "success" and not, as it was later interpreted, "triumph." It literally means "opening" and may also refer in particular to the opening of the Kaaba, which had been closed off to the Believers.[25]

In 'Urwa's narrative, municipal leaders such as Abu Sufyan and Khalid ibn al-Walid had already thrown in the towel, and when the Prophet arrived in the holy city, "The people stood before him to swear allegiance to him, and so the people of Mecca became Muslims." It is only in that sense that Mecca "fell." Obviously, that ending to the story is considerably too neat since the whole city did not convert in any meaningful sense all at once.

The Qur'an (*Help* 110:1–3), however, does concur that there was at some point some sort of mass conversion. It celebrates, "When comes the help of God, and success, and you see the people entering the religion of God in throngs, then proclaim the praise of your Lord, and seek his forgiveness; for he is ever ready to forgive."

Success rebukes the formerly combative leaders of the Quraysh: "They are the ones who paganized and barred you from the sacred shrine, preventing the sacrifice from reaching its altar."[26]

Why did the Believers not mount a military conquest of the traditionalists, given the enormity of their crimes? The Qur'an answers that Mecca was full of secret Believers, both men and women, of whose identity even the Prophet remained unaware, given that they had been cut off from Medina since the Emigration and had had to practice clandestinely.

Success continues, "God would not have prevented you from fighting the pagans had there not been believing men and believing women whose identity you did not know, and whom you might have trampled underfoot and unknowingly harmed."[27] Despite the presence of a casus belli, or legal cause of action for a just war, prudence had dictated that the Believers not risk a clash that would kill innocents, including underground Meccan followers of the Prophet.

The chapter goes on to contrast the berserk battle madness and indiscipline of the Meccans with the divinely bestowed serenity of the Believers: "Behold, the pagans instilled in their hearts a war fever, the war fever of the unruly. But God sent down his peace (*Sakina*) on his messenger and on the believers and constrained them with the word of piety, and they proved worthy and deserving of it. God is omniscient" (*Success* 48:26).

Mecca's welcoming of the Prophet on January 10, 630, when the formerly hostile Quraysh elite gave up and accepted Muhammad's leadership by acclamation was, from the scripture's point of view, not a military triumph but a success of inner divine peace. It allowed the Believers to demonstrate spiritual self-control in the face of the provocations of the reckless Quraysh. The underground surge of Meccans into the faith of Muhammad had created a substantial if furtive community, the very existence of which protected the city from any martial attack. The example of the Believers' composed steadfastness brought the Meccan traditionalists over to their side and brought social peace to the city.

Later Muslim civilization called the time before Islam the Jahiliyyah, which in classical Arabic meant not the age of ignorance but the age of wildness, when people were out of control. The Qur'an contrasts that indiscipline with the peace of God, the *Sakina*, that the Prophet had brought his people. Jewish rabbis had taught that at the end-time, the Shechinah, or divine presence, would return to Jerusalem.[28] Inasmuch as the scripture identified the Kaaba as a twin of the altar on the temple mount, Muhammad's return to Mecca was the equivalent of the Jews' return from exile to Jerusalem. There may be an apocalyptic implication to its use of this phrase here.

The relative geopolitical strength of Medina and Mecca may have changed dramatically in the year and a half leading up to these events. The son of the late Shiroyeh Kavad II, Ardashir III, was still a small child of seven on his father's death. His regents, including the chamberlain Farrukhzad and the notable Meh-Adur Goshnasp, placed him on the throne around September 628 and oversaw Iran's affairs.[29]

The Near Eastern question, however, remained unresolved for a while. An impatient Herakleios offered Shahr Varaz his support should he wish to relinquish Egypt and Syria and go to Ctesiphon to claim the White Palace. In July 629, the Iranian general, war weary, finally met the Roman emperor at a northern pass called Arabissos Tripotamos. They recognized the Euphrates as the border between the two empires, and Shahr Varaz agreed to begin withdrawing his troops. "They made peace with each other and they built a church there and named it Eirene [Peace]."[30] The Sasanian retreat took months to effect afterward. If pagan Mecca continued to seek an Iranian alliance, it saw a distinct ebbing of practical support in the fall of 629 as the Sasanians began trekking home from the Near East.

Speaking of the Prophet in Mecca, the Qur'an exclaims, "God truly vindicated the vision he vouchsafed to his messenger.... He knows what you know not, and appointed for you besides this an imminent success."[31] The climax of this account comes in *Success* 48:29, which says that the Prophet's Believers became heirs, on the fall of Mecca, to both the virtues of the Hebrew Bible and those of the New Testament. They have bowed so much in prayer that their foreheads developed a mark from being touched so often to a prayer stone, which the Qur'an identifies as an attribute of the Jewish scriptures. It may have in mind a passage such as Nehemiah 8:6: "Then Ezra blessed the Lord, the great God, and all the people answered, 'Amen, Amen,' lifting up their hands. Then they bowed their heads and worshiped the Lord with their faces to the ground."

Then the passage continues its comparison to the next dispensation: "The parable for them in the Gospel is as a seed that puts forth its shoot, and strengthens it, and it grows stout and rises straight upon its stalk, pleasing the sowers, that through them he may enrage the pagans. God has promised those of them who believe and perform righteous works forgiveness and a magnanimous recompense."[32] This latter is obviously a reference to Jesus's parable of the sower in Mark 4:5–8: "Other seed fell among thorns, and the thorns grew up and choked it, and it yielded no grain. Other seed fell into good soil and brought forth grain, growing up and increasing and yielding thirty and sixty and a hundredfold."

The homecoming in Mecca for the religion of Muhammad is the occasion for the Qur'an to celebrate in the Believers the culmination of Abrahamic piety since they brought together in themselves virtues from the Hebrew Bible (prostration all the way to the ground) and the New Testament (fertile receptivity to the Logos or Word). Above all, this piety or God fearing was exemplified in their peaceable approach to the holy city, which forestalled a gory conflict.

❧

BOTH THE QUR'AN and later biographers such as 'Urwa suggest that on Muhammad's advent in Mecca, its inhabitants underwent a sudden mass conversion. Christian sources in late antiquity also reported such phenomena among Arab pagans. A century and a half before, the ascetic Saint Simeon the Stylite in Syria brought to Christ pastoralist Arab worshippers of al-'Uzza by virtue of his self-denying life atop a pillar. As his biographer described it,

> As for the Ishmaelites, they arrived in bands, of two hundred or three hundred at once, sometimes a thousand. They renounced

with great cries their ancestral error, breaking before the great luminary the idols that their fathers had adored and giving up the orgies of Aphrodite—for they had long since adopted the cult of that demon—they participated in the divine mysteries, accepting the laws from that sacred tongue, bidding farewell to the customs of their fathers and abstaining from eating wild asses and camel.[33]

The smashing of the betyls by newly Christian Arabs in the Near East had the effect of freeing the new Believers from the shackles of their past.[34]

Muhammad's serene procession and his recitation of the Qur'an had a similar effect on pagan Mecca a century and a half later. Some of the earlier Christian saints, too, had been able to preach in eloquent Arabic or in Arabic-inflected Aramaic that the tribal notables understood. As an agent of religious change for the Arabs, Muhammad succeeded the Near Eastern Christian saints who had helped convert Banu Kalb and Banu Ghassan and was recognized as a late-antique holy man who spoke truth to the power of the Meccan establishment.[35] He offered a different model than the desert stylites, however, of social engagement and active peacemaking among warring clans. Tribal societies based on vendetta required an outside mediator, whose holiness guaranteed impartiality.

As with the Arab enthusiasts of Saint Simeon who had broken their god stones of al-ʿUzza outside Antioch in the fifth century, so the new Believers of Mecca are said to have turned on their former objects of devotion.[36] The later Muslim historians represent the destruction of the betyls as something the Helpers and Emigrants did to the Meccans, but it is more likely that an iconoclastic enthusiasm gripped the city across the board.

The Qur'an (Repentance 9:28) then outlawed the rites of polytheists at the Kaaba, in part because they were held to be ritually impure.[37]

Nevertheless, there is no evidence that the Qur'an altered its stance that inner conscience should not be coerced. Outside of the area around the Kaaba, traditionalists continued to exist in the Hejaz in fair numbers. Early Muslim polities in the Near East tolerated surviving pagan communities at Harran and elsewhere, and some Christian monks of the later seventh century were upset by the Muslim policy of religious pluralism.

Muhammad's religion was triumphant but not vindictive. The later biographers maintained that major pagan leaders such as Abu Sufyan were entirely amnestied, in accordance with the verses of the Qur'an that had repeatedly promised the Quraysh there would be no reprisals if they made an armistice. They even allege that the Prophet went so far as to bestow one hundred camels each on Abu Sufyan, his son Mu'awiya, and a few other civic leaders, for the purpose of "uniting the hearts." As we saw, the Qur'an (*Success* 48:24) celebrates the lack of bloodshed: "He it is who withheld their hands from you and your hands from them in the heart of Mecca after he made you ascendant over them."[38]

❧

THE QUR'AN IN the late 620s and into 630 begins to concentrate less on the themes of just war and to focus instead on the conditions under which tranquility could be restored to the Hejaz—that is, it moves from a concern with negative peace to a preoccupation with positive peace. It begins singling out neutral pagans who were willing to give strong evidence of their good intentions for special treatment by the Believers. Their greetings of "peace" must be returned in kind, and the Believers have no permission to treat them as hostile if they withdraw and decline to engage in combat. Muhammad's followers must even be fair and just toward those who had not assaulted them. The downfall of Khosrow II perhaps paved the way to an armistice with Mecca, which many Believers may have found hard to imagine or even, given that the pagans had killed their friends and families, may have viewed as distasteful. *The Woman Tested* 60:7, however, insisted that it was possible for God to create love between former enemies. The Treaty of Hudaibiya is not mentioned in the Qur'an but does not contradict the emphases in the late chapters. Perhaps, like the Constitution of Medina, it was seen as a secular document and outside the scripture. Or perhaps later biographers created the episode as a referent for the chapter of *Success* so that they could turn the accession of Mecca into a martial event.

Although the later biographical tradition saw the procession to Mecca and the Quraysh mass embrace of Muhammad's religion as a "conquest," the Qur'an describes a peaceful cavalcade, a campaign of nonviolent noncooperation, which ruled out beforehand violence or looting—a decision that determined potential bedouin allies to stay home. With the advent of the Believers in the sanctuary city, the Qur'an celebrates the mass conversion of the Quraysh and the cleansing of the shrine of God from the pollution of pagan worship. The Believers, imbued with the *Sakina*, or divine peace, demonstrated the self-discipline to avoid fighting in the sanctuary and the courage and faith to win over the hearts of their former deadly foes. The faith of Muhammad proved successful in Mecca not through war but by the Prophet's tactics of conciliation. While the Qur'an continues to warn polytheists of the torments of hellfire, it does not allow their conversion by force. The Qur'an and even Abbasid sources present significant evidence that some tribal groups remained pagan, even as some of them allied with Muhammad.[39]

✺

MECCA HAD ATTEMPTED three times to take Medina in all-out war and failed in all three attempts, leaving its elite in a quandary. The

Qur'an for its part had repeatedly emphasized that if the enemy sued for peace, the Believers would call off the hostilities. Moreover, it pledged that the Meccans would suffer no reprisals for having taken up arms. The missing ingredient was pagan willingness to compromise and to put away their swords. Their leaders ultimately did so when it became apparent that they could not have their way and could not even stop Meccan clans from swinging toward the Prophet's leadership. Their willingness to bargain may also have been increased by the precipitously declining fortunes of the Sasanians. The Qur'an indicates its support for the Roman cause allegorically, implicitly celebrating Herakleios as the new Alexander, charged with restoring the divine barricade against invasion from the East. It is also important for the history of religious ecumenism to underline that the Qur'an represents the Hejaz conflict not only as a just war of self-defense for the Believers but as having been waged to protect Christianity and its institutions as well.

Muhammad, for his part, having made the point that the Medinan Believers could not be militarily overwhelmed, turned to nonviolent collective action in order to shame the Meccan leadership. Muhammad's use of strategic nonaggression proved key to gaining readmission to Mecca for his followers and to winning over hearts and minds in the sanctuary city and among pastoral nomads outside it.

If chroniclers such as Tabari are right on this issue, Muhammad increasingly proved able to appeal to elites up and down the Tihama through the message of the Qur'an and his apocalyptic charisma. The descendants of the Sasanian officer corps in Yemen are said to have swung to the new religion as their own liege lord lost his victory halo. As later Muslims told the story, Yemen fell to the Prophet without any military engagement at all, a history consonant with the emphasis in the Qur'an on peace and debating members of other faiths "in the best of ways."

The narrative, in the chapter of *Success* (48), of the procession of the Believers to Mecca in 630 also points to the Prophet's increasing deployment of an Arabian form of nonviolent collective action. The Qur'an and the later accounts of `Urwa ibn al-Zubayr both suggest that Medina and Mecca competed for the loyalty of pastoralists in the region, who were impressed by qualities such as coolness under fire and willingness to take risks in upholding the conventions of peace centered on the Kaaba. The avoidance of fighting in the sanctuary city and the descent of the *Sakina* on the Believers, endowing them with serenity, formed a religious counterpart to the tribal virtue of even-temperedness. The poetry of Arab battle days commemorated reckless raids and pointless savagery. In contrast, the Qur'an celebrates the way in which God forestalled violence in the heart of the holy city. This sacred nonbelligerence promoted mass conversion in Mecca and among many of the bedouins, which confirmed Muhammad's spiritual leadership of the Hejaz. The Believers could not rest on their laurels, however; nor could they put behind them the necessity for just war, despite their moral victory over the Quraysh. The anarchic tribes of Arabia viewed that very leadership as a threat and gathered for another fierce military challenge to the Prophet and his followers.

§ 7 §

INTO THE WAY OF PEACE

IN LATE JANUARY 630, THE FUMING THAQIF TRIBE ASSEMBLED OUTSIDE the castellated walls of their adobe beehive of a city, Taif, perched high on the slopes of the Sarawat Mountains. Shivering in the dim winter dawn, they descended past sheer schist hills and occasional scraggly junipers toward Mecca, chanting hymns of loyalty ("Here I am!") to their patron warrior goddess, Allat. They sought to meet up with their rural tribal allies, the Hawazin, led by the fierce Malik ibn ʿAwf al-Nasri, who had conceived the campaign.

'Urwa ibn al-Zubayr explained that pagan tribes had gathered to launch a major war on Mecca, having heard that the holy city had welcomed Muhammad and accepted his leadership.[1] Most of the urban centers along the Arabian side of the Red Sea littoral—Medina, Mecca, Najran, Sana'a, and Aden—had by that time come under the sway of the Prophet, with the exception of Taif, according to later biographers. All had acquiesced to his leadership peacefully. Still, many in the more lightly populated countryside remained hostile.

The Hawazin tribe, which generally pastured northeast of Mecca on the way to Hira in the Sasanian Empire, instigated this battle. They came down from the Northeast as an entire people in the pastoralist manner, bringing their families and bleating livestock. By 630 the Iranians had been forced back out of Egypt and Palestine, but they still had Mesopotamia and remained a presence in inner Arabia. Sasanian generals would have been alarmed to see a potential challenger arising in the Hejaz, which had by its religious message stripped their empire of Yemen and so could equally well threaten them in the Tigris and Euphrates River valleys. Farrukhzad and other regents of child emperor Ardashir III in the Sasanian Empire, with which Hawazin conducted most of its trade, could well have put their clients up to this attack.

Muhammad's scouts brought back reports of the Hawazin advance on Mecca, where he and his companions were temporarily still based. On January 27, 630, a band of Meccans, along with a contingent of Helpers and Emigrants who had come with the Prophet from Medina that January, joined Muhammad in a defensive formation. Ironically, his old enemy Abu Sufyan now fought shoulder-to-shoulder with him, having become a Believer or at least having acknowledged Muhammad's political leadership.

The two forces clashed at Hunayn, a dry riverbed glinting with jasper and chalcedony. Brazen cavalrymen caracoled toward their foes, and infantrymen sought a footing on the loamy alluvial sand, swinging Damascene swords imbrued with the gore of the enemy. In the end, the joint Mecca-Medina forces put the Hawazin and Thaqif to flight. Muhammad then allegedly led his army up to Taif and besieged it for two weeks. His forces, however, could not breach its walls, though villagers and tribesmen in the area decided to transfer their allegiance to him. The Prophet returned to Medina without having taken the city, `Urwa wrote. On his way back, he halted at al-Ji`ranah, where the captives from Hawazin, along with their women and children, were being held. That tribe, however, had rethought its opposition and sent delegations pledging loyalty to the Prophet. He freed all the prisoners.

Muhammad then went on a lesser pilgrimage to Mecca. Thereafter, he returned to Medina, leaving others behind in charge of Mecca and of instructing its people in the faith (a telling detail that shows even later Muslim authors were aware that accepting Muhammad as a political leader and embracing his religion were not the same thing). After the Prophet arrived back at Medina, Taif municipal leaders, having repented of their attack, came up and gave him their pledge of fealty.

The Qur'an gives some details of a battle at Hunayn but mentions nothing about a siege of Taif, which may be a later fiction. The scripture indicates that bedouin tribes mounted an attack on the Believers. While some pastoralists clearly also felt the pull of the new religion, many remained outside its orbit at this point, and some who had made agreements with Medina reneged on them once it became clear that something like a state was forming around the Prophet.

Bedouins had been called "leaderless" by Roman historian Menander the Guardsman. Tribes preferred this condition and strove persistently for it. When the Banu Baghid of Ghatafan had attempted, just before Muhammad's birth, to create a sacred sanctuary and a

175

trucial system among local clans, Zuhayr ibn Janab of the Banu Kalb immediately struck them to forestall the establishment of any new center of authority.[2]

As of 630, Muhammad saw the region's pastoralists as a major challenge, reciting, "The Bedouin are the most egregiously pagan and hypocritical and more likely to remain unaware of the limits God has set by what he revealed to his messenger, and God is All-Knowing, All-Wise" (*Repentance* 9:97). Some of his reluctant nomadic allies, *Repentance* 9:98–99 avers, saw the extra expense incurred in the Prophet's defensive wars as a penalty, and secretly they eagerly awaited his downfall. Other bedouins believed in God and the Judgment Day and accounted their expenditures for the sake of the new religion a means of nearing the divine and obtaining the blessings and prayers of the Prophet. The pastoralists thus fell into four groups, comprising hostile pagans, those who sought a peace treaty with Muhammad, those who had such a covenant but broke it, and converts.

The Qur'an implies (*Repentance* 9:1–3) that traditionalists with whom Muhammad had made peace treaties, such as the Hawazin, had, in the aftermath of the accession of Mecca, reneged on them and declared war on the Believers. The noncompliance of the other parties had rendered these covenants void, and the Prophet and his followers washed their hands of the oath breakers. The Believers would continue to honor the ban on fighting them for four months, but thereafter Muhammad's faithful would treat them as the deadly enemies they had revealed themselves to be.[3]

The Qur'an (9:4) adds, however, an exception to this counter-declaration of war "for the pagans with whom you have concluded a treaty and who have not contravened it from their side or helped others against you. You must fulfill the commitments of the covenant with them according to its term. Surely God loves the pious."

Tribesmen who sought further such accords had to agree to them with the Prophet at the Kaaba (9:7), the center of peace, where former belligerents naturally concluded any treaty of nonaggression and the sanctity of which guaranteed it on both sides. The Believers were duty bound to honor any truce contracted with such well-meaning but unbelieving tribes. Indeed, the scripture insists on the principle of impartiality (*The Table* 5:8), even with regard to former enemies who sought peace: "Believers, be responsible before God and bear witness in fairness. Do not let hatred for a people move you not to be equitable. Be equitable—that is nearer to piety."

Pagans could also seek the Prophet's formal protection (9:6) and would be delivered to a safe place by the Believers if they did so (the Kaaba, which Muhammad now oversaw, had the offering of sanctuary as one of its functions). This verse does not say anything about first requiring such clients to convert. The Messenger entertained the severest doubts that most pagans would honor their contractual obligations, however. The Qur'an (9:10) lamented that they observe "neither bond of kinship nor pact with a believer; they are the transgressors."

The scripture urges the faithful to stand their ground in the face of hostile traditionalists, however: "Then, when the sacrosanct months have faded, fight the pagans with deadly force wherever you encounter them, and capture them, and besiege them, and sit keeping a watch for them at every look-out."[4] These pagans had announced their intention to mount a violent campaign against Medina and Mecca. As for the phrase "wherever you encounter them," Tabari said that it means "the fighters of the pagans who attack you, whenever they fall upon you, must be killed by the believers if you are able to kill them."[5] That is, this important early Muslim thinker interpreted "pagans" here as "malefic pagans." The chapter had already made clear that nonbelligerents could conclude a peace treaty. *Repentance* 9:36 demonstrates the defensive character of Muhammad's campaign, instructing the Believers, "Fight the pagans together, just as they fight you together." The scripture provides no warrant here for aggressive warfare.

As the Medinan polity became more formalized, the Prophet appears to have begun implementing a rule of law that often resembled Roman practice. Emperor Justinian's Novella 134.13 had specified, "If anyone commits a capital crime under the law, those who are guilty shall be put to death. If, however, they commit a crime not deserving of the death penalty, they will be physically punished or transported into exile." The emperor added, "When anyone openly commits a violent assault, either with or without weapons, whether in dwellings or on the highways or at sea, they will be punished in accordance with the law," which permitted amputation of a limb, adding, "If the crime is such as to require that a limb be cut off, only one hand shall be removed."[6] The Qur'an in this era portrays aggressive, unprovoked warfare on the part of the pagan tribes as a form of brigandage. *The Table* 5:33–34 proclaims, in a passage that uncannily resembles that imperial Novella, "The recompense of those who make war on God and his prophet and spread corruption in the land is to be killed, or crucified, or to have their hands or feet cut off, or to be exiled from the territory. That is a degradation for them in this world, and they face in the next life severe torment—save for those who repent before you gain power over them. Know that God is forgiving and merciful."

The building pagan assault provoked fear and consternation among some of the more lukewarm recent converts, the "Hypocrites." They beseeched the Prophet for permission to stay home, and he granted it, on the grounds that such fainthearted warriors would have been useless on the battlefield anyway (*Repentance* 9:42–47, 101).

Repentance 9:25 addressed those valiant Believers who did go out to the battlefield: "God has already helped you in many regions, and on the day of Hunayn, when your multitude was pleasing to you; but it did not avail you at all, and the earth, vast as it is, was made narrow for you, and you turned about, retreating." The battle began badly, with a rout of many of the Believers, despite what appear to have been their superior numbers.

This setback proved temporary since the next verse (9:26) says, "Then God sent down upon his messenger his Peace [*Sakina*], and upon the believers, and he sent down invisible hosts, and he chastised the pagans; and that is the recompense of the pagans." Here, as at the approach to Mecca the previous month, the peace of God's presence, his *Sakina*, enters the hearts of Muhammad and his followers and gives them the self-discipline and internal calm to prevail over the pagan attackers. Whereas at Mecca the *Sakina* enabled nonviolence, at Hunayn it stiffened the morale of the Believers, allowing them successfully to defend themselves and their sanctuary cities from predatory tribes.

The Qur'an requires warlike pagans who launched unprovoked assaults on the Believers but then wanted to reconcile to give reparations (*jizya*) for their war crimes. I read *Repentance* 9:29 to say of the aggressors at Hunayn, "Fight those who do not believe in God and the Last Day and do not forbid what God and his messenger have forbidden—and who do not follow the religion of truth comprising those given scripture—until they willingly pay reparations and have been humbled." Since the Hawazin and Thaqif had gathered pugnaciously to destroy the Believers, showing that they did "not forbid" the wars of aggression that "God and his messenger have forbidden," they would be amnestied only if they stood down and forfeited damages. (This verse was later applied to Jews and Christians, but that use of it is frankly bizarre.)[7]

Inimical pagans on the attack could also return to the status of noncombatants by thinking better of their aggression and converting (9:5): "But whenever they repent, and perform the prayer, and pay alms for the poor, then let them go their way; God is All-forgiving, All-compassionate." This verse does not require conversion at the point of a sword. Rather, it has been argued that it insists that the Believers not continue to treat repentant converts as hostile.[8] The Qur'an elsewhere (9:4, 9:7, 8:19) made provisions for confrontational traditionalists to renounce their campaign and go to the Kaaba to make a secular peace treaty with the Prophet, retaining their gods but incurring a monetary penalty for their previous aggression.

EVENTS IN THE Hejaz likely mirrored geopolitical struggles. The end of formal hostilities with Iran did not relieve the Romans of anxieties about the possibility of renewed Sasanian aggression. Constantinople sought Arab federates, and indeed its need for such allies was one of the strategic lessons of the world war. Emperor Herakleios did what he could to set a cat among the pigeons, whispering in the ear of General Shahr Varaz that Constantinople would back him were he to seek the Iranian throne. As he finally retreated entirely from the Near East early in 630, the Iranian general, enraged that the notables at court in Ctesiphon had not consulted him about installing little Ardashir III, went into rebellion.

In April 630 the Iranian general gathered an army of thousands in Mesopotamia and, with the covert help of allies at court, besieged the capital. Shahr Varaz of the House of Mehran, a descendant of the Arsacid ruling family of the old Parthian Empire, took control of Ctesiphon and deposed the child king, crowning himself emperor.

Provincial aristocrats often had Arsacid ancestry, and this division in the Iranian elite had weakened it. Instability and intrigue roiled the capital, where most notables found this act of rank insubordination by a non-Sasanian to be unacceptable. In early June 630, Shahr Varaz, conqueror of Jerusalem and the former master of Syria and Egypt, fell victim to assassination.

The court had run out of sons of Khosrow II to ensconce in power, and a faction turned to his elder daughter Poran, who acceded to the throne as the first Iranian empress in the midsummer of 630. She seems to have had trouble persuading her male nobles to obey her commands and was forced to make further territorial concessions to Herakleios. One of her coins shows her wearing her crown on which is perched two feathered wings, the symbol of Verathragna, the angel of victory. On the other side of the coin stand a Zoroastrian fire altar and two attendants. Another of her coins bears the inscription "Your world brings new glory." After only a few months, she appears to have been shunted aside by her sister Azarmig Dokht, who became the paramount queen and ruled into 632. Perhaps exiled to the eastern provinces, Poran continued to mint coins for three years before she is heard of no more.[9]

This period of extreme instability at the Sasanian center can only have left policy toward Arabia in disarray. We should not assume, however, that the empresses and the generals and great notables around them lacked interest in finding ways to shore up Iranian power in the West. A picture book of the Sasanians depicts a rather martial Empress Azarmig Dokht seated on her throne in an embroidered cherry-red tunic and deep-blue sequined pants, holding a battle ax in her right hand and supporting herself with the sword in her left hand. She established a castle at Asadabad in northwestern Iran, near the border with Rome, and continued to try to spread and support

Zoroastrianism, founding a fire temple at Abkhaz.[10] Some of the bedouin unrest of which the Qur'an complains may have been impelled
by Iranian officials dismayed at their shrinking geopolitical influence.

In the spring of 630, the Abbasid chronicler Tabari wrote, Herakleios walked on foot from Emesa (Homs) to Jerusalem to commem-
orate its restoration to Christian Rome. "Carpets were rolled out for
him and aromatic basil leaves were placed on them." He reached
Jerusalem with his "generals and the aristocracy of the Romans" and
"carried out his worship." The duke of the restored garrison of Bostra
then came to him with an Arab who had been in Mecca. They inter-
rogated him by means of an interpreter, and he reported, "A man has
arisen among us, asserting that he is a prophet. Some people have
become his adherents and have believed in him, while others have
gone against him, and in many locales there have been epic battles
between them. That is how it was when I left." Herakleios, according to this late account, then gave orders to his spies in Palestine to
bring him any Meccans who might have more recent and better intelligence. They accosted a Quraysh caravan then off-loading goods in
Gaza and brought them to Jerusalem for questioning. Muslims told
this tale, as with the anecdote about the monk Nestorios who maintained that the twenty-five-year-old Muhammad had sat under a tree
reserved for envoys of the divine, to demonstrate that Christians
had a presentiment of a new prophet who would challenge Roman
control of Syria. This point of view is anachronistic, since only after
Muhammad's death did conflict develop between Medina and Constantinople. Nevertheless, that Herakleios in Jerusalem might have
gained intelligence about the soft underbelly of his newly recovered
Near Eastern dominions is entirely possible. The rise of a new polity
in the Hejaz would have raised important questions for Roman security, especially given Iran's continued hold over nearby Mesopotamia
and its influence among the Arabian tribes. Later Muslim tradition

often vilified Herakleios because after Muhammad's death the Medi-nan state came into conflict with him.[11]

A few folk memories of an alliance between Herakleios and the Prophet may survive, incongruously, in the midst of these other accounts. There is the story that Herakleios's governor of Egypt, once it had been recovered from Shahr Varaz, sent a bride for Muhammad as a way of making an alliance with him. The Prophet is said to have married the half-Greek and half–Coptic Christian Maria, the daugh-ter of Simeon, and to have had a child with her, who died in infancy.[12] This tale implies that Muhammad thereby gave a very personal sign of his willingness to accede to the late Roman commonwealth.

Ibn Sa`d alleges that Herakleios on a different occasion sent Muhammad the gift of a brocade silk suit but that the Prophet had it sent to King Armah, the Negus or Christian king of Ethiopia, also a member of the Eastern Roman commonwealth. The folk process clearly has worked on the details of this story about the Prophet's investiture by the emperor, the most obvious interpretation of which is that Herakleios sought a vassal. The storyteller signals that victori-ous Constantinople viewed Muhammad as a potential client and suc-cessor to the Jafnids, yet in the same breath denies that the Prophet could have accepted such a status. The tale has him restore the bal-ance of prophetic honor by passing it on to a geopolitical client of the eastern Roman Empire.[13]

If Muhammad did show interest in a friendly alliance of equals with the Christians, it did not imply a willingness to become subor-dinate to them or their empire. *The Table* 5:51 warns, "You who have believed, do not take Jews and Christians as patrons. They are patrons of one another. Whoever among you takes them as patrons has joined them. God does not guide wrongdoers."[14] The precise meaning of *patron* (in Arabic *wali*) in pre-Islamic Arabian society is difficult to define since Arabs used the word in many ways, but it generally means something like "benefactor." Muhammad may have feared that by taking Jews or Christians as patrons, Believers thereby joined their tribes and so would have conflicting political loyalties.

The client typically had a lower social status and might be either Arab or non-Arab. If a client went into business and did well, he could buy out his agreement and become instead an ally of his former patron.[15] The Arabic word for *patron* bears another possible meaning, which is "political ally," but since the Qur'an seems happy enough to have equal Christian allies, it is most likely prohibiting taking them as superiors.

In the Roman Empire, the institution of patronage powerfully shaped social relations. The upper-class patron would perform favors for a client of lower socioeconomic and social status and arrange for employment or connections. In return, the client would perform services for the patron. Freedmen became clients of their former masters. Infantrymen were considered clients of their officers. It is hard to see how the practice of Arab patronage in Syria by, say, the Banu Ghassan could have been isolated from Roman influences.[16]

For those poorer individuals who had newly embraced the religion of Muhammad, taking a Christian or Jew as a formal patron posed a clear danger. The Believer would be in a socially subordinate position, seeking favors, and might be forced to participate in the patron's religious ceremonies or even convert. Some Hejazi Sabians, Jews, or Christians preferred for reasons of politics that Muhammad's Believers relapse into their paganism. *The Family of Amram* (3:100) warned, "You who have believed, if you follow one faction of those given scripture aforetime, they will cause you to revert to being pagans after your belief." *The Table* 5:51 does not imply bad relations or enmity between the Believers and the scriptural communities, only a desire to protect new proselytes from undue coercion of conscience, a constant theme in the Qur'an.[17]

Muhammad's concerns were hardly unique. Christian authorities in late antiquity also worried about their flock being subordinate to nonbelievers through the institution of patronage and the impact it might have on their faith. Two centuries before, in Roman Africa, Augustine (Sermon 62) had discouraged Christians from going to pagan temples to please their Roman patrons. The appointment of a high pagan official in Carthage enraged his congregation, who feared he would use his office against them, chanting, "Pagans should not be in charge; pagans should not boss Christians around!" Augustine had to quiet a near riot in his church.[18]

The later Muslim biographers alleged that Muhammad launched a last military expedition, in the fall of 630, to Tabuk, at the juncture of the Hejaz and Transjordan. They represent it as an attempt to fend off an attack from Rome, of which the Prophet had received intelligence. It is, however, highly unlikely that Herakleios's army had reasserted itself in rural southern Transjordan. The sources alleged that the Prophet went up to Tabuk with a strong force and no Roman army appeared, so after a month he simply returned to Medina. These later writers attributed to the Prophet treaties with Jews and Christians there, but these accounts show signs of anachronism.[19]

The Qur'an makes no reference to any battle of Tabuk or of any threat from Christian Rome. If such an episode occurred at all, it may have been a case of hostile Arab tribes akin to the Hawazin, who contemplated another attack on Muhammad's budding realm. Muhammad had allied with Constantinople and went to his grave that way in 632.[20] The commonwealth of Medina in the Tihama remained secure until the Prophet's death. The Tabuk campaign is likely a later fiction, perhaps offered as a warrant for the post-Muhammad Arab invasion of Syria. In contrast, the stories of Rome's attempts to reach out to the Muslims after the defeat of Iran may be remnants of a dim memory among later Muslims of an alliance between Rome and the

Prophet, which was otherwise suppressed once the Byzantines became the enemy.

❧

THE QUR'AN GIVES consistent evidence of good relations with Christians. In Muhammad's last two and a half years of life, 630–632, he continued to attempt to forge an alliance of monotheists, though very much on his own terms. *The Table* 5:69 reaffirmed, "Those who believed, and the Jews, and the Sabians and the Christians—whoever has believed in God and the Last Day, and performed good deeds— no fear is upon them and nor shall they grieve."[21]

Other late verses, such as *Iron* 57:27, reaffirm the Believers' friendly feelings toward the Christians, while underlining the Qur'an's prerogative of critiquing the shibboleths of these allies. Having mentioned Noah and Abraham among the patriarchs, it continues, "Then we sent messengers in their wake, and we sent Jesus the son of Mary and bestowed on him the Gospel. We put into the hearts of those who followed him kindness and mercy. As for monasticism, we did not prescribe it to them, but rather they invented it in a quest for the good-pleasure of God. But they did not pursue it in the right way. We gave those among them who believed their recompense. But many of them are corrupt."[22] This verse might be characterized as tough-love ecumenism. The Qur'an acknowledges the truth of Jesus Christ but locates him as one of a series of nondivine messengers dispatched by God. It warmly praises Christians for their compassion. It nevertheless censures monasticism, one of the major institutions of Near Eastern Christianity, apparently on the grounds that it took asceticism to an extreme. It clearly uses the verb *believed* here, since it is in the past tense, to speak of those who truly believed in Christianity, not to

186

refer to those monks who converted to Muhammad's religion (which cannot have been a large-enough category to be worth mentioning). Despite the Qur'an's clear desire to maintain the independence of Muhammad and his new religious tradition from its predecessor, the scripture expressed overall positive sentiments toward Christianity and Christians, with an obvious political import in the world of restored Christian Roman suzerainty circa 630–632.

That this theological and political project of ecumenism proved more successful with followers of Jesus seems clear. *The Table* 5:82 proclaimed,

> You will find that those most intensely hostile to the believers are Jews and pagans. And you will find that the nearest to them in love are those who say "We are Christians." That is because they have among them priests and monks, and they are not haughty. And when they hear what has been revealed to the messenger, you see their eyes overflowing with tears inasmuch as they recognize the truth and say, "Our lord, we have believed, so inscribe us among those who bear witness."[23]

Those among the Jews and pagans who evinced animosity had likely been allied with Iran, in contrast to pro-Roman Christians. This verse from the chapter of *The Table* merely describes the transitory political situation. That is, it concerns some factions of Arab Jews in the late 620s, not Jews or Judaism in general. The Qur'an has many verses praising Jews and speaking of good relations with some of them and other verses that criticize Christians and even the monks who are lauded here. *The Table* 5:12 reminds Medina's Jews of their obligations, saying, "God made a covenant with the children of Israel." It says he instructed them to perform prayers, give alms, and

"believe in my messengers and aid them." If they obey these directives, God says, "I will acquit you of your evil deeds and bring you
into the Garden, beneath which rivers flow." If Jews instead chase
after false gods and depart into pagan impiety, they will have gone
astray. In the event, it continues (5:13), many Jews broke this covenant, so God cursed them and made them hard-hearted. They came
to have a distorted interpretation of the Bible and forgot some of the
commandments, becoming treacherous, "all but a few." This accusa-
tion that Jews were misinterpreting the Bible, either through their
Mishna, or commentary tradition, or by reading scripture too literally,
also occurs in Emperor Justinian's Novella 146 of 553.[24] The Roman
ruler's implication was that their approaches to interpreting the Bible
were standing in the way of recognizing Jesus as the Messiah. The
Qur'an, unlike that law, issues no blanket condemnation since it
identifies some righteous Jews even among those who did not embrace
the faith of Muhammad.

Muhammad toward the end of his life, in 630–632, admittedly
criticized some Arabian Jewish beliefs. *Repentance* 9:30 complains,
"Jews say, 'Ezra is the Son of God'; Christians say, 'The Messiah is the
Son of God.' That is the utterance of their mouths, lapsing into paganism. God's imprecations be upon them! How they are perverted!"
Muhammad appears to have assumed that Jews and Christians took
this diction literally; if so, it would be a peculiarity of Hejazi sects of
those religions. The reference to Jews' identifying Ezra as the son of
God likely has to do with material found in 1 Enoch, 2 Esdras, and
other extracanonical works that were widely read in the early seventh
century. Deuteronomy 14:1 says, "You are children of the Lord your
God." The precise phrase "sons of God" occurs in the Hebrew Bible
but there refers to angels rather than to prophets. Still, monarchs in
the line of David also receive this epithet in some Jewish works, and

late wisdom books of the Septuagint use the phrase. Sirach 4:10 says, "Be a father to orphans, and be like a husband to their mother; you will then be like a son of the Most High." Wisdom 2:18 too uses this diction to refer to ordinary Israelites. The Qumran scrolls also contain this construction. That some Hejazi author at some point applied the term to Ezra is perfectly plausible.[25]

Even the Jews gone morally or doctrinally astray remain the objects of divine solicitude. God orders in *The Table* 5:13, "Nevertheless, pardon and forgive them. God loves the doers of good." Whatever it meant by saying that God had cursed those Jews who proved faithless and did not accept Jesus—thus contravening the Covenant of the Prophets—that sin did not forestall God's clemency.[26] Elsewhere, the Qur'an affirms the principle that the divine leniency can always be granted to monotheists. *The Women* 4:48 says, "God does not forgive anyone who makes him part of a pantheon, but forgives everything else in whomever he pleases—whoever gives God a divine associate has devised a heinous sin."

The Qur'an's rejection of the metaphor of God as father stands out as almost unique among the religious groups of late antiquity. Only the worshippers of the Most High God in the Near East, referred to by terms such as *Hypsistarians* (from the Greek for "most high"), also avoided this terminology. Gregory of Nyssa complained of "those who are called Hypsistiani, between whom and the Christians there is this difference, that they acknowledge that there is a God Whom they term the Highest or Almighty, but do not admit that he is Father; while a Christian, if he believe not in the Father, is no Christian at all."[27] This congruence of beliefs between the Qur'an and the "All-Highers," as I have argued throughout this book, strongly suggests that the latter formed one religious matrix out of which Muhammad's religion emerged.

❧

Now THAT THE Believers had come to dominate the Hejaz, the issue of conflicts within the community came to the fore. The Qur'an (*The Chambers* 49:9) urges a form of collective security as a way of dealing with internecine struggles: "If two factions among the believers fall to fighting, make peace between them. If one commits aggression toward the other, fight the aggressors until they comply with the commandment of God. Make peace between them equitably, and be fair, for God loves those who are fair."[28] The verse underlines that nonaggression forms a key Qur'anic teaching and that the Believers have a core duty of peacemaking, which is identified with the commandment of God. The next verse (49:10) asks them to dampen down conflicts within this spiritual family: "The believers are siblings, so make peace among your siblings and fear God, so that perhaps you will receive mercy."

The Qur'an differentiates between the urban, settled Believers, some of them literate and in personal contact with Muhammad, and the surrounding bedouin nomads. The bedouins, it implies (*The Chambers* 49:14), are like catechumens in the Christianity of that time, persons who indicated strong interest in the religion but had not yet been accepted into full membership: "The Bedouins assert, 'We have believed.' Say: 'Do not say, "we have believed." Rather, say: "We have submitted," for faith has not entered your hearts. If you obey God and his messenger, he will not undervalue your deeds. In truth, God is forgiving and merciful.'" This verse makes it clear that these bedouins had entered into only a generalized monotheism or submission (*islam*) but had not yet been accepted fully into the faith of Muhammad. The later biographical tradition went into excruciating detail about all the tribal leaders of Arabia who came in delegations to Muhammad at Medina in his last two years of life to pledge their fealty.

A story is told that late in Muhammad's life, Dimam ibn Tha'laba, "a muscular man with two long braids of hair," came to the Prophet on behalf of the Banu Sa'd, a sept of the Bakr tribe. "He came and made his camel kneel before the door of the mosque, then hobbled it. He went into the place of worship where the messenger was sitting with his companions." Dimam approached the group and asked, "which of you is the son of 'Abd al-Muttalib?"

Muhammad answered that he was.

"So you are Muhammad?"

"Yes."

"Son of Abd al-Muttalib, I am going to ask you an indelicate question, so do not be offended."

Muhammad said, "I will not be offended. Ask whatever it occurs to you to ask."

"I adjure you by God, your God and the God of your predecessors, and the God of those who will come after you, has God sent you to us as a Messenger?"

Muhammad replied that he had.

Dimam then inquired if the supreme deity had demanded that only he be worshipped.

Muhammad said, "Yes."

Dimam then embraced the new faith and, on returning to his tribe, spoke ill of the goddesses Allat and al-'Uzza.

"Oh, no," his kin exclaimed. "Beware lest you be struck by leprosy, or elephantiasis or insanity!"

Dimam insisted that the old goddesses could inflict neither "hurt nor harm."

Muhammad is said to have pronounced, "If this man with the two plaits of hair is sincere, he is destined for heaven."

The Banu Sa'd had kept their distance from the new religion for two decades, but according to Ibn Hisham, some of its members came to form part of Muhammad's growing sphere of political and spiritual authority in the Hejaz, what might be called his polity or commonwealth (it was too vague and informal to be called a state).[29]

Precisely because, as the Qur'an noted, these tribal adherents of the Prophet lacked the sort of knowledge and commitment truly to be called Believers, they had virtually no appreciation for his key teachings—the prohibitions on coercion of conscience and on aggressive warfare. After Muhammad's death on June 8, 632, some of these pastoralists (a militarily powerful population even if less numerous than Arabian sedentary people) relinquished their faith, while others, beginning two years later, launched raids into Roman and Iranian territory in disregard of the Prophet's option for peace.

Muhammad seems by the early 630s to have been increasingly philosophical about the likelihood that religious diversity would continue to be a fact of life. *The Table* 5:48 presents God as saying to the members of the various monotheistic faiths, "We have prescribed to each of you a law and a tradition. If God had desired, he could have made you a single community. Instead, he is testing you with regard to the revelations you received. So compete in doing good. You will all return to God, and he will inform you then concerning those things about which you argued." The Qur'an here turns away from the minutiae of theology and religious law, raising instead the question of how far a religious community achieves its own moral ideals and how much it helps those in need. The scripture reminds the monotheists that their ultimate charge is to do good and be charitable, and if they want to demonstrate their superiority to other faiths, they must show more kindness and philanthropy than others, not simply claim a superior doctrine or ritual exactitude.[30]

Alongside its heavenly ecumenism, the Qur'an points to the need of the very different people down on earth again to learn to live in peace. There were, after all, two sexes, various city-states, pagan and believing Arab tribes, eastern Romans, Iranian Zoroastrians, Christians of several denominations, and Jews. *The Chambers* 49:13 says, "People, we have created you male and female and made you nations and tribes so that you may come to know one another. The noblest of you in the sight of God is the most pious of you. God is knowing and aware."

The Qur'an here celebrates gender and ethnic diversity as an enrichment of the human experience. Encountering someone very different, it says, presents an opportunity to learn and should not be viewed as a source of potential bigotry or conflict. The verse makes explicit the idea that men have something to learn from women, which seems a progressive notion in late antiquity. Further, the Qur'an here puts forward the principle that social status is determined not by ascriptive identity, not by how powerful or wealthy a group one is born into, but by piety. Again, given the mention of women, it is implying that a pious woman is better than a powerful but impious man.

The Qur'an 49:11–12 points to some grounds for positive peace. These verses say that one people or ethnicity should not laugh at another or make sarcastic comments. Moreover, they should avoid obsessive suspicion of one another. Some suspicion, it observes, is a sin, and it compares paranoia and backbiting to cannibalism. In short, it urges all to avoid the pathological dynamics of any sort of chauvinism. Ensuring the dignity of all is a way, it says, to avoid the grudges and resentments that lead to faction fighting.

The scripture condemns violence and promotes social harmony. Naturally, then, it forbids murder, retelling the story of Cain and Abel and then quoting the Palestinian Talmud.[31] It says (*The Table* 5:32), "For this reason, we decreed for the children of Israel that those who kill another person—save in punishment for murder or the wreaking of corruption in the land—it is as though they had killed all humankind. And those who revive someone, it is as though they gave life to all humankind. Our messengers brought them clear proofs, but many of them thereafter committed excesses in the land." The reasoning of the rabbis had been that Adam was a single individual, and if he had been murdered, then the whole human race would have been prevented from existing. Muhammad preferred the universal form of this rabbinical teaching, equating the murder of anyone of any faith to genocide. Outside of formal defensive war on the battlefield, and outside the structured judicial context of a death penalty for murder or other capital crimes imposed by duly constituted authorities, killing is always wrong, according to the Qur'an. *The Women* 4:59 instructs, "Believers, obey God and obey the Messenger and those who enjoy authority among you." That is, the Qur'an forbids vigilante violence.

In *The Table* 5:15, the Qur'an tells the scriptural communities that a new messenger has come from God, who is explaining the Bible and abrogating parts of it. A new book has been revealed, full of light. It then proclaims (5:16), "God thereby guides those who follow his good-pleasure to the way of peace and delivers them from the shadows into light by his leave, and conducts them to the straight path." It has been shown that this verse is paraphrasing the prophecy of Zechariah in the Gospel according to Luke 1:77–79, in which the father of John the Baptist speaks of his impending birth.[32] Luke wrote, "And you, child, will be called the prophet of the Most High; for you will go before the Lord to prepare his ways, to give knowledge of salvation to his people by the forgiveness of their sins. By the tender mercy of our God, the dawn from on high will break upon us, to give light to those who sit in darkness and in the shadow of death, to guide our feet into the way of peace."

As with the prophecy of Zechariah, the Qur'an announces the advent of a new prophet of the Most High, acceptance of whom means adopting a preference for nonviolence. If the Qur'an has a Hypsistarian background, this talk of an envoy of the Highest God would have resonated especially powerfully with Muhammad and his followers. The passage has messianic and apocalyptic overtones. Muhammad is configured as a John the Baptist figure, calling in the wilderness and showing the people to the way of peace. God, the verse says, has given people the gift of a new prophet's mission, of bringing light in the place of the darkness of death and tranquility in the place of turmoil.

꙳

THE INCORPORATION OF Mecca into the Medinan commonwealth created a new polity in the Hejaz. While peace had been achieved between the two city-states, their union threatened the autonomy of surrounding bedouins and of other urban settlements. The Qur'an describes a further big battle, which the biographers maintain took place one month after the accession of Mecca. Later tradition explained this clash by saying that after Mecca embraced the faith, some large tribal federations such as Hawazin and Thaqif demonstrated persistent hostility to Muhammad and the Believers, determined to raid and fight them. It may be that they feared the emergence of a Mecca-Medina sanctuary complex would draw overwhelming resources to the Believers movement and reduce their own power and wealth.

By the same token, the Qur'an castigated as perfidious their willingness to cast aside the norms of the Hejaz and attack sanctuary cities. The scripture attempted to reform the tribal custom of constant raiding, defining violent assault as a crime and prescribing much the same punishments for it as are enumerated in the Code of Justinian. Some later anecdotes may point to Roman Christian attempts to cultivate the Prophet as an ally, which is no more implausible than the empire's dependence on Arian German and on pagan Arab federate troops at the frontiers.

The Qur'an rebukes Jews and Christians for their doctrinal lapses but offers them divine clemency if they show forth righteous faith and works within the framework of their traditions or as converts to the new message. Above all, it takes the spotlight off creed and ritual, making charity and beneficence the center of religion and challenging the scriptural communities to compete with one another in doing good, if they are so concerned to demonstrate their superiority over other faith communities. It implicitly compares Muhammad to John the Baptist as the prophet of a coming era of peace.

CONCLUSION

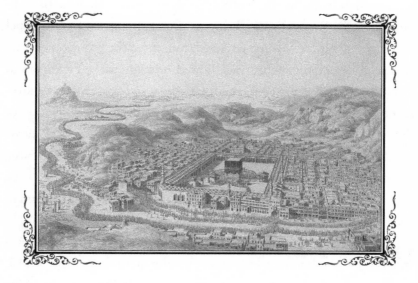

A RICH VEIN OF PEACE THOUGHT RUNS THROUGH THE QUR'AN. ITS earlier chapters celebrate the tranquility of heaven, depicting well-being and concord as its spiritual reality and its pinnacle. The Qur'an goes on in the subsequent decade to address the ways the beleaguered band of Believers in the one God could live among intolerant pagans in Mecca and elsewhere, insisting on repelling evil with good, wishing tranquility and welfare on one's enemies, and urging forgiveness. It counsels a mixture of firmly preaching hellfire to the heathen and forbearance in this world of their foibles. "To you your religion," the

Qur'an has Muhammad say to the pagans, "and to me mine." This tolerance grows naturally out of the conviction that it would be wrong to attempt to compel a person's conscience: "Will you then coerce the people to become believers?" (*Jonah* 10:99).

The Meccans may have deliberately maneuvered Muhammad and his followers out of Mecca, to remove them from the sanctuary city where physically attacking them would have brought shame on the Quraysh in the eyes of both city dwellers and bedouins throughout the Hejaz. Persecuting and threatening them just enough to impel them to emigrate to Medina removed from them the protection of the Kaaba's zone of nonviolence and allowed Abu Jahl and Abu Sufyan to declare war with the goal of taking Medina and crushing the movement entirely. They launched a concerted campaign of abduction of the Believers intended to deprogram them, return them to the ancestral religion of the Quraysh, and demoralize the remaining stalwarts. Some of this animosity likely derived from a Meccan alliance with the Sasanians and a war aim of defeating a Roman ally in the form of the new religious movement.

In multicultural Medina, the Prophet put together a diverse "nation" of Abrahamians in hopes of pitting monotheists (along with their pagan clients) against the militant traditionalists of Mecca. The Qur'an mirrored this political alliance in the city down on earth in a pluralist soteriology or doctrine of salvation, holding out hope of heaven to all those (Christians, Jews, or pagan monotheists) who lived righteous lives, worshipped the one God, and accepted the resurrection and Judgment Day.

In Medina in the 620s, the Qur'an consistently depicts the Prophet and the Believers as reluctant warriors, concerned primarily with defending themselves and winning reparations for their loss of property and loss of access to the blessings of pilgrimage as well as with resisting to the death any coercion of their consciences. The

Prophet deployed the rabbinical conception of the Shechinah, taken over into Arabic as *Sakina*, as a term for the spiritual peace that allowed the Believers calmly to withstand pagan persecution and face down the war fever of berserk warriors. The peace of God allowed them to enter Mecca in 630 without bloodshed. It also gave them the self-possession to vanquish the militant Hawazin on the battlefield at Hunayn. The Qur'an's sentiments on the necessity of just war parallel those in church fathers such as Augustine and Ambrose. The Medinans' goal was the reestablishment of the status quo ante and liberty of worship so that the religion would be God's.

The Qur'an depicts three major defensive battles against the invading Meccans, two smaller clashes with paganizers from among the people of the Book, and a big defensive action at Hunayn against bedouins who reneged on their earlier peace treaties with the Prophet. It implies some smaller defensive clashes as well, in which bedouin allies were accustomed to taking booty from the battlefield. It never explicitly mentions a caravan raid of the sort the later medieval martial biographies celebrate and never urges offensive warfare. It details no massacre of prisoners of war at Khaybar and indeed strictly forbids that sort of treatment of the captured, identifying it with the tyranny of Pharaoh.

Understanding that the chapter of *Success* (48) concerns the fall of pagan Mecca rather than the peace treaty of Hudaibiya allows us to see the Prophet's procession of January 630 to the sanctuary city as more resembling the Reverend Martin Luther King Jr.'s 1963 march on Washington than a military campaign. Muhammad had clearly announced that there would be no fighting or booty taken, which caused many bedouins to peel off. There was no violence in the sanctuary city: "He it is who withheld their hands from you and your hands from them in the heart of Mecca after he made you ascendant over them" (*Success* 48:24). A vigorous and large fifth column of secret

Believers and secret pagan partisans of Muhammad had so under-mined the Quraysh leadership that even militants such as Khalid ibn al-Walid and Abu Sufyan simply threw in the towel.

Even the later sources admit that none of the cities of the Hejaz fell to a big Muslim military campaign but rather gave in to the pow-erful appeal of the new religion. Most Hejazis were settled, not bed-ouins, so the spread of the religion peacefully among the sedentary population was decisive. Muhammad was invited into Medina by the Khazraj tribe. Mecca acquiesced when the Believers in 630 made a point of mounting a peaceful procession to it. The conversion of the Abna', or remnants of the Sasanian officer caste in Yemen, would have delivered Aden, Sana'a, and Najran. Taif's notables allegedly gave up after their allies, the Hawazin, and their own troops lost the battle of Hunayn and the Hawazin converted by acclamation. Despite all their importation into the biography of the Prophet of the motifs of Ara-bic poetry about battle days, the writers of the Umayyad and of the Abbasid eras seem to have felt unable to tinker with the narratives that reached them from earlier generations so radically as to make the Prophet and his armies conquerors of cities in the Tihama. The most they could accomplish was to provide the peaceful procession to Mecca with two battle standards and one minor skirmish, details that are contradicted by the Qur'an.

It is suspicious that `Urwa placed one of the alleged battle stan-dards in the hands of his own father, al-Zubayr ibn al-`Awwam, Khad-ija's nephew and the husband of Aisha's younger sister Asma'. This imagery was more than a claim on family honor. Al-Zubayr had mounted a rebellion against Ali when he became commander of the faithful in 656, along with his friend Talha and his sister-in-law Aisha, only to go down to defeat. Then two and a half decades later, `Urwa's brother Abdullah mounted an unsuccessful rebellion from Mecca against the Damascus-based Umayyad dynasty in the 680s, which ended in his death.[1] Although `Urwa is not known to have joined the revolt, he may have been influenced by it. For family tradition to put a military standard in al-Zubayr's hands as he led one of two bands into Mecca in 630 would have created a reputation helpful in his rebellion against Ali. Later on, it would have bolstered his son Abdullah's claim on leadership. Even if some traditions actually go back to the son of al-Zubayr and to Aisha, relying on them for early Islamic history is sort of like depending on the younger disciples of Leon Trotsky in Mexico for our understanding of the 1917 Russian Revolution. They were failed revolutionaries against the new order, which colored their accounts. `Urwa's family traditions may have begun the process of militarizing the procession to Mecca for political reasons, a tale that grew in the telling among later historians. The reality described by the Qur'an, that a ragtag band of Believers walked and rode unopposed into a Mecca suddenly seized with veneration for Muhammad, redounded to no one's military honor and supported no subsequent assertions of the prerogative to rule.

Given that the Prophet launched no large military campaigns to subdue the major population centers of the Tihama, the celebrators of his alleged "battle days" invented dozens of inconsequential rural raids and, implausibly, a Mu'ta campaign in the Sasanian Transjordan (where they alleged an anachronistic Roman military threat), or a Tabuk campaign in late 630, where they also portray nothing happening of any consequence. Some of these narratives may have aimed at providing a justification for the later Muslim invasions of the Near East. Other authors seem to have wanted to cover up the Prophet's alliance with the Roman Empire, which had by their days become the truncated Byzantine Empire and a perennial enemy of the Muslim state in the marches of Anatolia.

The image of the Qur'an and of the prophet Muhammad that emerges from a careful consideration of verses about peace and conciliation is 180 degrees away from that in Western polemics for the past nearly millennium and a half and differs significantly from the picture of the Prophet in most Muslim commentary. Soon after Muhammad's death, bedouins who had given him their political fealty but who probably knew virtually nothing of his teachings began raiding in the Levant and Mesopotamia, leading to the lightning-fast establishment of a new world empire. From the vantage point of even a decade after the Prophet's death, when Medina ruled from Alexandria to Ahvaz, the Qur'an looked different and was read as a warrant for the establishment of a new kingdom rather than as the words of an itinerant preacher of peace and conciliation who had occasionally been forced into defensive actions.

One question this book raises is how to explain these events after the Prophet's death in 632, given the Qur'an's condemnation of aggressive warfare and its emphasis on religious tolerance, even for nonbelligerent pagans. That a prophet of peace should found a movement that subsequently turned militant is hardly unprecedented. In a sense, the mid-seventh-century vicars of Muhammad such as Abu Bakr, Omar, and ʿUthman ibn ʿAffan simply put Islam to the same sorts of uses that Constantine and his successors had put Christianity. Not even a century after Constantine's 312 conversion, Augustine and Ambrose had already laid out justifications not only for Christian just war but even for Christian wars of conquest and coercion of others' consciences.

We might consider some other historical parallels here. The peaceful spiritual founder of the Sikh religion in medieval India, Guru Nanak (d. 1539), was succeeded by more militant figures such as the fifth Guru, Arjun, and then by the tenth, Gobind Singh (d. 1708), who instituted warlike rules for the religion. Historian Hew McLeod argued that the change in direction came about in part because large numbers of tribal Jats in the Punjab converted, bringing their pastoralist ethos of raiding and fighting into the religion and affecting the policies of the gurus. More recently, it has been argued that the Jats carried only one of several cultures of violence that influenced the community.[2]

The spread of allegiance to Muhammad among the bedouin populations of Arabia and the Near East likely functioned in a similar way. If the thesis is correct that Muhammad preached the Qur'an in Transjordan, Palestine, and Syria during his own lifetime, he may have attracted a substantial following among the bedouins and Arab peasants there, so that the transfer of these territories to Medina occurred not so much through an invasion from Arabia alone as through a set of local uprisings of a sort that had been common in this region in previous decades. Some of the sons of the tribesmen loyal to the Jafnids who ransacked Syria in the 580s after Tiberios II humiliated those phylarchs may well have declared for Muhammad in the 630s. That pastoralists should disregard the ban on aggressive warfare is not hard to understand. The Qur'an itself complains about the bedouins not being proper Believers, only basic monotheists who did not entirely understand the faith's values. In some instances, Miaphysite Christians with a tradition of ascetic militancy may have converted to Muhammad's Unitarianism and brought into the new religion their own long-standing practices of religious violence.[3]

One reason the peace verses of the Qur'an and its condemnation of aggressive war have been slighted in later Muslim intellectual history is that medieval Muslim clerics developed, and many misused, a theory of abrogation. The Qur'an shows evolution in its treatment of a few laws. It begins by forbidding Believers to come to prayers drunk, but later verses say there is more harm than good in alcohol. (It never did outlaw the latter, inasmuch as it mentions no punishment and, therefore, specifies no legal infraction.) Some clerics attempted to use what they called the "sword" verse (9:5) to abrogate all the passages about peace and peacemaking that came in the book previous to it. Many great Muslim scholars pushed back against this intellectual and spiritual travesty. Tabari pointed out that only a command can be abrogated. It would follow that values cannot be set aside, only specific laws. The eighteenth-century reformer Shah Wali Allah of Delhi limited the instances of abrogation in the text to five.[4] All this is not to mention that read in context, as it is in this book, 9:5 is speaking of a defensive action at Hunayn in the face of pagans reneging on previous peace treaties for a bellicose campaign against Mecca and Medina. These verses do not command aggressive war, much less abrogating all the peace verses.

Later Muslims also reinterpreted the words of the Qur'an in ways that enabled a new exclusivism. They appropriated for the religion of Muhammad the general term *islam*, which the Qur'an had used to refer to the perennial tradition of all the monotheistic prophets. They read the Qur'anic word for impious pagans (*kafir*) as referring to all those who declined to follow Muhammad. At some point many came to hold that only Muslims are saved. The Qur'an contains very little in the way of law, and it is not clear that it intended to establish an elaborate legal system; some of its prescriptions appear to me to involve simply observing in the Hejaz some elements of the Code of Justinian. The word *sharia* in the sense of Islamic law does not occur in the Qur'an, though the verbal root does. Later generations collected sayings and doings passed down orally and attributed to the Prophet and his vicars and imbued them with the force of law, part of what medieval Muslims meant by *sharia*. Many of these sayings are essentially folk literature or dubious, and some are transparent forgeries. Sayings that developed along the frontier between the Umayyad kingdom, ruled by the descendants of Abu Sufyan, and the Byzantine Empire, ruled by successors of Herakleios, often celebrated warfare, for which they appropriated the term *jihad* in a way the Qur'an does not.

Perhaps the Muslims borrowed the notion of holy war from their Byzantine foes, who had developed it during the war with Khosrow II. A saying falsely attributed to Muhammad prescribing stoning for adultery, which obviously derives from Jewish law (*halacha*), convinced many Muslim judges to overrule the Qur'an, which prescribes lashes, not death (*Light* 24:2). The Qur'anic punishment more resembles that of Justinian (Novella 134.10), who had reduced the penalty for the adulteress from death to being whipped and then relegated to a nunnery. Some of what later Muslims called the sharia is, of course, based on or compatible with the Qur'an, and most of it has parallels in Jewish, Roman, or Roman Catholic canon law.[5]

Both the empire of the commanders of the faithful (632–658) and that of the subsequent Umayyad kingdom (658–750) have suffered from a black legend with regard to issues of religious tolerance and violence. Just as Christian monks produced apocalyptic narratives of the Sasanian conquest of Jerusalem in 614 that spoke of ninety thousand dead and the entire city razed, so they or their successors wrote up alarming accounts of the rise of Islam that resorted to similar hyperbole. War is never without regrettable casualties, injuries, and forced population movements. Still, big intellectual struggles have been waged over whether the Muslim conquests had a negative impact on the economy and demographics of the Near East. A substantial amount of archaeological evidence has been marshaled for this debate. Hugh Kennedy initially argued in the 1980s that there was a seventh-century decline but that it had little or nothing to do with Muslim rule since it had begun in the sixth century under the late Roman Empire, long before the arrival of the Muslims. Others have more recently relegated this pattern to a few urban areas but elsewhere have seen continued prosperity throughout the late Roman and early Muslim periods in Transjordan and Palestine, with the advent of Muslim rule having produced no discernible adverse impact.

The old thesis of Belgian historian Henri Pirenne that the rise of Islam contributed to the onset of the western European Dark Ages has been disproved by archaeology, which finds instead that western Europe went into a profound economic tailspin in the two centuries before the rise of Islam and that trade and silver from the Umayyads revived the Carolingian economy in the eighth century. The Umayyad Berber and Arab Muslim migration into southern Spain in the 700s did not differ in any obvious respect from earlier Gothic and Slavic movements into Europe except that the Muslims' implementation of large-scale agricultural irrigation led to significant economic growth there.[6]

A consensus has been reached that Syriac Christian writers of the seventh century saw the Roman-Iranian war of 603–629 as far more destructive, and noteworthy, than the Arab Muslim conquest. Most of the military engagements of the latter took place in the thinly populated countryside, and most cities were allowed to surrender on terms (the earliest fragmentary Syriac account says that Homs/Emesa was given security). The Arab forces settled in garrisons outside the cities, and during the first decades of Muslim rule conversion appears to have been rare; there is no evidence that the Muslims demanded it of anyone. The system of poll tax was only gradually implemented, and it built on earlier taxation regimes. In my reading, Qur'an 9:29 does not have anything to do with a poll tax on Jews and Christians but rather demands reparations from pagans guilty of launching aggressive wars, but later Muslim exegetes used it to support the imposition of the tax, which was likely modeled on Sasanian practice. Non-Muslims who paid the poll tax were considered in later times *dhimmis*, or members of protected communities, but the only time the Qur'an mentions this word it uses it to mean something like treaty obligation, and it complains that pagan tribes refused to conclude peace treaties with the Believers (*Repentance* 9:8, 10).

Archaeologists digging the cities do not find layers of ash or other signs of destruction in the 630s and 640s, and their findings directly contradict the rather hysterical pronouncements of figures such as Bishop Sophronios. In Rihab, Transjordan, excavating teams proved that several churches were actually being constructed in the mid- to late 630s and recovered their mosaic floors, showing no damage. In contrast, Sophronios alleged that the Arab invaders were during those very years indiscriminately burning churches and causing the population to flee. Christians in Rihab instead were undisturbed by the arrival of new rulers and carried on with their church building unmolested.[7]

The patriarch of the church of the East, Isho'yab, writing after 637, remonstrated with Christians of Oman who had converted, pointing out that the Muslims had demanded no such thing (though they had allegedly threatened to take half the locals' property if they did remain Christians). He said that the Muslims did not attack the Christian religion but rather honored Christian clerics and saints and gave grants to churches and monasteries.[8]

Both the government of the commanders of the faithful and then that of the Umayyads presided over a population in the West that was largely Christian and over Zoroastrians in the East. The Muslim Arab Umayyads, having huge Christian constituencies, played ecclesiastical politics, favoring particular candidates for bishop. Their state officers were often Christian Arabs. Admittedly, the Muslims fought civil wars among themselves, and a growing sectarianism between partisans of Ali, the prophet's cousin and son-in-law, and supporters of Uthman and his Umayyad successors roiled the new empire (this was the origin of the Sunni-Shiite split that was to prove fateful for Islam). The evidence shows, however, that non-Muslims were treated well.

The Christian Yohannan bar Penkaye, writing in the 680s, some fifty years after Muhammad's death, said that the Umayyad ruler "had received, as I said, from the one who was their chief [Muhammad] an order in favor of Christians and of clerics." Some of the Arab ruling class, he averred, were Christian. He described the unprecedented peace that had been afforded by the rule of Abu Sufyan's son Mu'awiya (658–680) over the "Iranian and Roman Empires" and added, "From each person they only require the payment of tribute, and they leave him the liberty of embracing any belief at all; there are even Christians among them; some of them belong to the heretics and some are our own."[9]

The interesting thing here is not that the conquered paid tribute or taxes, since they used to pay taxes under the Romans as well. The interesting thing is that this Christian eyewitness says that the early Muslims allowed people to follow any belief they desired, which certainly had not been true under Christian Rome. Bar Penkaye implied that the early Muslim state tolerated the remaining Hellenes or pagans much better than had the Romans, and there is other evidence for the truth of this allegation, since the Umayyads appear to have left pagan Harran alone. At most, such pagans sometimes found it advisable to declare themselves "Sabians." Among Christians deprived of the levers of power and living under Muslim rule, he complained, "There was no longer any distinction between pagan and Christian, the believer was not distinguished from the Jew." He condemned his coreligionists in the Umayyad Empire for "commerce with infidels, union with the perverse, relations with heretics and friendship with Jews."[10] His witness is an unexpected confirmation of the continued salience of key Qur'anic values of tolerance and peace and of the way in which they had disturbed the late-antique order of things.

ACKNOWLEDGMENTS

THIS BOOK HAS BEEN GESTATING FOR DECADES, BUT I INCURRED SPECIAL debts during the later stages of research and writing. I am grateful to then librarian of Congress James Billington for appointing me to the John W. Kluge Chair for the Countries and Cultures of the South in May–August 2016 on the basis of this project. I would also like to express my deep appreciation to the great Qur'an scholar Jane Dammen McAuliffe, director of the John W. Kluge Center and Office of Scholarly Programs at the Library of Congress, for her intellectual hospitality during my tenure as well as to Jason Steinhauer for all his help. My thanks also to Mary-Jane Deeb, chief of the African and Middle Eastern Division there. I further benefited from a sabbatical granted by the College of Letters, Sciences, and Arts of the University of Michigan in the summer and fall of 2017. I had wonderful and sometimes challenging conversations, in person or by email, regarding this project with Adam H. Becker, Stephen Rutledge, Rudolf Ware, Azfar Moin, Michael Bonner, Samer Ali, Alexander Knysh, Karla Malette, Brian Schmidt, Ian Moyer, Michael Pregill, Olga Davidson, Gregory Nagy, and Jordan Pickett, though none of them bears any responsibility for any of the errors in this book. I'm grateful to them for their insights. This book could not have been written without the resources of the Hatcher Graduate Library at the University of

Michigan and its heroic interlibrary loan department. My thanks in particular to Middle East bibliographer Evyn Kropf.

My agent, Brettne Bloom, enthusiastically believed in this book from the beginning and went beyond the call of duty with her proposals for shaping it. I am deeply beholden to my editor at Nation Books, Alessandra Bastagli, for her judicious reading of the drafts and her innumerable key suggestions and improvements. Her sage advice and coolheaded responses to my authorial crises were crucial.

I taught an undergraduate course at the University of Michigan in the winter of 2017, Peace and Peace Movements in Islam, and am grateful to my students for their comments, which pointed the way to better communicating my findings.

Writing a book such as this one takes a heavy toll on leisure and family life, and I am deeply grateful to my wife, Shahin Cole, not only for her moral encouragement and for acting as an essential sounding board but also for the many unreasonable sacrifices she made.

Bible verses are quoted with permission from the New Revised Standard Version Bible, copyright 1989, Division of Christian Education of the National Council of the Churches of Christ in the United States of America; all rights remain reserved. Interpretations of Qur'an verses and renderings of many other Arabic sources quoted here are my own. I often quote late-antique Greek texts from nineteenth-century translations because they are out of copyright, but I also tried to cite recent apposite academic secondary work and consult originals for technical terms. Eastern Roman Greek names after about 400 CE are generally transliterated according to the system of the *Oxford Dictionary of Byzantium* (1991), except, as with Justinian, where a figure is so well known by a Latinized or English name that it would be pedantic to use any other form.

◊ Appendix ◊

QUR'AN VERSES ON PEACE RELEVANT TO THIS BOOK

These verses are listed in chronological order according to the Nöldeke schema.

The Night of Power 97:1–5.
In the Name of God, the Merciful, the Compassionate.
Behold, we revealed it on the night of power.
What will make you understand the night of power?
The night of power is better than a thousand months.
The angels and the spirit descend then, with the permission
of their Lord, in every affair.
And peace it is, until the breaking of the dawn.

The Event 56:15–26.
A crowd of ancients and a handful of moderns, sitting on ornamented thrones, reclining on them, facing one another; and immortal youths constantly serve them, cups and goblets and chalices filled to overflowing, but it won't give them a hangover and won't make them drunk. And there will be fruit platters from which to choose, and whatever fowl they have an appetite for, and wide-eyed heavenly maidens like hidden pearls—as a reward for their good deeds. Therein they will hear no words of abuse, nor any talk of sin, only the saying, "Peace, peace."

The Event 56:90–91.

And if they are among the companions of the right hand, then they will be greeted, "Peace be to you," by the companions of the right hand.

Qaf 50:32–34.

This is what you were promised, to all the contrite who are safeguarded, those who fear the All-Merciful in the Unseen and come with a penitent heart: "Enter in peace!" That is the day of eternity.

Y.S. 36:53–58.

Only a single cry will ring out, then behold, they shall all be gathered before me. On that day, no soul will be in any way wronged, and you will only receive the just deserts of your deeds. The dwellers in the garden on that day will delight in their affairs; they and their spouses will repose on couches in the shade. They will have fruit and whatever they call for. "Peace!" The word will reach them from a compassionate Lord.

Mary 19:33.

[Jesus]: "So peace be upon me, the day I was born, and the day that I die, and the day that I am raised."

Gilded Ornament 43:88–89.

"My Lord, these are a people who do not believe." Yet pardon them, and say, "Peace!" Soon they will know.

The Criterion 25:63.

And the servants of the All-Merciful who walk humbly upon the earth—and when the unruly taunt them, they reply, "Peace!"

Distinguished 41:33–34.

Whose discourse is more beautiful than one who summons others to God, and performs good deeds, and proclaims, "I am a monotheist"? Good and evil are not equal. Repel the latter with the highest good, and behold, your enemy will become a devoted patron.

Rome 30:22.

And among his signs is the creation of the heavens and earth and the variety of your languages and complexions. Surely in that are signs for all living beings.

The Bee 16:31–32.

The Garden of Eden that they will enter, beneath which run rivers. They will have whatever they want there; that is how God rewards the Godfearing—those among the good whom the angels take up. They say to them, "Peace be upon you: Enter the Garden by virtue of your deeds."

The Bee 16:125.

Call to the way of your lord with wisdom and exquisite counsel. Debate them in the best of ways. For your lord knows best who has strayed from his path, and he knows best who is guided.

Stories 28:52–54.

Those to whom we gave a Book before this one have believed in it. When it is recited to them they say, "we have believed in it, it is the truth from our lord. Even before this, we were monotheists." They will be given their reward twice over inasmuch as they patiently endured, and repel evil with good deeds and shared the provisions we gave them. And when they hear abusive talk, they turn away from it and say, "to us our deeds and to you yours; peace be upon you—we do not seek out the unruly."

The Spider 29:46.

Debate the scriptural communities only in the best of ways, except for those who do wrong. Say "We believe in the revelation sent down to us, and the revelation sent down to you; our God and your God is one, and to him we have submitted."

Consultation 42:40–43.

The retribution for a wrong is a wrong the like of it, but God will recompense whoever pardons and makes peace; surely he does not love wrongdoers. One who insists on retribution after being wronged cannot be reproved, but the way is only open against those who do wrong to people and transgress in the land without any right; there awaits them a painful chastisement. Still, truly the one who is patient and forgives displays steadfastness.

Jonah 10:25–26.

God summons all to the abode of peace, and guides whomever he will to the straight path. The doers of good shall have the loveliest recompense, and a windfall; neither dust nor abasement will cover their countenances. Those are the inhabitants of paradise, dwelling forever therein.

The Heights 7:22, 24, 35.

Did I not forbid that tree to you and say to you that Satan is a manifest enemy?...Descend, being enemies to one another...Children of Adam, if messengers come to you from among you, relating our verses, whoever fears God and makes peace will have no fear, nor will they sorrow.

The Heights 7:159.
Among the people of Moses is a nation that guides others by the truth and establishes justice.

The Cattle 6:54.
When those who believe in our verses come to you, say "Peace be upon you." God has prescribed for himself compassion. Whoever among you commits a sin out of ignorance, and then repents and makes restitution—God is forgiving, merciful.

The Cattle 6:126.
For them there will be an abode of peace with their lord; he will be their guardian, because of their deeds.

The Cow 2:62.
Those who believed, and the Jews, and the Christians, and the Sabians, and whoever has believed in God and the Last Day and performed good works, they shall have their reward with their Lord.

The Cow 2:111–112.
They maintain that no one will enter heaven but Jews or Christians. Such are their vain notions. Say: produce your proof, if you speak truly. Rather, all those who submit to God and do good works will receive their recompense with their Lord, and no fear will be upon them, nor will they sorrow.

The Cow 2:113–114.
The Jews say, "The Christians have nothing to stand on"; and the Christians say, "The Jews have nothing to stand on"—even though they both recite the Bible. Those who are ignorant say the same thing. God will

judge among them on the Resurrection Day regarding those matters over which they dispute. Who is more of a despot than one who forbids the mention of God's name in the houses of God, and strives to tear them down? They should not have entered them save in fearful reverence. Their lot in this world is disgrace, and in the next they face severe torment.

The Cow 2:135.
They say: "Become Jews and Christians and be guided." No, the philosophy of Abraham, the pious gentile. He was no polytheist.

The Cow 2:190.
Fight in the path of God those who enter into combat against you, but do not commit aggression. God does not love aggressors.

The Cow 2:192–193.
If they desist, God is forgiving and merciful. Fight them until there is no longer any coercion of conscience and until the religion is God's. If they cease, there is no enmity save toward wrongdoers.

The Cow 2:208.
You who have believed, enter into Peace all together. Do not follow in the footsteps of Satan, for he is an open enemy.

The Cow 2:248.
And their prophet said to them, "The sign of his sovereignty is that the Ark will come to you, within which is the Peace (*Sakina*) from your lord, a bequest left to you by the family of Moses and the family of Aaron, borne by the angels. In that is a sign for you, if you are believers."

The Cow 2:256.
There can be no compulsion at all in religion.

The Spoils 8:1.

They ask you about spoils. Say, "The spoils belong to God and the Messenger. Fear God, and make peace among yourselves, and obey God and his Messenger, if you are believers."

The Spoils 8:38.

Say to the pagans that if they desist they will be forgiven for what went before. But if they backslide, the way of the ancients has already passed.

The Spoils 8:61.

If they incline toward peace, you must incline toward it. Trust in God—he is all-hearing and omniscient.

The Spoils 8:62–63.

He is the one who supported you with his succor and with the believers, and united their hearts. Even if you had spent everything on the whole earth you could not have brought their hearts together, but God unified them. He is mighty and wise.

The Family of Amram 3:64.

Say: "People of the Book, come to a common Word between you and us, that we will only worship God and not associate anything with him, and that we will not take some of us as lords for others apart from God." If they turn away, say: "Bear witness that we are monotheists."

The Family of Amram 3:103.

Hold fast, all of you, to the cord of God, and do not divide into factions. Remember God's favor to you, inasmuch as you were enemies, but he united your hearts—so that by his blessing you became siblings. You were on the brink of a pit of fire, and he delivered you from it. In this way does God make clear his signs to you, so that you might be guided.

The Family of Amram 3:105.
Do not be like those who divided into sects and disputed, after clear verses came to them, for severe torment awaits them.

The Family of Amram 3:113–115.
They are not all the same: Some among the scriptural communities are an upstanding nation, who recite God's verses in the watches of the night while bowing in prayer. They believe in God and the Last Day, and enjoin what is right and forbid what is wrong, and compete in doing philanthropy. They are among the righteous. Whatever philanthropy they do, God will not blot it out. God knows all concerning the Godfearing.

The Gathering 59:23.
He is God, other than whom there is no god, the King, the Holy, the Peace, the Defender, the Guardian, the Mighty, the Omnipotent, the Supreme.

The Women 4:59.
Believers, obey God and obey the Messenger and those who enjoy authority among you...

The Women 4:89–90.
They want you to be pagans, just as they are pagans, so that you would be equal. Do not take patrons from among them unless they emigrate in the path of God. If they renege, take them, and fight them with lethal force wherever you encounter them, and do not take from among them either patrons or supporters. Make an exception for

those who seek refuge with a people who have a compact with you, or come to you with no desire to fight you or their own people. Had God wished, he could have ensconced them in power over you, such that they would have fought you. So if they withdraw and decline to engage you in combat, and offer you peace, God has not ordained for you any way to go against them.

The Women 4:94.
Believers, when you fight in the way of God, be discriminating. Do not say to one who greets you with "Peace!" "You are not a believer!" You aspire to the goods of this world, but with God are many riches. You were like them in the past, but God conferred his favor on you. So scrutinize carefully. God is aware of what you do.

The Pilgrimage 22:17.
The believers, the Jews, the Sabians, the Christians, the Zoroastrians, and the pagans—God will decide among them on the Resurrection Day. God sees all things.

The Pilgrimage 22:39–40.
He endorsed those who fought because they had been wronged, and in truth God is able to aid them—those who were expelled from their homes unjustly, solely for saying our lord is God. Had God not checked one people with another, then monasteries, churches, oratories and places of worship wherein God is much mentioned would have been razed to the ground. God aids those who aid him. God is powerful, mighty.

Success 48:3.
He is the one who sent down divine peace (*Sakina*) into the hearts of the believers, to increase their faith.

Success 48:23–24.

This is the tradition of God, as ever before, and you will find no change in the tradition of God. He it is who withheld their hands from you and your hands from them in the heart of Mecca after he made you ascendant over them. God sees the things you do.

Success 48:26.

Behold, the pagans instilled in their hearts a war fever, the war fever of the unruly. But God sent down his peace (*Sakina*) on his messenger and on the believers and constrained them with the word of piety, and they proved worthy and deserving of it. God is omniscient.

The Woman Tested 60:7–8.

Perhaps God will create love between you and those among whom were your enemies. God does not forbid you, with regard to those who have not fought you over religion nor expelled you from your homes, from being righteous and just toward them, for God loves those who are just.

The Chambers 49:9–10.

If two factions among the believers fall to fighting, make peace between them. If one commits aggression toward the other, fight the aggressors until they comply with the commandment of God. Make peace between them equitably, and be fair, for God loves those who are fair. The believers are siblings, so make peace among your siblings and fear God, so that perhaps you will receive mercy.

The Chambers 49:11–12.

Believers, let not one people ridicule another, for the latter may be better than they; nor should women ridicule other women, for the latter may be better than they. Do not insult each other, or call each other names. A corrupt name is a miserable thing after faith. Whoever will not repent, those are wrongdoers. Believers, avoid too much suspicion, for some suspicion is sin. Do not spy on others nor should some of you backbite others. Would any of you like to eat the flesh of your dead brethren? Fear God, for God is forgiving and merciful.

The Chambers 49:13.
People, we have created you male and female and made you nations and tribes so that you may come to know one another. The noblest of you in the sight of God is the most pious of you. God is knowing and aware.

Iron 57:27.
Then we sent messengers in their wake, and we sent Jesus the son of Mary and bestowed on him the Gospel. We put into the hearts of those who followed him kindness and mercy. As for monasticism, we did not prescribe it to them, but rather they invented it in a quest for the good-pleasure of God. But they did not pursue it in the right way. We gave those among them who believed their recompense. But many of them are corrupt.

Repentance 9:6.
If any of the pagans seeks your protection, protect him, so that he may hear the word of God. Then deliver him to his refuge. That is because they are a people who do not know.

Repentance 9:26.
Then God sent down upon his messenger his Peace (*Sakina*), and upon the believers, and he sent down invisible hosts, and he chastised the pagans; and that is the recompense of the pagans.

Repentance 9:40.

The pagans drove him away, the second of two, when both were in the cave. He said to his companion, "Do not sorrow; surely God is with us." Then God sent down on him his Peace (*Sakina*), and confirmed him with invisible hosts; and he made the word of the unbelievers the most abject; and God's word is most exalted; God is Almighty, All-Wise.

The Table 5:8.

Believers, be responsible before God and bear witness in fairness. Do not let hatred for a people move you not to be equitable. Be equitable—that is nearer to piety.

The Table 5:16.

God thereby guides those who follow his good-pleasure to the way of peace and delivers them from the shadows into light by his leave, and conducts them to the straight path.

The Table 5:31.

For this reason, we decreed for the children of Israel that those who kill another person—save in punishment for murder or the wreaking of corruption in the land—it is as though they had killed all humankind. And those who revive someone, it is as though they gave life to all humankind. Our messengers brought them clear proofs, but many of them thereafter committed excesses in the land.

The Table 5:46.

And we sent, following in their footsteps, Jesus the son of Mary, in confirmation of what was in the Torah, and we bestowed upon him the Gospel, in which is guidance and light, in verification of the Torah and as direction and admonition for the God-fearing.

The Table 5:48.

We have prescribed to each of you a law and a tradition. If God had desired, he could have made you a single community. Instead, he is testing you with regard to the revelations you received. So compete in doing good. You will all return to God, and he will inform you then concerning those things about which you argued.

The Table 5:69.

Those who believed, and the Jews, and the Sabians and the Christians—whoever has believed in God and the Last Day, and performed good deeds—no fear is upon them and nor shall they grieve.

The Table 5:82.

You will find that those most intensely hostile to the believers are Jews and pagans. And you will find that the nearest to them in love are those who say "We are Christians." That is because they have among them priests and monks, and they are not haughty.

NOTES

ABBREVIATIONS

BSOAS: *Bulletin of the School of Oriental and African Studies*

EQO: *Encyclopaedia of the Qur'an Online*, ed. Jane Dammen McAuliffe (Leiden: Brill Online, 2001–2006)

Ibn Rashid,   Ma`mar ibn Rashid, *Kitab al-Maghazi*, ed. and
Maghazi: trans. Sean W. Anthony as *The Expeditions: An Early Biography of Muhammad* (New York: New York University Press, 2014) (bilingual edition)

IJMES: *International Journal of Middle East Studies*

JAOS: *Journal of the American Oriental Society*

JESHO: *Journal of the Economic and Social History of the Orient*

JLA: *Journal of Late Antiquity*

JQS: *Journal of Qur'anic Studies*

JSAI: *Jerusalem Studies in Arabic and Islam*

Q.:   Qur'an

SLNPNF: Select Library of the Nicene and Post-Nicene Fathers, ed. Philip Schaff and Henry Wace

Tabari,   Abu Ja`far Muhammad ibn Jarir al-Tabari, *Tafsir*
Tafsir: *al-Tabari: Jami' al-bayan 'an ta'wil ay al-Qur'an*, ed. `Abd Alla¯h ibn `Abd al-Muh?sin al-Turki, 26 vols. (Cairo: Dar Hijr, 2001)

PREFACE

1. For recent academic work along these lines, see G. W. Bowersock, *The Crucible of Islam* (Cambridge, MA: Harvard University Press, 2017); Patricia Crone, *The Qur'anic Pagans and Related Matters: Collected Studies* (Leiden: E. J. Brill, 2016), vol. 1; Aziz al-Azmeh, *The Emergence of Islam in Late Antiquity: Allah and His People* (Cambridge: Cambridge University Press, 2014); Stephen J. Shoemaker, *The Death of a Prophet: The End of Muhammad's Life and the Beginnings of Islam* (Philadelphia: University of Pennsylvania Press, 2012); Peter Sarris, *Empires of Faith: The Fall of Rome to the Rise of Islam, 500–700* (Oxford: Oxford University Press, 2011), chap. 7; James Howard-Johnston, *Witnesses to a World Crisis: Historians and Histories of the Middle East in the Seventh Century* (Oxford: Oxford University Press, 2010); Fred Donner, *Muhammad and the Believers: At the Origins of Islam* (Cambridge, MA: Belknap Press of Harvard University Press, 2010); Angelika Neuwirth, *Der Koran als Text der Spätantike: Ein europäischer Zugang* (Frankfurt am Main: Verlag der Weltreligionen, 2010); and Fred Donner, "The Historical Context of the Qur'an," in *The Cambridge Companion to the Qur'an*, ed. Jane D. McAuliffe (Cambridge: Cambridge University Press, 2006), 21–39. See also Robert Hoyland, "Writing the Biography of the Prophet Muhammad: Problems and Solutions," *History Compass* 5, no. 2 (2007): 581–602.

2. That peace is an important theme in the Muslim tradition is of course not a new insight, though the scholarly literature on what might be called Islamic peace studies is remarkably thin. See Fred Donner, "Fight for God—but Do So with Kindness: Reflections on War, Peace, and Communal Identity in Early Islam," in *War and Peace in the Ancient World*, ed. Kurt Raaflaub (Oxford: Blackwell's, 2006), 297–311; Irfan A. Omar, "Peace," in *The Qur'an: An Encyclopedia*, ed. Oliver Leaman (London: Taylor and Francis, 2005), 489–491; Irfan A. Omar, "Jihad and Nonviolence in the Islamic Tradition," in *Peacemaking and the Challenge of Violence in World Religions*, ed. Irfan A. Omar and Michael K. Duffey (Chichester, West Sussex: John Wiley and Sons, 2015), 9–41; Qamar-ul Huda, ed., *Crescent and Dove: Peace and Conflict Resolution in Islam* (Washington, DC: US Institute of Peace, 2010); Amitabh Pal, *"Islam" Means Peace: Understanding the Muslim Principle of Nonviolence Today* (Santa Barbara: Praeger, 2011); Mohammed Abu-Nimr,

Nonviolence and Peace Building in Islam: Theory and Practice (Gainesville: University Press of Florida, 2003); Aida Othman, "'An Amicable Settlement Is Best': Sulh and Dispute Resolution in Islamic Law," *Arab Law Quarterly* 21, no. 1 (2007): 64–90; Rudolph T. Ware, *The Walking Qur'an: Islamic Education, Embodied Knowledge and History in West Africa* (Chapel Hill: University of North Carolina Press, 2014); and James L. Rowell, "Abdul Ghaffar Khan: An Islamic Gandhi," *Political Theology* 10, no. 4 (2009): 591–606.

3. For issues in the study of the Qur'an, see Anne-Sylvie Boisliveau, *Le Coran par lui-même: Vocabulaire et argumentation du discours coranique autoréférentiel* (Leiden: Brill, 2013); Carl Ernst, *How to Read the Qur'an: A New Guide, with Select Translation* (Chapel Hill: University of North Carolina Press, 2011); Muhammad Abdel Haleem, *Understanding the Qur'an: Themes and Style* (London: I. B. Tauris, 2010); Michael Sells, *Approaching the Qur'an: The Early Revelations*, 2nd ed. (Ashland, OR: White Cloud Press, 2006); Neal Robinson, *Discovering the Qur'an: A Contemporary Approach to a Veiled Text*, 2nd ed. (Washington, DC: Georgetown University Press, 2003); and Michael Cook, *The Koran: A Very Short Introduction* (Oxford: Oxford University Press, 2000). The revised classic in the field is Theodor Nöldeke et al., *The History of the Qur'an*, ed. and trans. Wolfgang H. Behn (Leiden: Brill, 2013), which set the chronological approach used in this book.

4. Comparative history has been fruitful for the study of late antiquity, and I deploy it here. See, for example, Peter Fibiger Bang, *The Roman Bazaar: A Comparative Study of Trade and Markets in a Tributary Empire* (Cambridge: Cambridge University Press, 2008); Chris Wickham, *The Inheritance of Rome* (New York: Penguin, 2009); J. Arnason and K. Raaflaub, eds., *The Roman Empire in Context: Historical and Comparative Perspectives* (Chichester: Wiley-Blackwell, 2011); and Garth Fowden, *Before and After Muhammad: The First Millennium Refocused* (Princeton, NJ: Princeton University Press, 2014). See also Philippa Levine, "Is Comparative History Possible?," *History and Theory* 53, no. 3 (2014): 331–347; and my introduction in Juan Cole, *Comparing Muslim Societies* (Ann Arbor: University of Michigan Press, 1992). For a complaint about the resistance to comparative studies of early Islam, see al-Azmeh, *Emergence of Islam*, 45.

5. Michael Lecker, "Were the Ghassanids and the Byzantines Behind Muhammad's Hijra?," in *Les Jafnides, des rois arabes au service de Byzance (VIe siècle de l'ère chrétienne)*, ed. Denis Genequand and Christian Robin (Paris: De Boccard, 2015), 277–293; Bowersock, *The Crucible of Islam*, chap. 6.

6. The old Western polemical tradition that Muhammad "learned" or appropriated ideas from the Near East is wrongheaded, in part because as a Near Easterner, that was his heritage. Everyone in late antiquity shared much common vocabulary about religion, and anyone who wished to convey religious ideas to that audience had to deploy it. The Qur'an is remarkable not for sharing in this discourse but for its original and creative uses of it. See Johann Fueck, "The Originality of the Arabian Prophet," in *Studies on Islam*, ed. and trans. Merlin Swartz (New York: Oxford University Press, 1981), 86–98.

7. Academics have all along, but especially since the 1970s, expressed unease with the lateness of most Muslim biographies of the Prophet (which were written down between 130 and 300 years and more after his death)—an unease I share. Indeed, here I have disregarded most such later material, including the biography of Muhammad ibn `Umar al-Waqidi, as being obviously very distant from the Qur'anic primary source. I have accepted from the later literature only the broadest of historical outlines and some dates. There have been two recent strands of this skepticism. One, that of Patricia Crone, rejected this corpus entirely. She remarked of Ibn Ishaq's biography (*sira*), "One can take the picture presented or leave it but one cannot *work* with it." Patricia Crone, *Slaves on Horses: The Evolution of the Islamic Polity* (Cambridge: Cambridge University Press, 2003), 4. Other philologists had also argued that since the later sources are not datable, we have to either accept them all or reject them all. As reported by Robert Hoyland, "Review of *Muslims, Jews and Pagans: Studies on Early Islamic Medina* by Michael Lecker," *BSOAS* 61, no. 1 (1998): 129–131. As a historian, I find this all-or-nothing approach baffling since there are indeed ways of analyzing and judging late textual reports. In fact, working from late sources is not unusual for late-antique and medieval historians. Chris Wickham pointed out, as a puzzled classicist, that in Islamics,

the revisionists had taken an extremely unusual position in completely jettisoning later works. He noted that mid-seventh-century Constantinopolitan history can only be known from early ninth-century writers such as Theophanes the Confessor, "without Byzantinists being more than regretful about it." See Wickham, *The Inheritance of Rome*, chap. 12. No one at all suggests we have to take Theophanes in toto or leave him entirely aside. The second form of revisionism, that of John Wansbrough, urged that the biographical literature be approached through the same tools that scholars use to study the Bible, including source and form criticism. I will be citing scholars who took him up on this proposed project (see the next note). I do reject the second part of Wansbrough's thesis, however, that the Qur'an is a late compilation of accumulated traditions, and I consider it early seventh century. In fact, this conclusion makes this book possible, since it gives me a primary source and fulcrum for judging other sources. For arguments for studying Muhammad from the Qur'an, see Alford T. Welch, "Muhammad's Understanding of Himself: The Koranic Data," in *Islam's Understanding of Itself*, ed. Richard G. Hovannisian and Speros Vryonis (Malibu, CA: Undena, 1983), 15–52; and Uri Rubin, *Muhammad the Prophet and Arabia*, Variorum Collected Studies Series (Farnham: Ashgate, 2011), chap. 1. The Cartesian moment of revisionism begun by Patricia Crone and Michael Cook's *Hagarism* (Cambridge: Cambridge University Press, 1977) has in some ways been salutary for the field, but the authors repudiated it and it is time to attempt a new synthesis.

8. My approach is that recommended by Angelika Neuwirth, who wrote that when seeking the significance of a Qur'anic theme, it is necessary first of all to trace its development throughout the text chronologically, but then also to listen for resonances with other works of late antiquity. See Angelika Neuwirth, "Wissenstransfer durch Typologie: Relektüren des Abrahamsopfers im Koran und im islamischen Kultus," in *Denkraum Spätantike: Reflexionen von Antiken in umfeld des Koran*, ed. Nora Schmidt, Nora K. Schmid, and Angelika Neuwirth (Wiesbaden: Harrassowitz Verlag, 2016), 170. I concentrate on the Qur'an and weight it as the only Arabic primary source. I bring in other, Roman and Iranian, late-antique primary sources for comparison and contrast with the Qur'an. I also compare and contrast the

Qur'an to the later reports of `Urwa ibn al-Zubayr and his student Ibn Shahab al-Zuhri that have been studied using the method of establishing thick chains of transmission by Andreas Görke and Gregor Schoeler, *Die ältesten Berichte über das Leben Muḥammads: Das Korpus `Urwa ibn az-Zubair* (Princeton, NJ: Darwin Press, 2008). I do not treat these `Urwa reports as primary or see most of them as AH first century and find that they sometimes contradict the Qur'an with regard to details and values, being substantially more warlike than it is. The `Urwa reports are, however, probably among our earliest Muslim sources for the life of the Prophet, and at least one of them does go back to 610, as I show below. I sometimes use anecdotes from other authors, but only if they seem compatible with the Qur'an or other seventh-century sources and largely for purposes of illustration. My major arguments about the theme of peace are built on the Qur'an itself.

CHAPTER 1: SANCTUARY

1. For Khadija and the trade commission, see Muhammad ibn Sa`d, *Al-Tabaqat al-Kubra*, 9 vols. (Beirut: Dar Sadir, 1960), 1:129–130. I say Muhammad was twenty-five in 692 because I think he was born in 567 rather than, as most authorities say, 570. The traditional date for Muhammad's birth is the "Year of the Elephant," when pagan Mecca repulsed a second major expedition by Abraha (d. ca. 568), then the Christian ruler of the Himyarite kingdom of Yemen. Recent scholarship is placing this campaign in the mid- to late 560s. See Christian Julien Robin, "Arabia and Ethiopia," in *The Oxford Handbook of Late Antiquity*, ed. Scott Fitzgerald Johnson (Oxford: Oxford University Press, 2012), 247–332, esp. 289–290. For Abraha, see Iwona Gajda, *Le Royaume de Himyar a l'époque monothéiste* (Paris: Mémoires de l'Académie des Inscriptions et Belles-Lettres, 2009), 116–150; and G. W. Bowersock, *Throne of Adulis: Red Sea Wars on the Eve of Islam* (Oxford: Oxford University Press, 2012).

2. Michael G. Morony, *Iraq After the Muslim Conquest* (Princeton, NJ: Princeton University Press, 1984), 181–213; Touraj Daryaee, *Sasanian Persia: The Rise and Fall of an Empire* (London: I. B. Tauris, 2009); Parvaneh Pourshariati, *Decline and Fall of the Sasanian Empire: The Sasanian-Parthian Confederacy and the Arab Conquest of Iran* (London: I. B. Tauris, 2008); Josef Wiesehöfer, "The Late Sasanian Near East,"

chap. 3 in *The New Cambridge History of Islam*, ed. Chase F. Robinson (Cambridge: Cambridge University Press, 2010), vol. 1. Western authors often call premodern Iran "Persia," after the province they called Persis, but Iranians used the term *Iran* for themselves as a people and for their realm.

3. For Muhammad's father, see Michael Lecker, "The Death of the Prophet Muhammad's Father: Did Waqidi Invent Some of the Evidence?," *Zeitschrift der Deutschen Morgenländischen Gesellschaft* 145 (1995): 9–27.

4. `Abd al-Malik ibn Hisham, *Sirat Rasul Allah*, ed. Ferdinand Wüstenfeld, 2 vols. (Gottingen: Dieterichsche Universitäts-Buchhandlung, 1858–1860), 1:107–108; Muhammad ibn Ishaq [`Abd al-Malik ibn Hisham], *The Life of Muhammad*, trans. Alfred Guillaume (1955; reprint, Karachi: Oxford University Press, 2002), 73; Ibn Sa`d, *Al-Tabaqat al-Kubra*, 1:118.

5. Ibn Sa`d, *Al-Tabaqat al-Kubra*, 8:15.

6. For trade and the white robes of peace, see Muhammad ibn Habib al-Baghdadi, *Kitab al-Muhabbar* (Beirut: Dar al-Afaq al-Jadidah, 1983), 263–268; and al-Azmeh, *Emergence of Islam*, 195. See also Uri Rubin, "The Ilaf of Quraysh: A Study of Sura CVI," *Arabica* 31, no. 2 (1984): 165–188; and Michael Bonner, "'Time Has Come Full Circle': Markets, Fairs and the Calendar in Arabia Before Islam," in *The Islamic Scholarly Tradition: Studies in History, Law, and Thought in Honor of Professor Michael Allan Cook*, ed. Asad Q. Ahmed et al. (Leiden: Brill, 2011), 15–47. The image of the bedouin children approaching a departing caravan is from Richard F. Burton, *Narrative of a Pilgrimage to Mecca and Medinah*, rev. ed. (London: William Mullan and Son, 1879), 397, which along with other Victorian travel literature such as Charles Doughty's *Travels in Arabia Deserta* (Cambridge: Cambridge University Press, 1888) suggested some descriptive passages below as well. Some of these descriptions derive from my own travels in Jordan, including to Petra and to the Eastern Desert. Others were provoked by ancient Arabic poetry.

7. Michael Lecker, "The Levying of Taxes for the Sasanians in Pre-Islamic Medina (Yathrib)," *JSAI* 27 (2002): 109–126.

8. Of their belief in the Creator God, the Qur'an (*Gilded Ornament* 43:87) asserts of the Hejazis, "If you ask them who created them, they

will certainly say, 'God.'" In Arabic they used a generic term, *Allah*, for this Creator, which just means "God," rather than being a personal name, and it is cognate to the Aramaic *Alaha* that Jesus used. Arab Christians in that era also called the God of the New Testament Allah, as is demonstrated by an inscription on a church built in 512 CE at Zabad in North Syria and another inscription near Dumat al-Jandal in Arabia. Those persons nowadays who insist on calling the Muslim God Allah as though the latter were his forename are thus committing an error. See Aziz al-Azmeh, "Linguistic Observations on the Theonym *Allah*," in *In the Shadow of Arabic: The Centrality of Language to Arabic Culture*, ed. Bilal Orfali (Leiden: Brill, 2011), 267–281, esp. 273. See also Laila Nehmé, "New Dated Inscriptions (Nabataean and Pre-Islamic Arabic) from a Site near Near al-Jawf, Ancient Dumah, Saudi Arabia," *Arabian Epigraphic Notes* 3 (2017): 121–164; David Kiltz, "The Relationship Between Arabic Allah and Syriac Allaha," *Der Islam* 88 (2012): 33–50; and Robert Hoyland, "Epigraphy and the Linguistic Background of the Qur'an," in *The Qur'an in Its Historical Context*, ed. Gabriel Said Reynolds (New York: Routledge, 2008), 51–69.

9. Antoninus Martyr, *Of the Holy Places Visited by Antoninus Martyr About the Year 570 A.D.*, trans. Aubrey Stewart (London: Committee of the Palestine Exploration Fund, 1885), para. 36; Antonini Placentini, *Itinerarium: Im unentstellten text mit deutscher Übersetzung*, ed. and trans. J. Gildemeister (Berlin: H. Reuters, 1889), para. 36. Hereafter, this source is cited with the paragraph number for all three texts, the Latin original and German and English translations. See also John Wilkinson, *Jerusalem Pilgrims: Before the Crusades* (Warminster, Wiltshire: Aris and Phillips, 2002), 146.

10. William Lancaster and Felicity Lancaster, "Concepts of Tribe, Tribal Confederation and Tribal Leadership," in *Les Jafnides, des rois arabes au service de Byzance (VIe siècle de l'ère chrétienne)*, ed. Denis Genequand and Christian Robin (Paris: De Boccard, 2015), 53–77; Bert de Vries, "On the Way to Bostra: Arab Settlement in South Syria Before Islam—the Evidence from Written Sources," in *Heureux qui comme Ulysse a fait un beau voyage: Movements of People in Time and Space*, ed. Nefissa Naguib and Bert de Vries (Bergen: BRIC, 2010), 69–92; Morony, *Iraq After the Muslim Conquest*, 214–235; Rudi Paul Lindner,

"What Was a Nomadic Tribe?," *Comparative Studies in Society and History* 24, no. 4 (1982): 689–711.

11. For trade routes, see Fanny Bessard, "The Urban Economy in Southern Inland Greater Syria from the Seventh Century to the End of the Umayyads," *Late Antique Archaeology* 10, no. 1 (2013): 377–421; Audrey Peli, "Les mines de la péninsule Arabique d'après les auteurs arabes (VIIe—XIIe siècles)," *Chroniques Yéménites* 13 (2006), http://journals.openedition.org/cy/1176; Mikhail D. Bukharin, "Mecca on the Caravan Routes in Pre-Islamic Antiquity," in *The Qur'an in Context: Historical and Literary Investigations into the Qur'anic Milieu*, ed. Angelika Neuwirth, Nicolai Sinai, and Michael Marx (Leiden: Brill, 2010), 115–134; al-Azmeh, *Emergence of Islam*, 134–162; U. Rubin, "Ilaf of Quraysh"; Gene W. Heck, "'Arabia Without Spices': An Alternate Hypothesis," *JAOS* 123, no. 3 (2003): 547–576; and R. B. Serjeant, review, "*Meccan Trade and the Rise of Islam*: Misconceptions and Flawed Polemics," *JAOS* 110, no. 3 (1990): 472–486. Some of these authors are replying to the late Patricia Crone's idiosyncratic skepticism in her youth about the Meccan caravans, which she revised in Patricia Crone, "Quraysh and the Roman Army: Making Sense of the Meccan Leather Trade," *BSOAS* 70, no. 1 (2007): 63–88. For Sasanian Iran in Yemen, see Robin, "Arabia and Ethiopia," 247–332, this point on 289–290; and Zeev Rubin, "Islamic Traditions on the Sasanian Conquest of the Himyarite Realm," *Der Islam* 84, no. 2 (2007): 185–199.

12. R. C. Blockley, *The History of Menander the Guardsman: Introductory Essay, Text, Translation and Notes* (Liverpool: Francis Cairns, 1985), 98 (quote). See also Greg Fisher, *Between Empires: Arabs, Romans, and Sassanians in Late Antiquity* (Oxford: Oxford University Press, 2011), 64–71; Irfan Shahid, *Byzantium and the Arabs in the Sixth Century*, 2 vols. (Washington, DC: Dumbarton Oaks Research Library and Collection, 1995–2010); Mark Whittow, "The Late Roman/Early Byzantine Near East," chap. 2 in *New Cambridge History of Islam*, ed. C. Robinson, vol. 1; and Isabel Toral-Niehoff, *Al-Hira: Eine arabische Kulturmetropole im spätantiken Kontext* (Leiden: Brill, 2013) and "Late Antique Iran and the Arabs: The Case of al-Hira," *Journal of Persianate Studies* 6, nos. 1–2 (2013): 115–126. A fifth-century Mesopotamian Arab chieftain is said to have been persuaded by a vision of

Saint Simeon the Stylite (d. 459) to allow his tribesmen to follow the cross but to have observed, "If I were not a subject of the Persian king, I too would have approached [Simeon] and have become a Christian." See Frank R. Trombley, *Hellenic Religion and Christianization, c. 370–529*, 2 vols. (Leiden: Brill, 1993), 2:198.

13. Burton, *Narrative of a Pilgrimage*, 385.

14. Ramsay MacMullen, *Christianizing the Roman Empire, AD 100–400* (New Haven, CT: Yale University Press, 1984), 54. For the poetry about swordplay, see Tarafa, "Qasidah," in *Kitab al-`Iqd al-Thamin fi Dawawin al-Shu`ara' al-Sitta al-Jahiliyyin*, ed. W. Ahlwardt (London: Trübner, 1870), 59. See also Michael Sells, "The Mu'allaqa of Tarafa," *Journal of Arabic Literature* 17 (1986): 21–33.

15. *Small Kindnesses* 107:2–3. See also Michael Bonner, "Poverty and Economics in the Qur'an," *Journal of Interdisciplinary History* 35, no. 3 (2005): 391–406.

16. U. Rubin, "Ilaf of Quraysh"; Harris Birkeland, "The Lord Guideth: Studies on Primitive Islam," *Skrifter Utgitt av Det Norske Videnskaps-Akademi i Oslo* 2, no. 2 (1956): 102–130.

17. For "bags of wheat," see Muhammad ibn Habib al-Baghdadi, *Al-Munammaq*, ed. Muhammad Khurshid Fariq (Beirut: `Alam al-Kitab, 1985), 42; Ibn Sa`d, *Al-Tabaqat al-Kubra*, 1:75–80; M. J. Kister, "Mecca and Tamim (Aspects of Their Relations)," *JESHO* 8, no. 2 (1965): 113–163; Mahmood Ibrahim, *Merchant Capital and Islam* (Austin: University of Texas Press, 1990), 42–43; and F. E. Peters, *Muhammad and the Origins of Islam* (Albany: SUNY Press, 1994), chap. 3. For Sasanian frontier tolls, see Stephen Mitchell, *A History of the Later Roman Empire, AD 284–641*, 2nd ed. (London: Wiley Blackwell, 2014), 373.

18. Mohammed Maraqten, "Dangerous Trade Routes: On the Plundering of Caravans in the Pre-Islamic Near East," *ARAM* 8 (1996): 213–236; Gene Heck, "Gold Mining in Arabia and the Rise of the Islamic State," *JESHO* 42, no. 3 (1999): 364–395; Heck, "'Arabia Without Spices'"; Robert G. Hoyland, *Arabia and the Arabs: From the Bronze Age to the Coming of Islam* (London: Routledge, 2001), 110–112. For Roman payment of gold to the Sasanians, see Blockley, *History of Menander the Guardsman*, 60–63, 160–161. For the corpse trade, see Yosef Tobi, "The Jews of Yemen in the Light of the Excavation of

the Jewish Synagogue in Qani`," *Proceedings of the Seminar for Arabian Studies* 43 (2013): 1–8.

19. Jacqueline Chabbi, *Les trois piliers de l'islam: Lecture anthropologique du Coran* (Paris: Éditions du Seuil, 2016), 100–106.

20. John F. Healey, *The Nabataean Tomb Inscriptions of Mada'in Salih* (Oxford: Oxford University Press, 1993), 154–155, 115; John F. Healey, *The Religion of the Nabataeans: A Conspectus* (Leiden: Brill, 2001), 13, 127–134; Peter Alpass, *The Religious Life of Nabataea* (Leiden: E. J. Brill, 2013), 123. For the intersection of Nabatean and Hejazi religion, see Carl Ernst, *How to Read the Qur'an: A New Guide, with Select Translation* (Chapel Hill: University of North Carolina Press, 2011), 84–88.

21. *Hijr* 15:80.

22. G. W. Bowersock, *Roman Arabia* (Cambridge, MA: Harvard University Press, 1983); Fergus Millar, *The Roman Near East, 31 BC–AD 337* (Cambridge: Cambridge University Press, 1993); Shahid, *Byzantium and the Arabs*; Fisher, *Between Empires*. Revising the older view that the Jafnids or "Ghassanids" ruled and administered Transjordan in the late sixth century and insisting that it was prosperous and well integrated into the Roman state is Robert Chrisman Caldwell III, "Between State and Steppe: New Evidence for Society in Sixth-Century Southern Transjordan" (PhD diss., University of Michigan, 2001), based on the Petra papyri. Petra paid no tribute to the Jafnids, only Roman taxes. The Jafnids were not a state but an auxiliary military force. See also Wolf Liebeschuetz, *East and West in Late Antiquity: Invasion, Settlement, Ethnogenesis and Conflicts of Religion* (Leiden: Brill, 2015), 248–249; J. H. W. G. Liebeschuetz, "Arab Tribesmen and Desert Frontiers in Late Antiquity," *JLA* 8, no. 1 (2015): 62–96; Fisher, *Between Empires*, 103–105; Geoffrey Greatrix, "Les Jafnides et la défense de l'empire au VIe siècle," in *Les Jafnides*, ed. Genequand and Robin, 121–154. For background and the evidence of inscriptions for the increasing density of Arab populations in eastern Syria and Transjordan, see Robert G. Hoyland, "Arab Kings, Arab Tribes and the Beginnings of Arab Historical Memory in Late Roman Epigraphy," in *From Hellenism to Islam: Cultural and Linguistic Change in the Roman Near East*, ed. Hannah M. Cotton et al. (Cambridge: Cambridge University Press, 2009), 374–400.

23. Christian Julien Robin, "Ghassan en Arabie," in *Les Jafnides*, ed. Genequand and Robin, 79–120.

24. For the Banu Judham of the Transjordan, see C. E. Bosworth, "Madyan Shu'ayb in Pre-Islamic and Early Islamic Lore and History," *Journal of Semitic Studies* 29 (1984): 56. For a survey of religion in the eastern Roman Empire in this era, see Averil Cameron, *The Mediterranean World in Late Antiquity, AD 395–700*, 2nd ed. (London: Routledge, 2012), chap. 8. For the survival of paganism among rural Arab populations, see Gideon Avni, *The Byzantine-Islamic Transition in Palestine* (Oxford: Oxford University Press, 2014), 191, 268–271, 283–285. For Father Nicholas and the pagan Arab kidnappers, see John Moschus, *Pratum Spirituale*, in *Patrologiae cursus completus, Series græca*, ed. Jacques-Paul Migne (1863), 87:3023–3026; John Moschos, *The Spiritual Meadow (Pratum Spirituale)*, trans. John Wortley (Collegeville, MN: Liturgical Press, 2008), 129; and Shahid, *Byzantium and the Arabs*, 1:597. For imperial persecution of pagans, see K. W. Harl, "Sacrifice and Pagan Belief in Fifth- and Sixth-Century Byzantium," *Past & Present*, no. 128 (August 1990): 7–27; and Polymnia Athanassiadi, *Damascius, the Philosophical History: Text with Translation and Notes* (Athens: Apameia, 1999). See also Glen Bowersock, *Hellenism in Late Antiquity* (Ann Arbor: University of Michigan Press, 1996); and Ramsay MacMullen, *Christianity and Paganism in the Fourth to Eighth Centuries* (New Haven, CT: Yale University Press, 1997), chap. 1. For background, see Robin Lane Fox, *Pagans and Christians* (New York: Alfred A. Knopf, 1987); Edward J. Watts, *The Final Pagan Generation* (Berkeley: University of California Press, 2015); James J. O'Donnell, *Pagans: The End of Traditional Religion and the Rise of Christianity* (New York: HarperCollins, 2015); and Christopher P. Jones, *Between Pagan and Christian* (Cambridge, MA: Harvard University Press, 2014), 31–32, 126–143.

25. For Allat inscriptions, see Healey, *Religion of the Nabataeans*, 56–59; Susanne Krone, *Die altarabische Gottheit al-Lat* (Frankfurt-am-Main: Peter Lang, 1992), 127–132, 329–336; Hans J. W. Drijvers, *The Religion of Palmyra* (Leiden: E. J. Brill, 1976), 16, 20; Hans J. W. Drijvers, "Sanctuaries and Social Safety: The Iconography of Divine Peace in Hellenistic Syria," in *Commemorative Figures: Papers Presented to Dr. Th. P. van Baaren* (Brill: Leiden, 1982), 66–73, this inscription

discussed on 66–67. For the inscription of Akh, see Trombley, *Hellenic Religion and Christianization*, 2:174–177. For the idea of *salam* or peace as individual, in contrast to the cognate *shalom* in the Hebrew Bible, which, it has been argued, primarily concerns groups of people, see Perry Yoder, "Introductory Essay," in *The Meaning of Peace: Biblical Studies*, ed. Perry B. Yoder and Willard M. Swartley and trans. W. Sawatsky, 2nd ed. (Elkhart, IN: Institute of Mennonite Studies, 2001), 1–13.

26. Placentini, *Itinerarium*, para. 38. See also Wilkinson, *Jerusalem Pilgrims*, 147.

27. Karl Gottfried Müller et al., *Fragmenta historicum graecorum*, 4 vols. (Paris: Didot Frères, 1853), 4:179–180; Nonnosus in Photius, *The Library of Photius*, trans. J. H. Freese (New York: Macmillan, 1920), 19. See also M. Gawlikowski, "The Sacred Space in Ancient Arab Religions," in *Studies in the History and Archeology of Jordan*, ed. Adnan Hadidi (Amman: Department of Antiquities, Hashemite Kingdom of Jordan, 1982), 301–303; and Harry Munt, *The Holy City of Medina: Sacred Space in Early Islamic Arabia* (Cambridge: Cambridge University Press, 2014), chap. 1.

28. *The Star* 53:49–50.

29. M. Leon de Laborde, *Journey Through Arabia Petraea* (London: John Murray, 1836), 168–171.

30. Epiphanius of Salamis, *The Panarion, Books II and III: De Fide*, trans. Frank Williams (Leiden: E. J. Brill, 2013), 51; Alpass, *Religious Life*, 57–58, 106; Shaher Rababeh and Rama al-Rabady, "The Crowsteps Motif in Nabataean Architecture: Insights into Its Meaning and Use," *Arabian Archaeology and Epigraphy* 25, no. 1 (2014): 29.

31. Fawzi Zayadine, François Larché, and Jacqueline Dentzer-Feydy, *Le Qasr al-Bint de Pétra: L'architecture, le décor, la chronologie et les dieux* (Paris: Recherche sur les Civilisations, 2003), 109; Walter D. Ward, "The 363 Earthquake and the End of Public Paganism in the Southern Transjordan," *JLA* 9, no. 1 (2016): 138–139; Javier Teixidor, *The Pagan God: Popular Religion in the Near East* (Princeton, NJ: Princeton University Press, 1977); Stephen Mitchell, "The Cult of Theos Hypsistos Between Pagans, Jews, and Christians," in *Pagan Monotheism in Late Antiquity*, ed. Polymnia Athanassidadi and Michael Frede (Oxford: Clarendon Press, 1999), 81–148; Stephen Mitchell, "Further

Thoughts on the Cult of Theos Hypsistos," in *One God: Pagan Monotheism in the Roman Empire*, ed. Stephen Mitchell and Peter van Nuffelan (Cambridge: Cambridge University Press, 2010), 167–208. Some sort of late-antique pagan monotheism of a Godfearer sort seems more likely to me as an immediate background for the Qur'an than straight Judaism or Christianity or a Jewish-Christian sect. The Qur'an nowhere commands circumcision, it considers Abraham and the patriarchs pre-Jewish, it is uninterested in the crucifixion and resurrection as soteriology, it never mentions baptism, and it denies the Fatherhood of God. That configuration is what you would get if Gentile monotheists with their own practices and theology appropriated texts from the Bible in isolation from the actual doctrinal and ritual life of Jews or Christians. As for Jewish Christians, there is no evidence for them in this era, and most such sects in an earlier period heavily emphasized baptism. See James Carleton Paget, *Jews, Christians and Jewish Christians in Antiquity* (Tübingen: Mohr Siebeck, 2010), 369–372; Daniel Boyarin, "Rethinking Jewish Christianity: An Argument for Dismantling a Dubious Category," *Jewish Quarterly Review* 99, no. 1 (2009): 7–36; and Joan E. Taylor, *Christians and the Holy Places: The Myth of Jewish-Christian Origins* (New York: Oxford University Press, 1993).

32. Leigh-Ann Bedal, "Desert Oasis: Water Consumption and Display in the Nabataean Capital," *Near Eastern Archaeology* 65, no. 4 (2002): 225–234; Mohammed Nasarat, Fawzi Abu Danah, and Slameh Naimat, "Agriculture in Sixth-Century Petra and Its Hinterland, the Evidence from the Petra Papyri," *Arabian Archaeology and Epigraphy* 23, no. 1 (2012): 105–115; Caldwell, "Between State and Steppe." For comparative economic issues, see Michael J. Decker, *The Byzantine Dark Ages* (London: Bloomsbury, 2016); Chris Wickham, *The Inheritance of Rome* (New York: Penguin, 2009), chaps. 1–7; Bryan Ward-Perkins, *The Fall of Rome and the End of Civilization* (Oxford: Oxford University Press, 2005); Cecile Morrisson and Jean-Pierre Sodini, "The Sixth-Century Economy," in *The Economic History of Byzantium: From the Seventh Through the Fifteenth Century*, ed. Angeliki E. Laiou (Washington, DC: Dumbarton Oaks, 2002), 171–220; and John Haldon, "The Resources of Late Antiquity," chap. 1 in *New Cambridge History of Islam*, ed. C. Robinson, vol. 1.

33. I am hypothesizing that although the Qur'an is grammatically in the Hejazi dialect, its more sophisticated vocabulary derives from urban Arabs in and around Damascus, Bostra, and Petra, who also knew Greek and Aramaic and had created neologisms for theological and philosophical discourse over centuries of living in the Roman Empire. Not only did they create new words, but they also gave existing Arabic terms new connotations, using them to substitute for a foreign notion, a phenomenon called by linguists a "loanshift." For Greek and Arabic bilinguality in Petra of a sort I suspect Muhammad shared, see Omar Al-Ghul, "Preliminary Notes on the Arabic Material in the Petra Papyri," *Topoi* 14, no. 1 (2006): 139–169. For sixth- and seventh-century Arabic, see Ernst A. Knauf, "Arabo-Aramaic and `Arabiyya': From Ancient Arabic to Early Standard Arabic, 200 CE–600 CE," in *The Qur'an in Context*, ed. Angelika Neuwirth et al. (Leiden: E. J. Brill, 2009). A survey of language use in the eastern Roman Empire in this era is Cameron, *Mediterranean World*, 176–181. For an argument that many in Egypt and the Levant spoke Greek as well as local languages in the eastern Roman Empire, see Fergus Millar, *A Greek Roman Empire: Power and Belief Under Theodosius II (408–450)* (Berkeley: University of California Press, 2006), chaps. 1 and 3; and Bowersock, *Hellenism*, chaps. 3, 5. For a model study of cultural interactions of this sort in antiquity, see Ian Moyer, *Egypt and the Limits of Hellenism* (Cambridge: Cambridge University Press, 2011). On the dynamics of multilinguality, see also Rachel Stroumsa, "Greek and Arabic in Nessana," in *Documents and the History of the Early Islamic World*, ed. Alexander T. Schubert and Petra Sijpesteinj (Leiden: E. J. Brill, 2015), 143–157. For loanshifts, see Fredric W. Field, *Linguistic Borrowing in Bilingual Contexts* (Amsterdam: J. Benjamins, 2002); and Joachim Grzega, "Lexical-Semantic Variables," in *The Handbook of Historical Sociolinguistics*, ed. Juan Manuel Hernández-Campoy et al. (London: John Wiley and Sons, 2012), chap. 15.

34. For Ethiopian merchants or pilgrims in Jerusalem, see Placentini, *Itinerarium*, para. 35. For the other remarks here, see Robert Schick, "A Christian City with a Major Muslim Shrine: Jerusalem in the Umayyad Period," in *Conversion in Late Antiquity: Christianity, Islam and Beyond*, ed. Arietta Papaconstantinou et al. (Farnham: Ashgate, 2015), 299–301; Dayna S. Kalleres, *City of Demons: Violence, Ritual*

and *Christian Power in Late Antiquity* (Berkeley: University of California Press, 2015), pt. 2; Cyril Mango, "The Temple Mount, AD 614–638," in *Bayt al-Maqdis*, ed. Julian Raby and Jeremy Johns (Oxford: Oxford University Press, 1992), 3; and Lee I. Levine, ed., *Jerusalem: Its Sanctity and Centrality to Judaism, Christianity and Islam* (New York: Continuum, 1999), pt. 3. For Jesus and Mary in the Kaaba, see Abu al-Walid Muḥammad al-Azraqi, *Akhbar Makkah wa ma ja'a fiha*, vol. 1 of Ferdinand Wüstenfeld, *Die Chroniken der Stadt Mekka*, 3 vols. (Leipzig: F. A. Brockhaus, 1857), 111; and G. R. D. King, "The Paintings of the Pre-Islamic Ka'ba," *Muqarnas* 21 (2004): 219–229.

35. Flavius Josephus, *Works*, trans. William Whiston, 2 vols. (Philadelphia: Grigg & Elliot, 1844), 1:30. For Genesis's incorporation of Ishmael and his descendants into the promise to Abraham, see Joseph Blenkinsopp, "Abraham as Paradigm in the Priestly History in Genesis," *Journal of Biblical Literature* 128, no. 2 (2009): 236–238. The Qur'anic chapter of *Abraham* 14:37 has the Patriarch Abraham say, "Our Lord! I have settled some of my posterity in an uncultivable valley near to your holy shrine." For this theme, see Reuven Firestone, *Journeys in Holy Lands: The Evolution of the Abraham-Ishmael Legends in Islamic Exegesis* (Albany: SUNY Press, 1990), chaps. 8–11; Joseph Witztum, "The Foundations of the House (Q 2: 127)," *BSOAS* 72, no. 1 (2009): 25–40; Gerald Hawting, "The Religion of Abraham and Islam," in *Abraham, the Nations and the Hagarites: Jewish, Christian, and Islamic Perspectives on Kinship with Abraham*, ed. Martin Goodman et al. (Leiden: Brill, 2010), 477–501; and Firestone, *Journeys in Holy Lands*.

36. John of Ephesus, *The Third Part of the Ecclesiastical History*, trans. R. Payne Smith (Oxford: Oxford University Press, 1860), 372–373; Shahid, *Byzantium and the Arabs*, 1:354–356.

37. Fisher, *Between Empires*, 175–178; John of Ephesus, *Ecclesiastical History*, 236. The view from Constantinople is given in Theophylact Simocatta, *Theophylacti Simocattae historiae*, ed. Peter Wirth and Carl de Boor (Stuttgart: B. G. Teubner, 1972), 144–146 (3.17); Theophylact Simocatta, *The History of Theophylact Simocatta: An English Translation with Introduction and Notes*, trans. Michael Whitby and Mary Whitby (Oxford: Clarendon Press, 1986), 99–101 (3.17); and Michael Whitby, *The Emperor Maurice and His Historian: Theophylact*

Simocatta on Persian and Balkan Warfare (Oxford: Oxford University Press, 1988), 272–274.

38. John of Ephesus, *Ecclesiastical History*, 241.

39. Michel le Syrien, *Le chronique de Michel le Syrien, Patriarche Jacobite Syrien (1166–1199)*, ed. and trans. J. B. Chabot, 4 vols. (Paris: Ernest Leroux, 1899–1905), 2:350–351; Robin, "Arabia and Ethiopia," 298.

40. Ibn Sa`d, *Al-Tabaqat al-Kubra*, 1:130. Another such tale is set in Muhammad's childhood, when he is said to have accompanied Abu Talib's caravan to Bostra. See Barbara Roggema, *The Legend of Sergius Bahira: Eastern Christian Apologetics and Apocalyptic in Response to Islam* (Leiden: Brill, 2009), 38–59; and Thomas Sizgorich, *Violence and Belief in Late Antiquity: Militant Devotion in Christianity and Islam* (Philadelphia: University of Pennsylvania Press, 2012), chap. 5.

41. *The Table* 5:82. For the puzzlement of the Muslim exegetical tradition about this verse and attempts to circumscribe its meaning, see Jane Dammen McAuliffe, *Qur'anic Christians: An Analysis of Classical and Modern Exegesis* (Cambridge: Cambridge University Press, 1991), chap. 7.

42. Maurice Sartre, *Bostra: Des origines a l'Islam* (Paris: Librairie Orientaliste Paul Geuthner, 1985); Trombley, *Hellenic Religion and Christianization*, vol. 2, chap. 11; William M. Johnston, ed., *Encyclopedia of Monasticism* (London: Routledge, 2000), 47; Abdulla al-Shorman et al., "Travel and Hospitality in Late Antiquity: A Case Study from Umm el-Jimal in Eastern Jordan," *Near Eastern Archaeology* 80, no. 1 (2017): 22–28. For monks' withdrawal from society, or *anachoresis*, see Peter Brown, *The Making of Late Antiquity* (Cambridge, MA: Harvard University Press, 1978), chap. 4.

43. Sartre, *Bostra*; Shahid, *Byzantium and the Arabs*; Clive Foss, "Syria in Transition, AD 550–750," in *Late Antiquity on the Eve of Islam*, ed. Averil Cameron (Farnham: Ashgate, 2013), 171–275, esp. 243–262; J. L. Porter, *Five Years in Damascus*, 2 vols. (London: John Murray, 1855), 2:164–168; Trombley, *Hellenic Religion and Christianization*, vol. 2, chap. 11; Michael Frede, "Monotheism and Pagan Philosophy," in *Pagan Monotheism in Late Antiquity*, ed. Athanassidadi and Frede, 41–68. For sixth-century pagan survivals in the eastern Roman Empire, see Anthony Kaldellis, "The Religion of Ioannes Lydos," *Phoenix* 57,

nos. 3–4 (2003): 300–316. Kaldellis also believes Justinian's chronicler Prokopios to have been a secret pagan.

44. Athanassiadi, *Damascius*, 114/115–116/117 (fragment 36) and 196/197 (fragment 76). For the context, see Christian Wildberg, "Philosophy in the Age of Justinian," in *Cambridge Companion to the Age of Justinian*, ed. Maas, chap. 13.

45. Peter Haddad, ed. and trans., *Sharbe medem men qlisiastiqe wadqosmostiqe*, with Arabic translation, *Al-Ta'rikh al-Saghir li al-Qarn al-Sabi` `Ashar* (Baghdad: Majma` al-Lughah al-Suriyaniyyah, 1976), 53–58 (I used the Arabic translation; for this source, also known as the "Khuzistan Chronicle," see Howard-Johnston, *Witnesses to a World Crisis*, 128–147); Sebeos, *The Armenian History Attributed to Sebeos*, trans. R. W. Thomson (Liverpool: Liverpool University Press, 1999), chaps. 10–11 (this source is not by Sebeos but has come to be so known; see Howard-Johnston, *Witnesses to a World Crisis*, chap. 3); A. Sh. Shahbazi, "Bahram VI Cobin," in *Encyclopaedia Iranica*, III/5, 514–522, http://www.iranicaonline.org/articles/bahram-06.

46. Frantz Grenet, ed. and trans., *La Geste d'Ardashir fils de Pabag: Karnamag i Ardaxser i Pabagan* (Die, France: Éditions a Die, 2003), 11: 13–15; Darab Dastur Peshotan Sanjana, *Karname i Artakshshir i Papakan* (Bombay: Education Society's Steam Press, 1896), 45–46 (my translation).

47. Abu al-Faraj al-Isfahani, *Kitab al-Aghani*, ed. Ihsan Abbas et al., 25 vols. (Beirut: Dar Sadr, 2008), 22:41; Hoyland, *Arabia and the Arabs*, 225–226; Ella Landau-Tasseron, "The Sinful Wars," *JSAI* 8 (1986): 37–59.

48. Michael Cook, "Early Medieval Christian and Muslim Attitudes to Pagan Law," in *Islam and Its Past: Jahiliyya, Late Antiquity, and the Qur'an*, ed. Carol Bakhos and Michael Cook (Oxford: Oxford University Press, 2017), 226; Muhammad al-Bukhari, *Sahih al-Bukhari*, ed. Abu Suhayb al-Karmi (Riyadh: Bayt al-Afkar al-Dawliya, 1998), 739, no. 3845; Sadik Kirazli, "Conflict and Conflict Resolution in the Pre-Islamic Arab Society," *Islamic Studies* 50, no. 1 (2011): 25–53. Cook argues that later Muslim authors may have attributed this story to Abu Talib in order to justify bringing into Muslim law from pagan times these principles of dispute settlement, which resemble those of other feuding societies. Cf. William Ian Miller, *Bloodtaking and Peacemaking:*

Feud, Law, and Society in Saga Iceland (Chicago: University of Chicago Press, 1990), chap. 8.

49. Ibn Saʿd, *Al-Tabaqat al-Kubra*, 1:131.

50. Ibid. There is also a story in these sources that Khadija had to get her uncle drunk to get permission to marry Muhammad. It doesn't strike me as a likely story, but in any case it would show that she was really in love.

51. For the quote from Jacob of Edessa, see Robert G. Hoyland, *Seeing Islam as Others Saw It* (Princeton, NJ: Darwin Press, 1997), 165; and Hoyland, "The Earliest Christian Writings on Muhammad: An Appraisal," in *The Biography of Muhammad: The Issue of the Sources*, ed. Harald Motzki (Leiden: Brill, 2000), 276–297. For the second quote on his trading missions to Palestine, see Chabot, *Le chronique de Michel le Syrien*, 2:403–404. For the argument about his travels to Yemen, see Chapter 3. For the religious situation in Yemen, see Iwona Gajda, "Remarks on Monotheism in Ancient South Arabia," in *Islam and Its Past*, ed. Bakhos and Cook, chap. 8.

52. Many of the reports attributed to Aisha were allegedly transmitted by her sister's son, ʿUrwa ibn al-Zubayr, and these have been studied recently as a corpus by a scholarly team. See Gregor Schoeler, *The Biography of Muhammed: Nature and Authenticity*, trans. Uwe Vagelpohl and ed. James E. Montgomery (New York: Routledge, 2011). See also Andreas Görke, Harald Motzki, and Gregor Schoeler, "First Century Sources for the Life of Muḥammad? A Debate," *Der Islam* 89, no. 1 (2012): 2–59, responding to Stephen J. Shoemaker, "In Search of ʿUrwa's Sira: Some Methodological Issues in the Quest for 'Authenticity' in the Life of Muhammad," *Der Islam* 85, no. 2 (2011): 257–344.

53. For the report from Aisha about Muhammad's quest, see Al-Bukhari, *Sahih al-Bukhari*, 21, no. 3. For the practice of retreats, see M. J. Kister, "Al-Tahannuth: An Inquiry into the Meaning of a Term," *BSOAS* 31, no. 2 (1968): 223–236; and al-Azmeh, *Emergence of Islam*, 235–236.

54. Eusebius Pamphilus, "Oration in Praise of Constantine Pronounced on the Thirtieth Anniversary of His Reign," in *The Church History of Eusebius*, SLNPNF, n.s. (Oxford: Parker, 1890), 1:606 (16.4); Thomas Renna, "The Idea of Peace in the West, 500–1150," *Journal of Medieval History* 6, no. 2 (1980): 144–145; Adrian Goldsworthy, *Pax Romana:*

War, Peace and Conquest in the Roman World (New Haven, CT: Yale University Press, 2016).

55. Ammianus Marcellinus, *The Roman History of Ammianus Marcellinus,* trans. C. Yonge (London: G. Bell, 1894), 283 (22.5.4).

56. Emran el-Badawi, *The Qur'an and the Aramaic Gospel Traditions* (London: Routledge, 2013); Emran el-Badawi, "The Impact of Aramaic (Especially Syriac) on the Qur'an," *Religion Compass* 8, no. 7 (2014): 220–228; Claude Gilliot, "Le Coran, production littéraire de l'Antiquité tardive ou Mahomet interprète dans le 'lectionnaire arabe' de la Mecque," *Revue des Mondes Musulmans et de la Méditerranée*, no. 129 (2012): 31–56. For Greek as a holy language even for some late Roman Jews (which has implications for Godfearers and for Muhammad), see Nicholas de Lange, "Jews in the Age of Justinian," in *The Cambridge Companion to the Age of Justinian*, ed. Michael Maas (Cambridge: Cambridge University Press, 2005), 403.

CHAPTER 2: PEACE IT IS

1. James Howard-Johnston, *Witnesses to a World Crisis: Historians and Histories of the Middle East in the Seventh Century* (Oxford: Oxford University Press, 2010), 436–460; Clive Foss, "The Persians in the Roman Near East (602–630 AD)," *Journal of the Royal Asiatic Society*, 3rd ser., 13, no. 2 (2003): 149–170; Foss, "The Persians in Asia Minor and the End of Antiquity," *English Historical Review* 90, no. 357 (1975): 721–747; Walter E. Kaegi, *Heraclius, Emperor of Byzantium* (Cambridge: Cambridge University Press, 2003).

2. *Chronicon Paschale*, ed. and trans. Ludwig Dindorf (Bonn: E. Weber, 1832), 694–698; *Chronicon Paschale*, trans. Michael Whitby and Mary Whitby (Liverpool: Liverpool University Press, 1989), 143–148; Michael Whitby, *The Emperor Maurice and His Historian: Theophylact Simocatta on Persian and Balkan Warfare* (Oxford: Oxford University Press, 1988), 24–28. For the *Chronicon Paschale*, see Howard-Johnston, *Witnesses to a World Crisis*, 36–59.

3. Beate Dignas and Engelbert Winter, *Rome and Persia in Late Antiquity: Neighbours and Rivals* (Cambridge: Cambridge University Press, 2007).

4. Hagith Sivan, "From Byzantine to Persian Jerusalem: Jewish Perspectives and Jewish/Christian Polemics," *Greek, Roman and Byzantine Studies* 41, no. 3 (2000): 287–288.

5. *Chronicon Paschale*, ed. and trans. Dindorf, 700–701; *Chronicon Paschale*, trans. Whitby and Whitby, 152. For Niketas's campaign in the Near East, see John Nikiu, *The Chronicle of John, Bishop of Nikiu*, trans. R. H. Charles (London: Williams and Norgate, 1916), chaps. 107–110. See also Umberto Roberto, "The Circus Factions and the Death of the Tyrant: John of Antioch on the Fate of the Emperor Phocas," in *Byzanz: Das Römerreich im Mittelalter*, ed. F. Daim and J. Drauschke (Mainz: Römisch-Germanisches Zentralmuseum, 2010), 1:55–77.

6. Nikiu, *Chronicle of John, Bishop of Nikiu*, 176.

7. Thomas Renna, "The Idea of Peace in the West, 500–1150," *Journal of Medieval History* 6, no. 2 (1980): 144–150. See also the useful comments of Kurt A. Raaflaub, ed., *War and Peace in the Ancient World* (London: Blackwell, 2007), 66–80, esp. 67; and Johan Galtung, "Positive and Negative Peace," in *Johan Galtung: Pioneer of Peace Research*, ed. Johan Galtung and Dietrich Fischer (New York: Springer, 2014), chap. 17.

8. Galtung, "Positive and Negative Peace," chap. 17; Paul F. Diehl, "Exploring Peace: Looking Beyond War and Negative Peace," *International Studies Quarterly* 60 (2016): 1–10.

9. Despite the prominence of skeptical revisionists in the academy in the last third of the twentieth century, who saw the Qur'an as a later-eighth- or ninth-century compilation of accumulated traditions, by this point in the twenty-first century most specialists have reached a consensus that the Qur'an is from the first third of the seventh century. Good overviews of the controversy are Nicolai Sinai, *Der Koran: Eine Einführung* (Stuttgart: Reclam, 2017), chap. 1; Bowersock, *The Crucible of Islam*; Jonathan E. Brockopp, "Islamic Origins and Incidental Normativity," *Journal of the Academy of Religion* 84, no. 1 (2016): 28–43; Howard-Johnston, *Witnesses to a World Crisis*, 355–358; and Jonathan A. C. Brown, *Muhammad: A Very Short Introduction* (Oxford: Oxford University Press, 2011). For specific studies, see Behnam Sadeghi and Uwe Bergmann, "The Codex of a Companion of the Prophet and the Qur'ān of the Prophet," *Arabica* 57, no. 4 (2010): 343–436; Behnam Sadeghi and Mohsen Goudarzi, "San'a' 1 and the Origins of the Qur'an," *Der Islam* 87, no. 1 (2012): 1–129; and Michael J. Marx and Tobias Jocham, "Zu den Datierungen von Koranhandschriften durch die ^{14}C-Methode," *Frankfurter Zeitschrift für islamisch-theologische*

Studien 2 (2015): 9–43. As François Déroche, *Qur'ans of the Umay-yads: A First Overview* (Leiden: E. J. Brill, 2014), notes, carbon dating is inexact and cannot absolutely prove that these manuscripts are early seventh century—but they do refute the Wansbrough thesis of a very late Qur'an. For a philological argument for the Qur'an's earliness, see Marijn van Putten, "The Feminine Ending -at as a Diptote in the Qur'ānic Consonantal Text and Its Implications for Proto-Arabic and Proto-Semitic," *Arabica* 64 (2017): 695–705. I visited the Sana'a Dar al-Qur'an in 1994, and Ursula Dreibholz kindly gave me a detailed overview of her team's work there, tipping me to evidence that the Qur'an is seventh century. Some scholars had rejected revisionism on other bases even earlier: John Burton, *The Collection of the Qur'an* (Cambridge: Cambridge University Press, 1979); Estelle Whelan, "Forgotten Witness: Evidence for the Early Codification of the Qur'an," *JAOS* 118 (1998): 1–14; and F. M. Donner, *Narratives of Islamic Origins: The Beginnings of Islamic Historical Writing* (Princeton, NJ: Darwin Press, 1998), chap. 1.

10. `Urwa passed his own reports of what Aisha said to his son and students. As noted above, I recount these narratives for the purpose of comparing and contrasting them to the Qur'an, which likely predates most of them by more than a century. I depend on the work of Schoeler, *Biography of Muhammed*; and Andreas Görke and Gregor Schoeler, *Die ältesten Berichte über das Leben Muḥammads: Das Korpus `Urwa ibn az-Zubair* (Princeton, NJ: Darwin Press, 2008).

11. Muhammad al-Bukhari, *Sahih al-Bukhari*, ed. Abu Suhayb al-Karmi (Riyadh: Bayt al-Afkar al-Dawliya, 1998), 21, no. 2. The phrase "in the form of a man" recalls the description of the angel in Daniel 7:13: "There came one like a son of man." See also Ibn Rashid, *Maghazi*, 12–15; `Abd al-Malik ibn Hisham, *Sirat Rasul Allah*, ed. Ferdinand Wüstenfeld, 2 vols. (Gottingen: Dieterichsche Universitäts-Buchhandlung, 1858–1860), 1:151–154; Muhammad ibn Ishaq [`Abd al-Malik ibn Hisham], *The Life of Muhammad*, trans. Alfred Guillaume (1955; reprint, Karachi: Oxford University Press, 2002), 105–107; Muhammad ibn Jarir al-Tabari, *Ta'rikh al-Rusul wa al-Muluk*, ed. M. J. de Goeje (Leiden: E. J. Brill, 1879), 1146–1149; and Muhammad ibn Jarir al-Tabari, *The History of al-Tabari (Ta'rikh al-Rusul wa al-Muluk)*, 40 vols. (Albany: SUNY Press, 1989–2007), 6:67–70. See also Görke

and Schoeler, *Die ältesten Berichte*, chap. 2; and Schoeler, *Biography of Muhammed*, chap. 2.

12. Al-Bukhari, *Sahih al-Bukhari*, 21, no. 2.

13. Q. 96:1–5. See Uri Rubin, "Iqra' bi-smi rabbika...: Some Notes on the Interpretation of Surat al-ʿAlaq," *Israel Oriental Studies* 13 (1993): 213–230.

14. Al-Bukhari, *Sahih al-Bukhari*, 21, no. 3. Cf. Ibn Hisham, *Sirat Rasul Allah*, 1:153; and Ibn Ishaq [Ibn Hisham], *The Life of Muhammad*, 106–107. For an excellent survey of the historiographical issues regarding the sayings and doings attributed to Muhammad or hadith, see A. Kevin Reinhart, "Review: Juynbolliana, Gradualism, the Big Bang, and Hadith Study in the Twenty-First Century," *JAOS* 130, no. 3 (2010): 413–444.

15. Michael Bonner, *Jihad in Islamic History: Doctrines and Practice* (Princeton, NJ: Princeton University Press, 2006), 41–42.

16. The Christian church fathers who commented on this chapter of Isaiah maintained that Jesus unsealed the book, and Christians saw the menace to Jerusalem mentioned in Isaiah 29:1 as having been a prediction of the Roman torching of the second Jewish temple in 70 CE. *Doctrina Jacobi nuper Baptizati*, 96–97; Matthew R. Crawford, "Scripture as 'One Book': Origen, Jerome, and Cyril of Alexandria on Isaiah 29:11," *Journal of Theological Studies*, n.s., 64, no. 1 (2013): 137–153; Katherine M. Hayes, "A Spirit of Deep Sleep: Divinely Induced Delusion and Wisdom in Isaiah 1–39," *Catholic Biblical Quarterly* 74, no. 1 (2012): 47–52; Robert L. Wilken et al., *Isaiah: Interpreted by Early Christian Medieval Commentators* (Grand Rapids, MI: Wm. B. Eerdmans, 2007), 245–252. For the *Doctrina Jacobi nuper Baptizati*, see Pieter van der Horst, "A Short Note on the *Doctrina Jacobi nuper Baptizati*," *Zutot* 6, no. 1 (2009): 1–6. It probably consists of two or three works dating from sometime late in the seventh century that were assembled into a single text during the ninth or tenth century during the Byzantine Renaissance. Paul Speck, *Beiträge zum Thema Byzantinische Feindseligkeit gegen die Juden im frühen siebten Jahrhundert* (Bonn: Rudolf Habelt GMBH, 1997), 6:264–439, esp. 436–439. Islamicists have in contrast tended to date it much earlier but are likely mistaken. See Sean W. Anthony, "Muhammad, the Keys to Paradise, and the Doctrina Iacobi: A Late Antique Puzzle," *Der Islam* 91, no. 2 (2014): 243–265.

17. Joseph Blenkinsopp, *Isaiah 1–39: The Anchor Bible* (New York: Double-day, 2000), 398–410; Ariel Goran Eidevall, *Prophecy and Propaganda: Images of Enemies in the Book of Isaiah* (Winona Lake, IN: Eisenbrauns, 2009), chap. 2; M. Bagg, "Palestine Under Assyrian Rule: A New Look at the Assyrian Imperial Policy in the West," *JAOS* 133, no. 1 (2013): 119–144.

18. The choice of Isaiah 29, which evokes an ancient threat from Mesopotamia to the Holy Land parallel to that of the Sasanians in order to contextualize Muhammad's own revelation in 610, demonstrates that Aisha's narrative here goes back to the teens of the seventh century, and perhaps to Muhammad himself. This sort of reading of scripture against current events is ephemeral, and the likelihood that later seventh-century Muslims would invent it when they already controlled Jerusalem, as well as Mesopotamia and Iran, is nil. For other points in this paragraph, see Joseph Blenkinsopp, *Opening the Sealed Book: Interpretations of the Book of Isaiah in Late Antiquity* (Grand Rapids, MI: Wm. B. Eerdmans, 2006), 9–15; *Doctrina Jacobi nuper Baptizati*, ed. Vincent Déroche, in G. Dagron and V. Déroche, "Juifs et chrétiens dans l'Orient du VIIe siècle," *Travaux et Mémoires* 11 (1991): 146–147; and *The Septuagint Version of the Old Testament*, ed. and trans. L. Brenton (London: S. Bagster & Sons, 1879), 863. See also Csaba Balogh, "Blind People, Blind God: The Composition of Isaiah 29:15–24," *Zeitschrift für die Alttestamentliche Wissenschaft* 121, no. 1 (2009): 48–69. Muhammad's circles likely knew the Septuagint, which was used by Greek-speaking Christians and which Justinian permitted to those Jews who preferred it to the Hebrew text. Catherine Brewer, "The Status of the Jews in Roman Legislation: The Reign of Justinian, 527–565 CE," *European Judaism: A Journal for the New Europe* 38, no. 2 (2005): 127–139.

19. For the kinship of the books of Isaiah and Daniel, see Blenkinsopp, *Opening the Sealed Book*, 8–27. For the last point about Daniel, see Paul L. Redditt, "Daniel 11 and the Sociohistorical Setting of the Book of Daniel," *Catholic Biblical Quarterly* 60, no. 3 (Jul 1998): 463–474.

20. Al-Bukhari, *Sahih al-Bukhari*, 21–22, no. 3. The later Muslim traditions say he knew Hebrew, but since they go on to quote him using a Greek word, we may conclude that it was Greek that he had studied— as would be natural for an Arab Christian on the fringes of the Christian Roman Empire.

21. Ahmad ibn Hajr al-`Asqalani, *Hidayat al-Ruwah*, ed. Muhammad Nasir al-Din Albani, 6 vols. (Dammam: Dar ibn al-Qayyim, 2001), 1:60; Ellen Muehlberger, *Angels in Late Ancient Christianity* (Oxford: Oxford University Press, 2013), 136. See also Debbie Hunn, "'Why Therefore the Law?': The Role of the Law in Galatians 3:19–20," *Neotestamentica* 47, no. 2 (2013): 355–372. Waraqah is playing the role in this story of the "interpreting angel." See David P. Melvin, *The Interpreting Angel Motif in Prophetic and Apocalyptic Literature* (Minneapolis: Fortress Press, 2013).

22. Eduard Schwartz, ed., *Kyrillos von Skythopolis* (Leipzig: J. C. Hinrichs Verlag, 1939), 97–101; Cyril of Scythopolis, *Lives of the Monks of Palestine*, trans. R. M. Price (Kalamazoo, MI: Cistercian, 1991), 106–109. For the late-antique holy man, see Peter Brown, "The Rise and Function of the Holy Man in Late Antiquity," *Journal of Roman Studies* 61 (1971): 80–101; Peter Brown, "The Rise and Function of the Holy Man in Late Antiquity, 1971–1997," *Journal of Early Christian Studies* 6, no. 3 (1998): 353–376; and his revision, Peter Brown, *Authority and the Sacred: Aspects of the Christianisation of the Roman World* (Cambridge: Cambridge University Press, 1995), chap. 3.

23. Saba Farès, "Christian Monasticism on the Eve of Islam: Kilwa (Saudi Arabia)—New Evidence," *Arabian Archaeology and Epigraphy* 22, no. 2 (2011): 243–252.

24. I both agree and disagree with the interpretation of Nicolai Sinai, "'Weihnachten im Koran' oder 'Nacht der Bestimmung'? Eine Interpretation von Sure 97," *Der Islam* 88, no. 1 (2012): 11–32. I concur with him that the proposal of "Christoph Luxemberg" and other Christianizing scholars to read the chapter as based on an Aramaic Christmas hymn is unconvincing, but Sinai's own suggestion that the Night of Power is actually a preexisting Night of Predestination (apparently similar to the Celtic Samhain) seems speculative. I see this chapter instead as one of four Danielic vision texts, with two others involving ascents of the Prophet to the precincts of paradise and a fourth a vision at the Temple Mount in Jerusalem.

25. For examples of God speaking directly to prophets, see Amos 1:1, 4, 7, and 8:1. For angels and maintaining God's transcendence, see Muehlberger, *Angels in Late Ancient Christianity*, 2.

26. The Psalms plead of God, "Cast me not away from your presence, and take not your holy Spirit from me" (Ps. 51:11). In the Gospels, Luke

says the Holy Spirit descended on Jesus in the form of a dove (Luke 3:22). For spirit in the Qur'an, see John O'Shaughnessy, *The Development of the Meaning of Spirit in the Koran* (Rome: Pontificum Institutem Orientalium Studiorum, 1953).

27. John Chrysostom, *The Homilies of S. John Chrysostom, Archbishop of Constantinople, on the Second Epistle of St. Paul the Apostle to the Corinthians*, trans. J. Ashworth (London: W. Smith, 1885), 32. See also Rangar Cline, *Ancient Angels: Conceptualizing Angeloi in the Roman Empire* (Leiden: E. J. Brill, 2011), 156n50; and Robin Lane Fox, *Pagans and Christians* (New York: Alfred A. Knopf, 1987), chap. 8.

28. Ibn Hisham, *Sirat Rasul Allah*, 1:155–165; Ibn Ishaq [Ibn Hisham], *The Life of Muhammad*, 111–117.

29. First quote in this paragraph: Ibn Hisham, *Sirat Rasul Allah*, 1:166 (my translation); cf. Ibn Ishaq [Ibn Hisham], *The Life of Muhammad*, 117; the second quote is from Muhammad ibn Sa`d, *Al-Tabaqat al-Kubra*, 9 vols. (Beirut: Dar Sadir, 1960), 1:199.

30. For Zayd, see Muhammad ibn Habib al-Baghdadi, *Al-Munammaq*, ed. Muhammad Khurshid Fariq (Beirut: `Alam al-Kitab, 1985), 152–154; Ibn Hisham, *Sirat Rasul Allah*, 1:143–149; and Ibn Ishaq [Ibn Hisham], *The Life of Muhammad*, 98–103. For Abraham and Hellenistic pagans, see J. S. Siker, "Abraham in Graeco-Roman Paganism," *Journal for the Study of Judaism in the Persian, Hellenistic, and Roman Period* 18, no. 2 (1987): 188–208; and Pieter W. van der Horst, *Studies in Ancient Judaism and Early Christianity* (Leiden: Brill, 2014), chap. 9. For Qusayy, see Khalil `Abd al-Karim, *Quraysh min al-qabila ila al-dawla al-markaziyya* (Cairo: Sina li al-Nashr, 1993), 119–120, 122–123. For the Hanifs, see Uri Rubin, "Hanifiyya and Ka`ba: An Inquiry into the Arabian Pre-Islamic Background of din Ibrahim," *JSAI* 13 (1990): 85–112, reprinted in Uri Rubin, *Muhammad the Prophet and Arabia*, Variorum Collected Studies Series (Farnham: Ashgate, 2011), chap. 10. For the Hanifs as Gentile or pagan monotheists, see François de Blois, "Nasrani (Ναζωραῖος) and Hanif (ἐθνικός): Studies on the Religious Vocabulary of Christianity and of Islam," *BSOAS* 65, no. 1 (2002): 1–30. I don't find the other half of de Blois's argument, about *nasara* being Jewish Christians, persuasive. Christelle Jullien and Florence Jullien, "Aux frontières de l'iranité," *Numen* 49, no. 3 (2002): 282–335, suggests that *nasara*, or Nazarenes in Sasanian usage, are local

Eastern Christians inside the empire and "Christians" are Catholics abroad. In the Qur'an, *nasara* seem just to be Christians in general.

31. See the essays in Polymnia Athanassiadi and Michael Frede, eds., *Pagan Monotheism in Late Antiquity* (Oxford: Clarendon Press, 1999), esp. Stephen Mitchell, "The Cult of Theos Hypsistos Between Pagans, Jews, and Christians," 81–148; and in Stephen Mitchell and Peter van Nuffelan, eds., *One God: Pagan Monotheism in the Roman Empire* (Cambridge: Cambridge University Press, 2010), esp. Stephen Mitchell, "Further Thoughts on the Cult of Theos Hypsistos," 167–208; Anna Collar, *Religious Networks in the Roman Empire: The Spread of New Ideas* (Cambridge: Cambridge University Press, 2013), chap. 5; and Richard Gordon, "Monotheism, Henotheism, Megatheism: Debating Pre-Constantinian Religious Change," *Journal of Roman Archaeology* 27 (2014): 665–676. For another textual tradition where pagan Greek, Jewish, and Christian themes are sampled and mixed, see Timothy A. Gabrielson, "A Pagan Prophetess of the Jewish God: Religious Identity and Hellenization in the Third Sibyl," *Journal for the Study of the Pseudepigrapha* 24, no. 3 (2015): 213–233.

32. For Qur'anic evidence of Meccans' devotion to God, see *Gilded Ornament* 43:87. See also *The Groups* 39:38: "If indeed you ask them who it is that created the heavens and the earth, they would be sure to say, 'God.'" For the second paganism, see H. S. Versnel, *Inconsistencies in Greek and Roman Religion*, vol. 1, *Ter Unus: Isis, Dionysos, Hermes— Three Studies in Henotheism* (Leiden: Brill, 1990). For a henotheistic interpretation of the Meccans, see Patricia Crone, "The Religion of the Qur'anic Pagans: God and the Lesser Deities," *Arabica* 57, nos. 2–3 (2010): 151–200. An inscription from Rawwafa in the northern Hejaz, found in a second-century CE Thamud temple built with Roman encouragement, says, "The temple which Shiddat, the priest of God [*Alaha*], son of Megido, who is from Rabato, made for God... with the encouragement of our lord the governor." The Roman governor in Bostra clearly attempted to attract Thamud young men as border guards (*limitanei*) for the Roman army and encouraged temple building in the outpost. Another inscription at this temple says, "For the well-being [or peace] of [Marcus] Aurelius Antoninus and Lucius Aurelius [Verus]...This is the temple which the brigade of Thamud made." See Michael C. A. Macdonald et al., "Arabs and Empire

Before the Sixth Century," in *Arabs and Empire Before Islam*, ed. Greg Fisher (Oxford: Oxford University Press, 2015), 50–51, 55–56; Michael C. A. Macdonald, "On Saracens, the Rawwafah Inscription and the Roman Army," in *Literacy and Identity in Pre-Islamic Arabia* (Farnham: Ashgate, 2009), chap. 8; John F. Healey, *The Religion of the Nabataeans: A Conspectus* (Leiden: Brill, 2001), 55–56; David Kiltz, "The Relationship Between Arabic Allah and Syriac Allaha," *Der Islam* 88 (2012): 33–50; and Crone, "Religion of the Qur'anic Pagans," 154.

33. Some Hypsistarians in the 200s CE appear to have adopted the oracle of Apollo at Klaros for themselves. It describes the supreme deity this way: "Born of itself, untaught, without a mother, unshakeable; not contained in a name, known by many names, dwelling in fire; This is God; We, his angels, are a small part of God. To you who ask this question about God, what his essential nature is, He has pronounced that Aether is god who sees all, on whom you should gaze and pray at dawn, facing toward the sunrise." Mitchell, "Cult of Theos Hypsistos," 86. It sounds to me a great deal like the Qur'an chapter of *Sincerity* 112.

34. Tilman Seidensticker, "Sources for the History of Pre-Islamic Religion," in *The Qur'an in Context: Historical and Literary Investigations into the Qur'anic Milieu*, ed. Angelika Neuwirth, Nicolai Sinai, and Michael Marx (Leiden: Brill, 2010), 308.

35. Al-Tabari, *Ta'rikh al-Rusul wa al-Muluk*, 1185–1187; al-Tabari, *History of al-Tabari*, 6:101–103. I omit the alleged threat reported by `Urwah—`Amr ibn al-`As by Muhammad of bringing "sacrifice" or "slaughter" (*al-dhibh*) to Quraysh because there is nothing like it in the Meccan suras and it is inappropriate to a sanctuary city.

36. The notion, met with in Abbasid-era Muslim works and in modern scholarship alike, that the god of the Kaaba was the obscure North Arabian deity Hubal is incorrect. The Qur'an mentions no such figure; he appears in only four ancient inscriptions, and the Qur'an points to Allah being the deity of the Kaaba. Nor can they be conflated since they are very different sorts of deity. See Ibn Sa`d, *Al-Tabaqat al-Kubra*, 2:136–137; Healey, *Religion of the Nabataeans*, 128–129; and Aziz al-Azmeh, *The Emergence of Islam in Late Antiquity: Allah and His People* (Cambridge: Cambridge University Press, 2014), 216.

37. For the alleged pressure on Abu Talib and his rejection of it, see Yunus ibn Bukayr, *Kitab al-siyar wa al-maghazi*, ed. Suhail Zakkar (Beirut: Dar al-Fikr, 1978), 154. For Abu Talib as a lifelong pagan, see Al-Tabari, *Ta'rikh al-Rusul wa al-Muluk*, 1177; al-Tabari, *History of al-Tabari*, 6:95; Ibn Hisham, *Sirat Rasul Allah*, 1:167–168; and Ibn Ishaq [Ibn Hisham], *The Life of Muhammad*, 119.

38. *Jonah* 10:41 says, for example, "And if they impugn your veracity, say 'To me my works and to you your works. You are not responsible for what I do, and I am not responsible for what you do.'" See Fred Donner, "Fight for God—but Do So with Kindness: Reflections on War, Peace, and Communal Identity in Early Islam," in *War and Peace in the Ancient World*, ed. Kurt Raaflaub (Oxford: Blackwell's, 2006), 303.

39. These ascensions show that the Qur'an falls in part into the genre of the apocalypse, which literally means the revelation of a mystery. Martha Himmelfarb, *The Apocalypse: A Brief History* (London: Wiley-Blackwell, 2010); David Brady, "The Book of Revelation and the Qur'an: Is There a Possible Literary Relationship?," *Journal of Semitic Studies* 23, no. 2 (1978): 216–225; Todd Lawson, "Duality, Opposition and Typology in the Qur'an: The Apocalyptic Substrate," *JQS* 10, no. 2 (2008): 23–49; Todd Lawson, "Paradise in the Quran and the Music of Apocalypse," in *Roads to Paradise: Eschatology and Concepts of the Hereafter in Islam*, ed. Sebastian Günther and Todd Lawson, 2 vols. (Leiden: E. J. Brill, 2016), vol. 1, chap. 6. John J. Collins, *The Apocalyptic Imagination: An Introduction to Jewish Apocalyptic Literature*, rev. ed. (Grand Rapids, MI: William B. Eerdmans, 1998), esp. 5–6, notes that apocalyptic works fell into two main categories—those that recounted a journey into another realm and others that presented a vision of history. In books falling into the first category, the seer either experiences visions on earth or voyages to another, celestial, world. This passage is most often a "rapture" (Martha Himmelfarb, *Ascent to Heaven in Jewish and Christian Apocalypses* [Oxford: Oxford University Press, 1993], 5), something that comes unbidden upon the visionary rather than something sought. In the course of the voyage, the seeker holds converse with supernatural beings, who reveal mysteries of the natural world or, in the second category of apocalypses, interpret history and future history. Typically, an angel appears who either descends to interpret a vision or accompanies the clairvoyant on a

heavenly quest. The seer or prophet faints or falls ill and is filled with dread and terror or shows other signs of human frailty and vulnerability before the awesome appearance of the supernatural.

40. Nicolai Sinai, "An Interpretation of Surat al-Najm (Q. 53)," *JQS* 13, no. 2 (2011): 1–28. For the possibility that Muhammad is depicted as seeing God in either passage, see Josef van Ess, "Vision and Ascension: Surat al-Najm and Its Relationship with Muhammad's Mi`raj," *JQS* 1 (1999): 47–62.

41. Abbasid Muslim historians placed this passage later in Muhammad's life and connected it to Jerusalem, but the Qur'an indicates no such context, and I concur with Sinai, "Interpretation of Surat al-Najm," in seeing it rather as a recounting of one of Muhammad's early apocalyptic visions.

42. Contrast Himmelfarb, *Ascent to Heaven*, chaps. 1–3. The Qur'an at one point translates the Greek *angelos* with the Arabic *rasul*, meaning "envoy" and I think here indicating "archangel." It also calls Muhammad a *rasul*, or "messenger," but my suspicion is that this second usage is a loanshift from Middle Persian and translates *payghambar*, a term Zoroastrians applied to Zarathustra. Prophets are not generally called "messengers" or "apostles" in the Jewish or Greek Christian tradition, and in Greek *apostolos* was typically a secular word for an overseas ambassador until it was applied to the disciples of Jesus. The late-antique Arabic appropriation of ideas from surrounding cultures often created what were essentially homonyms, words that sounded the same but bore entirely different meanings depending on context.

43. Cf. Mark Golden, "Demography and the Exposure of Girls at Athens," *Phoenix* 35, no. 4 (1981): 316–331.

44. For the widespread medieval Muslim conviction that those sentenced to hell will not stay there for eternity, see Mohammad Hassan Khalil, *Islam and the Fate of Others: The Salvation Question* (Oxford: Oxford University Press, 2012). For the Qur'an's heaven, see Christian Lange, *Paradise and Hell in Islamic Traditions* (Cambridge: Cambridge University Press, 2016), 21–26.

45. Cf. Q. 50:34. See C. Lange, *Paradise and Hell*, chap. 2; Günther and Lawson, eds., *Roads to Paradise*, esp. vol. 1, chaps. 4–7; Muhammad Abdel Haleem, *Understanding the Qur'an: Themes and Style* (London: I. B. Tauris, 2010), chap. 7; and Toshihiko Izutsu, *Ethico-Religious*

Concepts in the Qur'an (1959; reprint, Montreal: McGill-Queen's University Press, 2002), 108–116. See also J. Edward Wright, *The Early History of Heaven* (Oxford: Oxford University Press, 2000); and Jacqueline Chabbi, *Les trois piliers de l'islam: Lecture anthropologique du Coran* (Paris: Éditions du Seuil, 2016), chap. 7.

46. *The Event* 56:8–14, 42–43. For the prophets, see *The Women* 4:69. For an argument that the Qur'an has a pluralist soteriology, see Reza Shah-Kermani, "Beyond Polemics and Pluralism: The Universal Message of the Qur'an," in *Between Heaven and Hell: Islam, Salvation and the Fate of Others*, ed. Muhammad Hassan Khalil (Oxford: Oxford University Press, 2013), 85–107. It is probably a minority sentiment among contemporary Muslims.

47. *The Event* 56:15–26.

48. For "painless wine," see N. P. Milner, "Notes and Inscriptions on the Cult of Apollo at Oinoanda," *Anatolian Studies* 50 (2000): 141 (the Greek phrase is *analgei oinō*). Himmelfarb, *Ascent to Heaven*, 73; and Brad E. Kelle, "Dealing with the Trauma of Defeat: The Rhetoric of the Devastation and Rejuvenation of Nature in Ezekiel," *Journal of Biblical Literature* 128, no. 3 (2009): 469–490. Angelika Neuwirth also compares the Qur'an on paradise to Psalm 23:5, which speaks of the "cup," and Micah 4:4, which speaks of the vineyard whose shade is enjoyed by the just, as well as to the eschatological banquet expected in the Qumran scrolls. Neuwirth, "Paradise as a Quranic Discourse: Late Antique Foundations and Early Quranic Developments," in *Roads to Paradise*, ed. Günther and Lawson, 1:74–75.

49. *Al-Hijr* 15:47; *Smoke* 44:53.

50. "*En ouranō eirēnē kai doxa en hypsistois.*" For the Qur'an's "Abode of Peace," see *Jonah* 10:25–26: "God summons all to the abode of peace, and guides whomever he will to the straight path. The doers of good shall have the loveliest recompense, and a windfall; neither dust nor abasement will cover their countenances. Those are the inhabitants of paradise, dwelling forever therein." See also *The Cattle* 6:126.

51. For *Y.S.* 36:53–58 and the four levels it implies, see Abdullah Yusuf Ali, *The Holy Qur'an: Text, Translation and Commentary* (New York: McGregor and Werner, ca. 1970), 1182n4001. In his 1918 classic, Miguel Asin Palacios argued, controversially, that the Qur'an influenced Dante. Palacios, *Islam and the Divine Comedy*, trans. and

abridged by Harold Sutherland (1926; reprint, London: Routledge, 2013). For contemporary considerations of the controversy, see Jan M. Ziolkowski, ed., *Dante and Islam* (New York: Fordham University Press, 2014).

52. Ruth Webb, *Ekphrasis, Imagination and Persuasion in Ancient Rhetorical Theory and Practice* (London: Routledge, 2009); Robyn J. Whitaker, *Ekphrasis, Vision, and Persuasion in the Book of Revelation* (Tübingen: Mohr Siebeck, 2015); Daniel L. Schwartz, *Paideia and Cult: Christian Initiation in Theodore of Mopsuestia* (Washington, DC: Center for Hellenic Studies, 2013), 120, 138–140. For the observation about Middle Platonism being the spiritual commonwealth, see Polymnia Athanassiades, "The Chaldean Oracles: Theology and Theurgy," in *Pagan Monotheism in Late Antiquity*, ed. Polymnia Athanassidadi and Michael Frede (Oxford: Clarendon Press, 1999), 180–181. For a New Testament parallel to the notion of the Kaaba as reflecting the heavenly sanctuary, see Scott D. Mackie, "Heavenly Sanctuary Mysticism in the Epistle to the Hebrews," *Journal of Theological Studies*, n.s., 62, no. 1 (2011): 77–117.

53. Muehlberger, *Angels in Late Ancient Christianity*, 183–186. See Cyril of Jerusalem, *The Catechetical Lectures of S. Cyril, Archbishop of Jerusalem* (Oxford: John Henry Parker, 1839), 8; E. J. Yarnold, *Cyril of Jerusalem* (London: Routledge, 2002), 85.

54. Maria J. Stephan and Erica Chenoweth, "Why Civil Resistance Works: The Strategic Logic of Nonviolent Conflict," *International Security* 33, no. 1 (2008): 7–44. I prefer the term *preferential nonviolence* to their *strategic nonviolence* because the latter sounds to me too instrumental and because it discounts the real commitment to peaceful social action by persons who do not rule out resort to just war under some circumstances. The Qur'an's report of mainly oral harassment, which contrasts with some of Ibn Hisham's violent anecdotes, was noted as long ago as 1905: Leone Caetani, *Annali dell'Islām compilati da Leone Caetani, principe di Teano*, 10 vols. (Milan: U. Hoepli, 1905), 1:243–244, 248–249. See also William Montgomery Watt, *Muhammad at Mecca* (Oxford: Clarendon Press, 1953), 123–133; and Reuven Firestone, *Jihad: The Origin of Holy War in Islam* (Oxford: Oxford University Press, 1999), 106–109. These authors do not, however, tie this lack of violence, as I do, to Mecca's status as a sanctuary city.

55. The later Muslim interpreters ignored the compromise offered in the last verse of this chapter and attempted to depict this as a vehement rejection of Meccan overtures and an insistence on uncompromising monotheism. See Tabari, *Tafsir*, 24:702–704.

56. For "beautiful words," see Tabari, *Tafsir*, 18:282. For "peace be upon you" as a prayer of ritual blessing, see Sharon R. Keller, "An Egyptian Analogue to the Priestly Blessing," in *Boundaries of the Ancient Near Eastern World*, ed. Cyrus H. Gordon et al. (Sheffield: Sheffield Academic Press, 1998), 338–345; and Jacob Kremer, "Peace—God's Gift: Biblical-Theological Considerations," in *The Meaning of Peace: Biblical Studies*, ed. Perry B. Yoder and Willard M. Swartley and trans. W. Sawatsky, 2nd ed. (Elkhart, IN: Institute of Mennonite Studies, 2001), 22.

57. Arnobius of Sicca, *The Seven Books of Arnobius' Adversus gentes*, trans. Archibald Hamilton Bryce and Hugh Campbell (Edinburgh: T. & T. Clark, 1871), 133–135 (2.64–65); Maijastina Kahlos, *Forbearance and Compulsion: The Rhetoric of Religious Tolerance in Late Antiquity* (London: Duckworth, 2009), 48–49.

58. Lactantius, *The Works of Lactantius*, trans. William Fletcher, 2 vols. (Edinburgh: T. & T. Clark, 1871), 1:339–340 (5:19); Kahlos, *Forbearance and Compulsion*, 49–55. See also Mar Marcos, "Persecution, Apology and the Reflection on Religious Freedom and Religious Coercion in Early Christianity," *Zeitschrift für Religionswissenschaft* 20, no. 1 (2012): 35–69.

59. Renna, "Idea of Peace in the West," 147–148.

CHAPTER 3: REPEL EVIL WITH GOOD

1. Via `Amr, the grandson of `Urwa ibn al-Zubayr, quoted in `Abd al-Malik ibn Hisham, *Sirat Rasul Allah*, ed. Ferdinand Wüstenfeld, 2 vols. (Gottingen: Dieterichsche Universitäts-Buchhandlung, 1858–1860), 1:276–277; Muhammad ibn Ishaq [`Abd al-Malik ibn Hisham], *The Life of Muhammad*, trans. Alfred Guillaume (1955; reprint, Karachi: Oxford University Press, 2002), 191. This form of harassment shows up in other late-antique literary accounts of conflict between Near Eastern pagans and monotheistic faiths. When Porphyry, having become the bishop of Gaza, tried to enter the largely pagan city in 395, his biographer Mark the Deacon alleged, "Hard by Gaza there are villages beside

the road which are given to the madness of idols. So the dwellers in these villages agreed together and strewed all the road with thorns and prickles, so that one could not pass by." Marcus Diaconus, *Vita Porphyrii*, ed. and trans. Anna Lampadaridi, in *La conversion de Gaza au christianisme: La Vie de S. Porphyre* (Brussels: Société de Bollandistes, 2016), para. 17; Marcus Diaconus, *Life of Porphyry, Bishop of Gaza*, trans. G. F. Hill (Oxford: Clarendon Press, 1913), 23. See Raymond Van Dam, "From Paganism to Christianity at Late Antique Gaza," *Viator* 16, no. 1 (1985): 1–20; and Frank R. Trombley, *Hellenic Religion and Christianization, c. 370–529*, 2 vols. (Leiden: Brill, 1993), vol. 1, chap. 3.

2. Ibn Hisham, *Sira*, 1:282; *Life*, 195; Muhammad ibn Habib al-Baghdadi, *al-Munammaq*, ed. Muhammad Khurshid Fariq (Beirut: `Alam al-Kitab, 1985), 58–72; Uri Rubin, *Muhammad the Prophet and Arabia* (Farnham: Ashgate, 2011), chap. 12, 94–95.

3. *The Criterion* 25:3, 42.

4. Monotheists in late antiquity frequently deployed this argument against the existence of a multitude of deities. Bishop Athanasios of Alexandria (d. 373) had written, "For just as we said that polytheism was atheism, so it follows that the rule of more than one is the rule of none. For each one would cancel the rule of the other, and none would appear ruler, but there would be anarchy everywhere." See Athanase d'Alexandrie, *Contre les Païens*, ed. and trans. Pierre Thomas Camelot, 2nd ed. (Paris: Cerf, 1977), 178 (38.3); English quote from Athanasius, "Against the Heathen," in *Select Works and Letters*, by Saint Athanasius, vol. 4 of SLNPNF, 2nd ser. (Oxford and London: Parker, 1892), 24 (38.3). For the struggle of the Titans and Olympians and its Near Eastern background, see Hesiod, *The Homeric Hymns and Homerica*, trans. Hugh G. Evelyn-White (Cambridge, MA: Harvard University Press, 1914), lines 115–130, http://data.perseus.org/citations/urn:cts:greek Lit:tlg0020.tlg001.perseus-eng1:104–138; Bernard C. Dietrich, *The Origins of Greek Religion* (Liverpool: Liverpool University Press, 2004), 54–56; Albert A. Baumgarten, *The Phoenician History of Philo of Byblos: A Commentary* (Leiden: E. J. Brill, 1981), 15/181; Harold W. Attridge and Robert A. Oden Jr., *Philo of Byblos: The Phoenician History: Introduction, Critical Text, Translation, Notes* (Washington, DC: Catholic Biblical Association of America, 1981), 46–47; Donald E. Gowan, *When Man Becomes God: Humanism and Hybris in the Old*

Testament (Pittsburgh: Pickwick Press, 1975), 61–62; Tim Whitmarsh, *Battling the Gods: Atheism in the Ancient World* (New York: Alfred A. Knopf, 2015), chap. 3; Bruce Louden, "The Gods in Epic; or, The Divine Economy," in *A Companion to Ancient Epic*, ed. John Miles Foley (Oxford: Blackwell, 2006), 90–104. For the use of irony and ridicule in Christian-pagan polemics, see Maijastina Kahlos, *Debate and Dialogue: Christian and Pagan Cultures, c. 360–430* (Aldershot: Ashgate, 2007), 72–75.

5. Yemeni influence is also possible. See Christian Robin, "Les 'filles de dieu' de Saba' à la Mecque: Réflexions sur l'agencement des panthéons dans l'Arabie ancienne," *Semitica* 50 (2001): 113–192.

6. The later Muslim biographical tradition asserts that Muhammad wavered and initially praised the goddesses as "swans" but that this verse was then repudiated. I think the whole thing was made up out of whole cloth, given what else is in the Qur'an. See J. Burton, "Those Are the High-Flying Cranes," *Journal of Semitic Studies* 15 (1970): 246–265.

7. Dayna S. Kalleres, *City of Demons: Violence, Ritual and Christian Power in Late Antiquity* (Berkeley: University of California Press, 2015); Kahlos, *Debate and Dialogue*, 172–181; Robin Lane Fox, *Pagans and Christians* (New York: Alfred A. Knopf, 1987), 137, 326–320, 443–444.

8. While it is possible that some in the Hejaz were moving toward a pagan monotheism, it should be noted that adherents of Near Eastern religions in the Hellenistic and late-antique periods routinely asserted that the gods had divine envoys. In pre-Christian Palmyra the god Bel had a Malakbel, or angel, whom locals made an object of worship. Likewise, the popular god Baalshemim or Lord of the Heavens had an angel. In the Syrian town of Maloula, an Aramaic inscription transliterated into Greek script and dated 107 CE speaks of the angel of God the Most High (*Mal'ak 'el-'aliyan*), which is suggestive in the context of these Qur'an verses. Thamud inscriptions of North Arabia contain supplications to angels. See Javier Teixidor, *The Pagan God: Popular Religion in the Near East* (Princeton, NJ: Princeton University Press, 1977), 14–15; Spencer L. Allen, *The Splintered Divine: A Study of Istar, Baal, and Yahweh; Divine Names and Divine Multiplicity in the Ancient Near East* (Berlin: Walter de Gruyter, 2015), 232n106;

Azis al-Azmeh, *The Emergence of Islam in Late Antiquity: Allah and His People* (Cambridge: Cambridge University Press, 2014), 294; and Rangar Cline, *Ancient Angels: Conceptualizing Angeloi in the Roman Empire* (Leiden: E. J. Brill, 2011).

9. Augustine argued that the Neoplatonic pagans believed in a single "first cause" and held other gods to be mere angels of this one. The bishop cautioned, however, against seeing these angels as having any autonomy or ability to intercede with the Almighty, just as did the Qur'an: "Whatever we call these immortal and blessed spirits, who yet are only creatures, they do not act as mediators to introduce to everlasting felicity miserable mortals." Augustine, *The City of God*, in *Works of St. Augustine*, ed. Marcus Dods, 15 vols. (Edinburgh: T. & T. Clark, 1871–1876), 1:378, 380 (9.23). See also Augustine's dialogue with Longianianus, summarized in Kahlos, *Debate and Dialogue*, 81–82. See also Michael Frede, "Monotheism and Pagan Philosophy in Later Antiquity," in *Pagan Monotheism in Late Antiquity*, ed. Polymnia Athanassidadi and Michael Frede (Oxford: Clarendon Press, 1999), 59. It is not that Muhammad would have been aware of the *City of God* in particular, a Latin work from the west of the Roman Empire, but that monotheist polemics against polytheism shared some common arguments. See also Arnobius of Sicca, *Seven Books of Arnobius' "Adversus gentes,"* trans. Archibald Hamilton Bryce and Hugh Campbell (Edinburgh: T. & T. Clark, 1871), 150–151 (3.3). The Council of Laodicia in the mid-fourth century had also tried to forbid Christian worship of angels, though with indifferent success. Frank R. Trombley, "Christianity and Paganism, II: Asia Minor," in *Cambridge History of Christianity*, ed. A. Casiday and F. Norris (Cambridge: Cambridge University Press, 2007), 2:192–193.

10. Muhammad ibn Jarir al-Tabari, *Ta'rikh al-Rusul wa al-Muluk*, ed. M. J. de Goeje (Leiden: E. J. Brill, 1879), 1180–1182; Muhammad ibn Jarir al-Tabari, *The History of al-Tabari (Ta'rikh al-Rusul wa al-Muluk)*, 40 vols. (Albany: SUNY Press, 1989–2007), 6:98–99; Andreas Görke and Gregor Schoeler, *Die ältesten Berichte über das Leben Muḥammads: Das Korpus ʿUrwa ibn az-Zubair* (Princeton, NJ: Darwin Press, 2008), 38–44.

11. Ibn Hisham, *Sirat Rasul Allah*, 1:205–206; Ibn Ishaq [Ibn Hisham], *The Life of Muhammad*, 143–144.

12. I am arguing that *kāfir* was inflected by the Greek *asēbes* ("impious" or "irreverent"). See, for example, Athanase, *Contre les Païens*, 100 and passim. The classical Arabic dictionaries say the word *kāfir* originally meant "ungrateful" (Muhammad ibn Manzur, *Lisan al-`Arab*, 15 vols. [Beirut: Dar al-Sadir, 1956], 5:144), which is close to the Greek notion of rejecting the reverence properly owed to God. In Jeremiah 6:7 in the Septuagint, *asebeia* translates the Hebrew word for "violence" (*ḥamās*) and implies active hostility to the truth. In the New Testament, 2 Peter 2:6 gives as the reason for the catastrophe that befell the people of Sodom and Gomorrah that they lived impious lives (*asebesin*), a verb I think would be *kafara* in Qur'anic Arabic.

The Qur'an also uses the word *mushrikun*, which literally means "those who attribute to God partners" in his divinity, referring to polytheists. I will usually also translate it as "pagan." I am here rejecting the argument of G. R. Hawting, *The Idea of Idolatry and the Emergence of Islam: From Polemic to History* (Cambridge: Cambridge University Press, 1999), that the Qur'an is late, developing in seventh- and eighth-century Damascus, and that its polemics are primarily with Jews and Christians rather than with pagans.

13. The verb *ṣafaḥa* in 43:89, translated as "pardon" here, can also mean to "turn away from," but it makes more sense to forgive them and then wish them peace than angrily to turn one's back on them and do so, and in other similar passages the word clearly means "forgive," as in 2:109. I am differing here with David Marshall, *God, Muhammad and the Unbelievers: A Qur'anic Study* (Richmond, Surrey: Curzon Press, 1999), 80–89, who makes a Christian theological argument to the effect that in the Qur'an, God's justice predominates over his mercy toward the Meccan pagans; this is a common understanding of medieval Muslim exegetes as well. I am arguing here that while God may be punitive toward unrepentant polytheists in the next life, the Qur'an instructs the human Believers to treat them with kindness, pray for their peace and well-being, and forgive them their sins here on earth.

14. Simon Corcoran, "Anastasius, Justinian, and the Pagans: A Tale of Two Law Codes and a Papyrus," *JLA* 2, no. 2 (2009): 183–208; Simon Corcoran, "From Unholy Madness to Right-Mindedness," in *Conversion in Late Antiquity: Christianity, Islam and Beyond*, ed. Arietta Papaconstantinou et al. (Farnham: Ashgate, 2015), 89–93; Ramsay

MacMullen, *Christianity and Paganism in the Fourth to Eighth Centuries* (New Haven, CT: Yale University Press, 1997), 14–15, 27–29; Wolf Liebeschuetz, *East and West in Late Antiquity: Invasion, Settlement, Ethnogenesis and Conflicts of Religion* (Leiden: Brill, 2015), 363–366. For Christian policy toward pagans in the fourth and fifth centuries, see Michael Gaddis, *There Is No Crime for Those Who Have Christ: Religious Violence in the Christian Roman Empire* (Berkeley: University of California Press, 2005), 1–2, 15, 210, chaps. 5–6; John Chrysostom, *The Homilies of S. John Chrysostom on the Statues* (Oxford: J. H. Parker, 1842), 28 (1.30); Socrates Scholasticus, *The Ecclesiastical History* (London: Bell & Sons, 1874), 348–349; and Fergus Millar, *A Greek Roman Empire: Power and Belief Under Theodosius II (408–450)* (Berkeley: University of California Press, 2006), 116–122.

15. For the first embassy, see Agapius of Manbij, *Kitab al-'Unvan* (2.2), ed. and trans. A. Vasiliev, *Patrologia Orientalis* 7 (1912): 450. For the second one, see *Chronicon Paschale*, ed. and trans. Ludwig Dindorf (Bonn: E. Weber, 1832), 707–709; *Chronicon Paschale*, trans. Michael Whitby and Mary Whitby (Liverpool: Liverpool University Press, 1989), 160–162; Walter E. Kaegi, *Heraclius, Emperor of Byzantium* (Cambridge: Cambridge University Press, 2003), 65, 83; Albert de Jong, "Sub Specie Maiestatis: Reflections on Sasanian Court Rituals," in *Zoroastrian Ritual in Context*, ed. M. Stausberg (Leiden: Brill, 2004), 345–366; and Djalal Khaleghi-Motlagh, "Etiquette in the Sasanian Period," in *Encyclopaedia Iranica*, http://www.iranicaonline.org/articles/etiquette.

16. Géorgios de Sykéon, *Vie de Théodore de Sykéon*, ed. and trans. André-Jean Festugière, Subsidia Hagiographica no. 48, 2 vols. (Brussels: Société de Bollandistes, 1970), para. 153; Kaegi, *Heraclius, Emperor of Byzantium*, 68, 74–77.

17. Touraj Daryaee, *Sasanian Persia: The Rise and Fall of an Empire* (London: I. B. Tauris, 2009), chap. 4.

18. Agapius of Manbij, *Kitab al-'Unvan*, 450–451; "A Chronicle Composed in AD 640," in *The Seventh Century in the West-Syrian Chronicles*, trans. Andrew Palmer, Sebastian Brock, and Robert Hoyland (Liverpool: Liverpool University Press, 1993), 17. See for this work James Howard-Johnston, *Witnesses to a World Crisis: Historians and Histories of the Middle East in the Seventh Century* (Oxford: Oxford University Press, 2010), 59–66.

19. This verse is controversial and could be read in the active voice to say that "the Romans are victorious" instead. That, however, is not the earliest or most widespread reading and seems to grow in popularity during and after the Crusades. Because of the clear signs of Qur'anic preference for Herakleios, including its adoption of the allegorical "Alexander Romance," its complaints against threats to churches, and its explicit statement that Christians are closer in love to the Believers, I prefer the reading given here. I gloss the Arabic *ard* here as "province" (that is, eparchy). In general, I think Qur'anic Arabic is more sophisticated and more underlain by Greek, Aramaic, and Persian "loanshifts" than has generally been recognized. For varying later Muslim views of the significance of this chapter, see Nadia Maria El Cheikh, "Surat al-Rum: A Study of the Exegetical Literature," *JAOS* 118, no. 3 (1998): 356–364. For a vindication of the standard reading of the verse, see Tommaso Tesei, "'The Romans Will Win!': Q 30:2–7 in Light of 7th c. Political Eschatology" (forthcoming).

20. "*Deus adiuta Romanis*": Kaegi, *Heraclius, Emperor of Byzantium*, 90; Geoffrey Greatrex and Samuel N. C. Lieu, *The Roman Eastern Frontier and the Persian Wars, AD 363–628*, 2 vols. (London: Routledge, 2002), 2:196.

21. Theophylact Simocatta, *The History of Theophylact Simocatta: An English Translation with Introduction and Notes*, trans. Michael Whitby and Mary Whitby (Oxford: Clarendon Press, 1986), 153 (5.15). See also Philip Wood, "Sophronius of Jerusalem and the End of Roman History," in *History and Identity in the Late Antique Middle East* (Oxford: Oxford University Press, 2013), 9; *Doctrina Jacobi nuper Baptizati*, ed. Vincent Déroche, in G. Dagron and V. Déroche, "Juifs et chrétiens dans l'Orient du VIIe siècle," *Travaux et Mémoires* 11 (1991): 166–167; and Andrew Palmer, ed., *The Seventh Century in West-Syrian Chronicles* (Liverpool: Liverpool University Press, 1993), xv.

22. Muqatil b. Sulayman [al-Balkhi], *Tafsir*, ed. ʿAbdallah Mahmud Shihata, 5 vols. (Beirut: Muʾassat al-Taʾrikh al-ʿArabi, 2002), 3:402. See also Thomas Sizgorich, "Sanctified Violence: Monotheist Militancy as the Tie That Bound Christian Rome and Islam," *Journal of the American Academy of Religion* 77, no. 4 (2009): 900–902; El Cheikh, "Surat Al-Rum," 357–358; Garth Fowden, *Empire to Commonwealth: Consequences of Monotheism in Late Antiquity* (Princeton, NJ:

Princeton University Press, 1993), 100–137; and Bowersock, *Crucible of Islam.*

23. For the Arab *limitanei*, see M. J. Kister, "Mecca and Tamim (Aspects of Their Relations)," *JESHO* 8, no. 2 (1965): 113–163; and al-Azmeh, *Emergence of Islam*, 157–158. Cf. E. B. Banning, "Peasants, Pastoralists and 'Pax Romana': Mutualism in the Southern Highlands of Jordan," *Bulletin of the American Schools of Oriental Research*, no. 261 (1986): 25–50. For Jewish critiques of the Roman Empire in this era, see Alexei M. Sivertsev, *Judaism and Imperial Ideology in Late Antiquity* (Cambridge: Cambridge University Press, 2011); and David Biale, "Counter-history and Jewish Polemics Against Christianity: The 'Sefer toldot yeshu' and the 'Sefer zerubavel,'" *Jewish Social Studies*, n.s., 6, no. 1 (1999): 130–145.

24. For Colossians 3:11, see Harry O. Maier, "A Sly Civility: Colossians and Empire," *Journal for the Study of the New Testament* 27, no. 3 (2005): 344.

25. Shaul Shaked, "Eschatology i. In Zoroastrianism and Zoroastrian Influence," in *Encyclopedia Iranica Online*, http://www.iranicaonline .org/articles/eschatology-i.

26. For Zoroastrians in Mesopotamia, a likely proxy for those in Yemen, see Michael G. Morony, *Iraq After the Muslim Conquest* (Princeton, NJ: Princeton University Press, 1984), 280–305. The Persian word for religion is *dēn*, which should not be confused with the Semitic *dīn*, meaning "judgment," though the two become homonyms in Qur'anic Arabic.

27. Iwona Gajda, "Remarks on Monotheism in Ancient South Arabia," in *Islam and Its Past: Jahiliyya, Late Antiquity, and the Qur'an*, ed. Carol Bakhos and Michael Cook (Oxford: Oxford University Press, 2017), chap. 8; Christian Robin, "Himyar et Israël," *Comptes rendus des séances de l'Académie des Inscriptions et Belles-Lettres* 148, no. 2 (2004): 831–908; G. W. Bowersock, *Throne of Adulis: Red Sea Wars on the Eve of Islam* (Oxford: Oxford University Press, 2012); Zeev Rubin, "Islamic Traditions on the Sasanian Conquest of the Himyarite Realm," *Der Islam* 84, no. 2 (2007): 185–199. I am following the most recent findings of Gajda here rather than Robin and Bowersock. If Abraha invaded Mecca in 567 and died shortly thereafter in 568— the last year for which we have an inscription for his reign—and if

his sons reigned two to three years as later Muslim sources estimated, then the Iranian invasion could have begun as early as 570–571 rather than 575; this dating, based on new work by Robin, above, would revise the discussion in Iwona Gajda, *Le Royaume de Himyar a l'époque monothéiste* (Paris: Mémoires de l'Académie des Inscriptions et Belles-Lettres, 2009), 152–153. Although the Qur'an says that the Meccans did not recognize "the All-Merciful" as a name for God, it was used in North Arabia and of course in the Hebrew Bible. John F. Healey, "The Kindly and Merciful God: On Some Semitic Divine Epithets," in *"Und Mose schrieb dieser lied auf": Studien zum Alten Testament und zum Alten Orient*, ed. Manfried Dietrich and Igo Kottsieper (Munster: Ugarit-Verlag, 1998), 350–356.

28. Seth Ward, "The Qur'an, Chosen People and Holy Land," in *Coming to Terms with the Qur'an*, ed. Khaleel Mohammad and Andrew Rippin (North Haledon, NJ: Islamic Publications International, 2007), 63–74. For contrasts between the Qur'an's views of Jews and the later Abbasid Muslim traditions, see Uri Rubin, *Between Bible and Qur'an: The Children of Israel and the Islamic Self-Image* (Princeton, NJ: Darwin Press, 1999), esp. 59–62. I do not agree with Rubin's assertion that the Qur'an ultimately withdraws from the Jews their status as God's chosen; it does point to episodes where they proved faithless, but then so does the Bible. See also Angelika Neuwirth, "The House of Abraham and the House of Amram: Genealogy, Patriarchal Authority, and Exegetical Professionalism" and "Qur'anic Readings of the Psalms," both in *The Qur'an in Context: Historical and Literary Investigations into the Qur'anic Milieu*, ed. Angelika Neuwirth, Nicolai Sinai, and Michael Marx (Leiden: Brill, 2010), 499–532 and 733–778, respectively. Likewise, it is clear that Muhammad knew some of the Palestinian Talmud, and Yemeni Jews often went for pilgrimage to Palestine or carried the bones of deceased loved ones up to the Holy Land for burial, staying a while to interact with Jews in Transjordan and the provinces of Palestine. Muhammad's winter trade journeys to Yemen, with its substantial Jewish population, are the most likely context for such interactions earlier in his life. See Robin, "Himyar et Israël"; and Yosef Tobi, "The Jews of Yemen in the Light of the Excavation of the Jewish Synagogue in Qani`," *Proceedings of the Seminar for Arabian Studies* 43 (2013): 1–8.

29. The Arabic for this script is *zubūr*, which can also mean the Psalms of David, but that would make no sense here, as is argued by Jan Retsö, "Arabs and Arabic in the Age of the Prophet," in *The Qur'an in Context: Historical and Literary Investigations into the Qur'ānic Milieu*, ed. Angelika Neuwirth, Nicolai Sinai, and Michael Marx (Leiden: Brill, 2010), 289. See also Alan Jones, "The Word Made Visible: Arabic Script and the Committing of the Qur'an to Writing," in *Texts, Documents, and Artefacts: Islamic Studies in Honour of D. S. Richards*, ed. Chase F. Robinson (Leiden: Brill, 2003), 1–15. The Nöldeke tradition focused on *when* the Qur'an was, assuming that new subjects were broached when Muhammad found out about them. I am arguing that the new subjects were dictated instead by a change in audience addressed by a peripatetic Muhammad and that we should attend in our exegesis to *where* the Qur'an was.

30. Angelika Neuwirth, "Jerusalem and the Genesis of Islamic Scripture," in *Jerusalem: Its Sanctity and Centrality to Judaism, Christianity and Islam*, ed. Lee I. Levine (New York: Continuum, 1999), 315–325.

31. *Doctrina Jacobi nuper Baptizati*, 180–181. See also Sebeos, *The Armenian History Attributed to Sebeos*, trans. R. W. Thomson (Liverpool: Liverpool University Press, 1999), 68–69.

32. Antiochus, *Expugnationis Hierosolymae A.D. 614: Recensiones Arabicae*, ed. Gerardo Garitte, vols. 1A–1B (Louvain: Secretariat du Corpus SCO, 1973), 1A:9–12; F. C. Conybeare, "Antiochus Strategos: The Capture of Jerusalem by the Persians in 614 AD," *English Historical Review* 25 (1910): 506; *Chronicon Paschale*, ed. and trans. Dindorf, 704–705; *Chronicon Paschale*, trans. Whitby and Whitby, 156–157.

33. Antiochus, *Expugnationis Hierosolymae*, 1A:14–16; Conybeare, "Antiochus Strategos," 506–507.

34. Antiochus, *Expugnationis Hierosolymae*, 1A:16–17; Conybeare, "Antiochus Strategos," 507; Kaegi, *Heraclius, Emperor of Byzantium*, 78; Yuri Stoyanov, *Defenders and Enemies of the True Cross: The Sasanian Conquest of Jerusalem in 614 and the Byzantine Ideology of Anti-Persian Warfare* (Vienna: Östereichische Akademie der Wissenschaften, 2011), chap. 1; G. W. Bowersock, *Empires in Collision in Late Antiquity: The Menahem Stern Jerusalem Lectures* (Waltham, MA: Brandeis University Press, 2012), chap. 2; Clive Foss, "The Persians in the Roman Near East (602–630 AD)," *Journal of the Royal Asiatic*

Society, 3rd ser., 13, no. 2 (2003): 149–170; Gideon Avni, "The Persian Conquest of Jerusalem (614 C.E.): An Archaeological Assessment," *Bulletin of the American Schools of Oriental Research* 357 (2010): 35–48; Gideon Avni, *The Byzantine-Islamic Transition in Palestine* (Oxford: Oxford University Press, 2014), 302–311; Doron Ben-Ami, Yana Tchekhanovets, and Gabriela Bijovsky, "New Archaeological and Numismatic Evidence for the Persian Destruction of Jerusalem in 614 CE," *Israel Exploration Journal* 60, no. 2 (2010): 204–221; Greatrex and Lieu, *Roman Eastern Frontier*, 2:190–193.

35. Sebeos, *Armenian History*, 69–70; J. W. Allan, "Armor," in *Encyclopedia Iranica*, http://www.iranicaonline.org/articles/armor; Brannon M. Wheeler, "Imagining the Sasanian Capture of Jerusalem: The 'Prophecy and Dream of Zerubbabel' and Antiochus Stratehos' 'Capture of Jerusalem,'" *Orientalia Christiana Periodica* 57, no. 1 (1999): 74n22; Agapius, *Kitab al-'Unvan*, 451; Khaleghi-Motlagh, "Etiquette in the Sasanian Period."

36. For the 561–562 peace treaty, see R. C. Blockley, *The History of Menander the Guardsman: Introductory Essay, Text, Translation and Notes* (Liverpool: Francis Cairns, 1985), 74–77, 144–147. For the other points, see Matthew Canepa, *The Two Eyes of the Earth: Art and Ritual of Kingship Between Rome and Sasanian Iran* (Berkeley: University of California Press, 2009), 13–17; Philip Wood, "The Christian Reception of the Xwaday-Namag: Hormizd IV, Khusrau II and Their Successors," *Journal of the Royal Asiatic Society* 26, no. 3 (2016): 417–420; Richard E. Payne, *A State of Mixture: Christians, Zoroastrians and Iranian Political Culture in Late Antiquity* (Berkeley: University of California Press, 2015), chap. 1, esp. 23. It is worth noting that the chief priest of the third century, Kerdir, left behind an inscription, saying, "The Jews, Buddhists, Hindus, Nazarenes, Christians, Baptists and Manicheans were struck in the empire. Idols were destroyed, and the residences of demons were annihilated and became the throne and seat of the angels." See David Neil McKenzie, "Kerdir's Inscription," in *Iranica Diversa*, ed. McKenzie (Rome: Istituto Italiano per l'Africa e l'Oriente, 1999), 1:217–274, this passage in Pahlevi and English on 244–245. It has been argued that *struck* here means "strictly subordinated" to the state religion and that in contrast polytheist idols were "destroyed." See Christelle Jullien and Florence Jullien, "Aux

frontières de l'iranité," *Numen* 49, no. 3 (2002): 286–287. Their research suggests that here, "Nazarenes" are local Eastern Christians inside the empire and "Christians" are Catholics abroad.

37. The verb translated as "make peace" (*aslaha*) here could also mean "to do good" or "to reform." But since this course of action is being suggested as an antidote to post-Edenic conflict ("Descend, being enemies to one another"), I think this reading is justified. For Jerusalem, see Lawrence E. Stager, "Jerusalem as Eden," *Biblical Archaeology Review* 26, no. 3 (2000): 36–47.

38. Tabari, *Tafsir*, 2:443–446, says that some later Muslim commentators took this Qur'an verse to be referring to Roman Christians who denied Jews the right to worship at the temple mount. The verse, however, mentions places of worship in the plural, and anyway Christians were not in control of the temple mount—Iran was.

39. Callinicum is today's Raqqa, Syria. See Ambrose, Bishop of Milan, "Letter 40.14," in *On the Duties of Clergy*, SLNPNF (New York: Christian Literature, 1890), 10:442; Maria Doerfler, "Ambrose's Jews: The Creation of Judaism and Heterodox Christianity in Ambrose of Milan's *Expositio evangelii secundum Lucam*," *Church History: Studies in Christianity and Culture* 80, no. 4 (2011): 749–772; Gaddis, *There Is No Crime*, 194–196; Thomas Sizgorich, *Violence and Belief in Late Antiquity: Militant Devotion in Christianity and Islam* (Philadelphia: University of Pennsylvania Press, 2012), chap. 3.

40. For points about the sixth century, see Catherine Brewer, "The Status of the Jews in Roman Legislation: The Reign of Justinian, 527–565 CE," *European Judaism: A Journal for the New Europe* 38, no. 2 (2005): 127–139. Less sanguine are Peter Schäfer, *The History of the Jews in the Greco-Roman World: The Jews of Palestine from Alexander the Great to the Arab Conquest*, 2nd ed. (London: Taylor and Francis, 2003), 192–195 (which insists Jews were excluded from higher administrative offices and that the prohibition on owning slaves who converted to Christianity was economically ruinous for tradesmen); and Louis H. Feldman, *Jew and Gentile in the Ancient World: Attitudes and Interactions from Alexander to Justinian* (Princeton, NJ: Princeton University Press, 1993). For the fourth and fifth centuries, see Seth Schwartz, *Imperialism and Jewish Society, 200 B.C.E. to 640 C.E.* (Princeton, NJ: Princeton University Press, 2001), chaps. 7–10. Overviews are

Guy Stroumsa, *The Making of the Abrahamic Religions in Late Antiquity* (Oxford: Oxford University Press, 2015), chap. 6; and Paula Fredriksen and Oded Irshai, "Christian Anti-Judaism: Polemics and Policies," in *The Cambridge History of Judaism*, vol. 4, *The Late Roman-Rabbinic Period*, ed. Steven T. Katz (Cambridge: Cambridge University Press, 2006): 977–1034.

41. Peter Haddad, ed., *Sharbe medem men qlisiastiqe wad-qosmostiqe*, with Arabic translation, *Al-Ta'rikh al-Saghir li al-Qarn al-Sabi` `Ashar* (Baghdad: Majma` al-Lughah al-Suriyaniyyah, 1976), 95. The Christian work *Jacob the Newly Baptized* alleges an incident that occurred at the turn of the seventh century in what is today Akka: "In the name of God, do you remember in our youth the day we were in Ptolemais in the reign of the emperor Maurikios, at the mill near the place where the ships and customs were—you, me, your father—master Samuelos, my teacher—and a crowd of Jews? While we were walking some Jews said that in Tiberias the rabbi of our community had had a great revelation in a vision that told him that the Anointed, the king of Israel, the Messiah, would come in eight years, that he would be born of a virgin and would raise up the Jewish nation. We were so joyful." *Doctrina Jacobi nuper Baptizati*, 194–195. See also Judith M. Lieu, *Christian Identity in the Jewish and Graeco-Roman World* (Oxford: Oxford University Press, 2004), 226–230.

42. Ibn Hisham, *Sirat Rasul Allah*, 1:276–277; Ibn Ishaq [Ibn Hisham], *The Life of Muhammad*, 191.

43. Many such stories are told about Omar's conversion; this one is from Ibn Rashid, *Maghazi*, 18–23. A more elaborate account is in Ibn Hisham, *Sirat Rasul Allah*, 1:225–227; and Ibn Ishaq [Ibn Hisham], *The Life of Muhammad*, 156–157.

44. Al-Tabari, *Ta'rikh al-Rusul wa al-Muluk*, 1180–1182; al-Tabari, *History of al-Tabari*, 6:98–99; Görke and Schoeler, *Die ältesten Berichte*, 38–44.

45. Irfan A. Omar, "Jihad and Nonviolence in the Islamic Tradition," in *Peacemaking and the Challenge of Violence in World Religions*, ed. Irfan A. Omar and Michael K. Duffey (Chichester, West Sussex: John Wiley & Sons, 2015), 22.

46. For the range of medieval views on this verse, see Tabari, *Tafsir*, 17: 489–493. The later commentators saw this approach as a sign of having the quality of being "even-tempered" (*hilm*), a trait tribal peoples

prized because it could prevent unnecessary feuding. Some of them also used words like *meek* and *pure* to characterize this attitude, saying these early Believers were not haughty or overbearing.

47. For these themes, see Michel Desjardins, *Peace, Violence and the New Testament* (Sheffield: Sheffield Academic Press, 1997); and Philip L. Tite, "Pax, Peace and New Testament," *Religiologiques* 11 (Spring 1995): 301–324.

48. For Ibn Zayd, see Tabari, *Tafsir*, 17:470–471. For Greek equivalents of *jihad*, consider *spoudaios*. See Alexandrine Schiewind, "The Social Concern of the Plotinian Sage," in *The Philosopher and Society in Late Antiquity: Essays in Honour of Peter Brown*, ed. Andrew Smith (Swansea: Classical Press of Wales, 2005), 55–61. Another possibility is that *jihad* parallels *agōn* with its sense of an athletic contest. See, for example, Timothy 6:12, "Fight the good fight (*agōnizou ton kalon agōna*) of the faith; take hold of the eternal life, to which you were called." For the latter possibility, see Omar, "Jihad and Nonviolence," 36.

49. See Fred Donner, "Fight for God—but Do So with Kindness: Reflections on War, Peace, and Communal Identity in Early Islam," in *War and Peace in the Ancient World*, ed. Kurt Raaflaub (Oxford: Blackwell's, 2006), 302; and Mohammed Abu-Nimr, *Nonviolence and Peacebuilding in Islam: Theory and Practice* (Gainesville: University Press of Florida, 2003), 67–69. There is a long Western history of ignoring that the Qur'an makes these recommendations of mercy over justice. See Clinton Bennett, "Retribution in Islam (Qur'an 2:178): Fact and Fiction in Victorian Literature," *Victorian Review* 37, no. 2 (2011): 13–16.

50. Asma Afsaruddin, "Recovering the Early Semantic Purview of *Jihad* and Martyrdom: Challenging Statist-Military Perspectives," in *Crescent and Dove: Peace and Conflict Resolution in Islam*, ed. Qamar-ul Huda (Washington, DC: US Institute for Peace, 2010), 39–62; the author discusses this passage of the Qur'an, *Consultation* 42:43, on 42–43. *Patience* had also been a technical term for tolerance or forbearance in the philosophy of Lactantius. See also for the verses cited in this paragraph Abu-Nimr, *Nonviolence and Peacebuilding in Islam*, 71–73; Donner, "Fight for God," 302; and Mohammed Abu-Nimr, *Nonviolence and Peacebuilding in Islam: Theory and Practice* (Gainesville: University Press of Florida, 2003), 67–69. For patience as avoidance

of conflict see also *The Robed* 73:10: "Be patient with what they say and take your leave of them graciously."

51. *The Cattle* 6:136: "They render to God a portion of what he created from their crops and cattle, asserting 'This is for God,' as they say, 'and this is for our associated deities.' So what is for their associates does not reach God; but what is for God reaches their associates. How evil is their judgment!" That Muhammad was preaching to villagers in the Transjordan, Palestine, and Syria in conjunction with trade missions up north would help make sense of Patricia Crone's finding that the Qur'an depicts Muhammad's Believers as merchants and his pagan opposition as farmers, a situation unlikely to have obtained in Mecca. Patricia Crone, "How Did the Quranic Pagans Make a Living?," *BSOAS* 68, no. 3 (2005): 387–399. For what it is worth, Jacob of Edessa says Muhammad undertook trade journeys to Palestine in 617–619 CE. See Robert G. Hoyland, *Seeing Islam as Others Saw It* (Princeton, NJ: Darwin Press, 1997), chap. 4, n. 180.

52. Antoninus Martyr, *Of the Holy Places Visited by Antoninus Martyr About the Year 570 A.D.*, trans. Aubrey Stewart (London: Committee of the Palestine Exploration Fund, 1885), para. 15; Antonini Placentini, *Itinerarium: Im unentstellten text mit deutscher Übersetzung*, ed. and trans. J. Gildemeister (Berlin: H. Reuters, 1889), para. 15. See Michael Cook, *Muhammad* (Oxford: Oxford University Press, 1983), chap. 7; Sinai, *Der Koran*, chap. 1; and Geneviève Gobillot, "Histoire et géographie sacrées dans le Coran: L'exemple de Sodome," *Mélanges de l'Institut Dominicain d'Études Orientales* 31 (2016): 1:54; cf. Strabo, *The Geography of Strabo: An English Translation*, trans. Duane W. Roller (Cambridge: Cambridge University Press, 2014), 713. For the Banu Judham, see C. E. Bosworth, "Madyan Shu'ayb in Pre-Islamic and Early Islamic Lore and History," *Journal of Semitic Studies* 29 (1984): 56.

53. Cf. Jane Dammen McAuliffe, *Qur'anic Christians: An Analysis of Classical and Modern Exegesis* (Cambridge: Cambridge University Press, 1991), chap. 8.

54. Fred M. Donner, *Muhammad and the Believers: At the Origins of Islam* (Cambridge, MA: Belknap Press of Harvard University Press, 2010), chap. 2.

55. What is likely the first non-Muslim mention of an "Islam" of Muhammad, in the 680s or 690s, translates it by the Aramaic cognate *mashlmanuta*, which means "tradition" rather than "submission." S. P. Brock, "North Mesopotamia in the Late Seventh Century: Book XV of John Bar Penkaye's Ris Melle," *JSAI* 9 (1987): 61. See also R. Payne Smith, *A Compendious Syriac Dictionary: Founded upon the Thesaurus Syriacus of R. Payne Smith* (Winona Lake, IN: Eisenbrauns, 1998), 307. The Aramaic *mashlmanuta* in turn translates the Greek *paradosis*, from the verb *paradidomi*. See Daniel L. Schwartz, *Paideia and Cult: Christian Initiation in Theodore of Mopsuestia* (Washington, DC: Center for Hellenic Studies, 2013), 101–102; and Everett Ferguson, "Paradosis and Traditio: A Word Study," in *Tradition & the Rule of Faith in the Early Church: Essays in Honor of Joseph T. Lienhard, S.J.*, ed. R. Rombs and A. Hwang (Washington, DC: Catholic University of America Press, 2010), 3–29. In the Qur'an, *islam* is the monotheistic tradition of the prophets.

56. Cf. Galatians 3:7–9, "So, you see, *those who believe* (*hoi ek pisteōs*) are the descendants of Abraham. And the scripture, foreseeing that God would justify the Gentiles by faith, declared the gospel beforehand to Abraham, saying, 'All the Gentiles shall be blessed in you.' For this reason, *those who believe* are blessed with Abraham who believed" (emphasis added).

57. Placentini, *Itinerarium*, para. 17. See also Abdulla al-Shorman et al., "Travel and Hospitality in Late Antiquity: A Case Study from Umm el-Jimal in Eastern Jordan," *Near Eastern Archaeology* 80, no. 1 (2017): 22–28.

58. U. Rubin, "Between Arabia and the Holy Land." For the possibility of renewed Jewish worship at the Temple Mount when the city was under Jewish rule, see Hagith Sivan, "From Byzantine to Persian Jerusalem: Jewish Perspectives and Jewish/Christian Polemics," *Greek, Roman and Byzantine Studies* 41, no. 3 (2000): 277–306.

59. Frederick S. Colby, *Narrating Muḥammad's Night Journey: Tracing the Development of the Ibn ʿAbbās Ascension Discourse* (Albany: SUNY Press, 2008).

60. Sophronius, Saint Patriarch of Jerusalem, *Sophronii Anacreontica*, ed. and trans. Marcello Gigante (Rome: Gismondi, 1957), 102–107, 171–173; Sophronios in A. Couret, "La prise de Jerusalem par les

Perses," *Révue de l'Orient Chrétien*, ser. 1, 2 (1897): 139–143. For this figure, see Philip Booth, *Crisis of Empire: Doctrine and Dissent at the End of Late Antiquity* (Berkeley: University of California Press, 2014), chap. 2; and Philip Wood, "Sophronius of Jerusalem and the End of Roman History," in *History and Identity in the Late Antique Middle East* (Oxford: Oxford University Press, 2013), 3–8.

61. Indeed, the phrase "holy war" was explicitly used in this period, though a little tongue in cheek. Some pieces of the relic of the true cross had come from Apamea in central Syria, whose citizens initially so fiercely resisted the Roman authorities' determination to transfer the wood to Jerusalem that one historian said they had mounted a "holy war" (*hieron . . . polemon*) to prevent it. Blockley, *History of Menander the Guardsman*, 154–155.

62. Sivan, "From Byzantine to Persian Jerusalem," 295. Sivan sees the mention of "Ishmaelites" in this poem as a later interpolation and reads the verses as originally about the Sasanid period in Jerusalem, based on internal evidence. For the seal, see F. Dexinger and W. Seibt, "A Hebrew Seal from the Period of the Sasanian Occupation of Palestine (614–629 A.D.): A Contribution to the Position of the Jews Between Byzantium and the Persians in the Seventh Century," *Revue des Études Juives* 140, no. 3 (1981): 303–317. For Nehemiah, see "Sefer Zerubbabel," in *Trajectories in Near Eastern Apocalyptic: A Postrabbinic Jewish Apocalypse Reader*, trans. John C. Reeves (Atlanta: Society of Biblical Literature, 2005), 57–58; and Martha Himmelfarb, *Jewish Messiahs in a Christian Empire: A History of the Book of Zerubbabel* (Cambridge, MA: Harvard University Press, 2017), 28–29, 114–119, 151.

63. The early commentator Muqatil b. Sulayman reviews assaults on the temple by Nabuchadrezzar, the Seleukid Antiochus IV, and the Roman general Titus. Muqatil, *Tafsir*, 2:521–523. See also Tabari, *Tafsir*, 14:479–484. Some early Muslim commentators thus retained a memory of the actual historical referents of this verse. See also Uri Rubin, "Between Arabia and the Holy Land: A Mecca-Jerusalem Axis of Sanctity," *JSAI* 34 (2008): 345–362; Uri Rubin, "Muhammad's Night Journey (*isra'*) to al-Masjid al-Aqsa: Aspects of the Earliest Origins of the Islamic Sanctity of Jerusalem," *al-Qantara* 29 (2008): 147–165, both reprinted in Uri Rubin, *Muhammad the Prophet and Arabia*,

Variorum Collected Studies Series (Aldershot: Ashgate, 2011), chaps. 7 and 11; Brannon Wheeler, *Moses in the Quran and Islamic Exegesis* (London: RoutledgeCurzon, 2002), 114–115; and Ward, "The Qur'an, Chosen People and Holy Land," 67.

64. The original word for temple here, *masjid*, also exists in cognate form (*msgd*) in Nabatean inscriptions, where it can refer to a place of worship but can also bear the more specific meaning of "a tall votive altar." See Robert Wenning, "The Betyls of Petra," *Bulletin of the American Schools of Oriental Research*, no. 324 (2001): 82–83n9; and Teixidor, *Pagan God*, 85–87. De Vries translates it as "cult-stone." See Bert de Vries, "Between the Cults of Syria and Arabia: Traces of Pagan Religion at Umm al-Jimal," *Studies in the History and Archaeology of Jordan* X (Amman: Department of Antiquities of Jordan, 2009): 179. *Masjid* later came to mean "mosque" in Arabic, but at the time of this verse there were no mosques.

65. Angelika Neuwirth, "From Sacred Mosque to the Remote Temple," chap. 8 in her *Scripture, Poetry and the Making of a Community: Reading the Qur'an as a Literary Text* (Oxford: Oxford University Press, 2014).

66. 2 Chronicles 36:16–17 says that the Babylonians were able to destroy the first temple in 586 BCE as a result of moral lapses on the part of the Jews: "They kept mocking the messengers of God, despising his words, and scoffing at his prophets, until the wrath of the Lord against his people became so great that there was no remedy. Therefore he brought up against them the king of the Chaldeans, who killed their youths with the sword in the house of their sanctuary, and had no compassion on young man or young woman, the aged or the feeble; he gave them all into his hand." The phrase in Qur'an 17:5, "penetrated into your edifices," with regard to the destruction of the first temple, seems close to 2 Chronicles' "killed their youths with the sword in the house of their sanctuary."

67. The divine "return" is an idiomatic way of speaking about divine forgiveness in Semitic languages. Aicha Rahmouni and Baruch A. Levine, "Deities Who 'Turn Back' from Anger," *JAOS* 136, no. 2 (2016): 235–245.

68. John Chrysostom, *Discourses Against Judaizing Christians*, trans. Paul W. Harkins (Washington, DC: Catholic University of America Press, 1979), 132–134 (5:10.1–3); *Doctrina Jacobi nuper Baptizati*, 97–98. See

also Paul L. Redditt, "Daniel 9: Its Structure and Meaning," *Catholic Biblical Quarterly* 62, no. 2 (2000): 236–249.

69. Since most Jews in the Near East rooted for the Iranians at the time, this work was likely penned after their defeat in 628, so that the prophecy is after the fact, and the author is looking beyond Roman restoration to a spiritual reward for the long-suffering Jews. "Sefer Elijah," in *Trajectories in Near Eastern Apocalyptic*, trans. Reeves, 38–39.

70. Wheeler, "Imagining the Sasanian Capture," is attentive to the way in which the imaginary of such works is shaped by cultural tradition.

71. Theodore Syncellus, *Traduction et commentaire de l'homélie écrite probablement par Théodore le Syncelle sur le siège de Constantinople en 626*, ed. L. Sternbach, trans. Ferenc Makk (Szeged: Acta Universitatis de Attila József Nominatae, 1975), paras. 3, 40–43. See also *Chronicon Paschale*, ed. and trans. Dindorf, 716–726; *Chronicon Paschale*, trans. Whitby and Whitby, 169–181; and David Olster, *Roman Defeat, Christian Response, and the Literary Construction of the Jew* (Philadelphia: University of Pennsylvania Press, 1994), 44, 77–78, 125–126, 147. Likewise, thinkers such as the fourth-century bishop John Chrysostom had asserted that the Jewish temple could never be rebuilt. John Chrysostom, *Discourses Against Judaizing Christians*, 98 (5:3). See also Martin Hurbanič, "Adversus Iudaeos in the Sermon Written by Theodore Syncellus on the Avar Siege of AD 626," *Studia Ceranea* 6 (2016): 271–293, http://www.academia.edu/32700558 /Adversus_Iudaeos_in_the_Sermon_Written_by_Theodore_Syncellus _on_the_Avar_Siege_of_AD_626.

72. Haddad, *Sharbe medem*, with Arabic translation, *Al-Ta'rikh al-Saghir*, 82–83.

73. Tertullian, *Tertullian: Apologetic and Practical Treatises*, trans. Charles Dodgson, ed. E. Pusey, 2nd ed. (Oxford: J. H. Parker, 1854), 70–72; Tertullian, "The Shows; or, de Spectaculis," in *The Ante-Nicene Fathers: Latin Christianity: Its Founder, Tertullian*, ed. Alexander Roberts and Sir James Donaldson (New York: C. Scribner's Sons, 1903), 91. For Muhammad as treading a path between the spirituality of the monks and the worldliness of bishops, see Peter Sarris, *Empires of Faith: The Fall of Rome to the Rise of Islam, 500–700* (Oxford: Oxford University Press, 2011), 266.

74. El Cheikh, "Surat Al-Rum"; Bowersock, *Empires in Collision*, chap. 3.

75. Walid A. Saleh, "End of Hope: Suras 10–15, Despair and a Way Out of Mecca," in *Qur'anic Studies Today*, ed. Angelika Neuwirth and Michael A. Sells (London: Routledge, 2016), chap. 4.

CHAPTER 4: CITY OF THE PROPHET

1. `Abd al-Malik ibn Hisham, *Sirat Rasul Allah*, ed. Ferdinand Wüsten-feld, 2 vols. (Gottingen: Dieterichsche Universitäts-Buchhandlung, 1858–1860), 303–313; Muhammad ibn Ishaq [`Abd al-Malik ibn Hisham], *The Life of Muhammad*, trans. Alfred Guillaume (1955; reprint, Karachi: Oxford University Press, 2002), 208–212.

2. Marcus Diaconus, *Vita Porphyrii*, ed. and trans. Anna Lampadaridi, in *La conversion de Gaza au christianisme: La vie d S. Porphyre* (Brussels: Société de Bollandistes, 2016), para. 21; Marcus Diaconus, *Life of Porphyry, Bishop of Gaza*, trans. G. F. Hill (Oxford: Clarendon Press, 1913), para. 21. For theoretical issues in conversion, see Ramsay MacMullen, *Christianizing the Roman Empire, AD 100–400* (New Haven, CT: Yale University Press, 1984), 2–5, 87; Daniel L. Schwartz, *Paideia and Cult: Christian Initiation in Theodore of Mopsuestia* (Washington, DC: Center for Hellenic Studies, 2013), 9–13; Maijastina Kahlos, *Debate and Dialogue: Christian and Pagan Cultures, c. 360–430* (Aldershot: Ashgate, 2007), 26–34, 83–88. See also the essays by Arietta Papaconstantinou, Averil Cameron, and Polymnia Athanassiadi in *Conversion in Late Antiquity: Christianity, Islam and Beyond*, ed. Arietta Papaconstantinou et al. (Fanham: Ashgate, 2015), xv–48.

3. Giorgio di Pisidia, *Carmi*, ed. Luigi Tartaglio (Torino: Editrice Torinese, 1998), 100–102/101–103 (2.2.17–19); Michael Lecker, "Were the Ghassanids and the Byzantines Behind Muhammad's Hijra?," in *Les Jafnides, des rois arabes au service de Byzance (VIe siècle de l'ère chrétienne)*, ed. Denis Genequand and Christian Robin (Paris: De Boccard, 2015), 277–293; G. W. Bowersock, *The Crucible of Islam* (Cambridge, MA: Harvard University Press, 2017), chap. 6; James Howard-Johnston, "Heraclius' Persian Campaigns and the Revival of the East Roman Empire, 622–630," *War in History* 6 (1999): 1–44; Walter E. Kaegi, *Heraclius, Emperor of Byzantium* (Cambridge: Cambridge University Press, 2003), 111–131.

4. Muhammad ibn Jarir al-Tabari, *Ta'rikh al-Rusul wa al-Muluk*, ed. M. J. de Goeje (Leiden: E. J. Brill, 1879), 1234–1241; Muhammad ibn Jarir

al-Tabari, *The History of al-Tabari (Ta'rikh al-Rusul wa al-Muluk)*, 40 vols. (Albany: SUNY Press, 1989–2007), 6:145–149; Andreas Görke and Gregor Schoeler, *Die ältesten Berichte über das Leben Muḥammads: Das Korpus ʿUrwa ibn az-Zubair* (Princeton, NJ: Darwin Press, 2008), chap. 3; Andreas Görke and Gregor Schoeler, "Reconstructing the Earliest Sira Texts: The Higra in the Corpus of ʿUrwa b. al-Zubayr," *Islam—Zeitschrift für Geschichte und Kultur des Islamischen Orients* 82, no. 2 (2005): 209–220.

5. See T. Fahd, "Sakina," in *Encyclopaedia of Islam*, ed. P. Bearman et al., 2nd ed., http://dx.doi.org.proxy.lib.umich.edu/10.1163/1573-3912 _islam_SIM_6505; Reuven Firestone, "Shekhinah," in *EQO*, Arnold M. Goldberg, *Untersuchungen über die Vorstellung von der Schekhinah in der frühen rabbinischen Literatur: Talmud und Midrasch* (Berlin: Walter de Gruyter, 1969); Ephraim E. Urbach, *The Sages: Their Concepts and Beliefs*, trans. Israel Abrahams, 2 vols. (Jerusalem: Magnes Press of Hebrew University, 1975), 1:37–65.

6. The Mishna (oral teachings) of the great rabbis recounts that Rabbi Hanina ben Teradion (second century CE) said, "When two sit and there are not between them words of Torah, lo, this is 'the seat of the scornful'... But when two sit and there are between them words of Torah, the Shechinah rests between them." Rabbi Ishmael, *Mekhilta de-Rabbi Ishmael*, trans. Jacob Z. Lauterbach, 2 vols. (1933; reprint, Philadelphia: Jewish Publication Society, 2004), 1:78–79; Reuven Firestone, *Journeys in Holy Lands: The Evolution of the Abraham-Ishmael Legends in Islamic Exegesis* (Albany: SUNY Press, 1990), 68–71, 82–91. Likewise, medieval Muslims held that the cloud of the *Sakina* (the Arabic form) had helped Abraham decide where to build the Kaaba. Brannon Wheeler, *Moses in the Qur'an and Islamic Exegesis* (London: RoutledgeCurzon, 2002), 91.

7. He goes on to speak of the exiles in Egypt, Babylon, and Edom. R. H. Charles, ed., *The Apocrypha and Pseudepigrapha of the Old Testament*, vol. 2, *Pseudepigrapha* (Oxford: Clarendon Press, 1913), 698 (tractate of the "Words of the Fathers," edited in the early 200s CE).

8. Uri Rubin, "The Life of Muhammad and the Qur'an: The Case of Muhammad's Hijra," *JSAI* 28 (2003): 40–64, reprinted in Uri Rubin, *Muhammad the Prophet and Arabia*, Variorum Collected Studies Series (Aldershot: Ashgate, 2011), chap. 8.

9. The details of these accounts have been carefully constructed in light of later Muslim history. Both Abu Bakr and Ali later served as vicars of Muhammad, and both are given a role in the migration to foreshadow that later leadership. Other versions of the story show signs of such adjustments in the light of later events; one has Ali give orders to Abu Bakr. U. Rubin, "Hijra," 49ff.

10. Muhammad ibn al-Zabalah, *Akhbar al-Madinah*, ed. Salah `Abd al-`Aziz Salamah (Medina: Markaz Buhuth wa Dirasat, 2003), 185–192; Ali ibn `Abd Allah Samhudi, *Wafa' al-Wafa bi-Akhbar dar al-Mustafa*, 4 vols. (1984; reprint, Beirut: Dar al-Kutub al-`Alamiyah, 1984), 1:75–77; Harry Munt, *The Holy City of Medina: Sacred Space in Early Islamic Arabia* (Cambridge: Cambridge University Press, 2014), chap. 2.

11. Alan Jones, "The Dotting of a Script and the Dating of an Era: The Strange Neglect of PERF 558," *Islamic Culture* 72, no. 4 (1998): 95–103. See also A. Ghabban and R. Hoyland, "The Inscription of Zuhayr, the Oldest Islamic Inscription (24 AH/AD 644–645): The Rise of the Arabic Script and the Nature of the Early Islamic State," *Arabian Archaeology and Epigraphy* 19, no. 2 (2008): 210–237; Patricia Crone, "The First-Century Concept of 'Hiğra,'" *Arabica* 41, no. 3 (1994): 352–387; Muhammad al-Faruque, "Emigrants and Helpers," in *EQO*.

12. `Umar ibn al-Shabba, *Kitab Ta'rikh al-Madina al-Munawwara*, ed. Fahim Muhammad Shaltut, 4 vols. (Mecca: H. M. Ahmad, 1979), 2:459–460. For analysis, see Michael Lecker, "Glimpses of Muḥammad's Medinan Decade," in *Cambridge Companion to Muhammad*, ed. Jonathan E. Brockopp (Cambridge: Cambridge University Press, 2010), 65.

13. Samhudi, *Wafa' al-Wafa*, 1:142–169; C. J. Robin and S. Tayran, "Soixante-dix ans avant l'Islam: L'Arabie toute entière dominée par un roi chrétien," *Comptes rendus des séances de l'Académie des inscriptions et belles-lettres* (2012): 525–553; G. W. Bowersock, *Throne of Adulis: Red Sea Wars on the Eve of Islam* (Oxford: Oxford University Press, 2012), 115–116; Michael Lecker, "The Levying of Taxes for the Sassanians in Pre-Islamic Medina (Yathrib)," *JSAI* 27 (2002): 109–126.

14. Michael Lecker, "Zayd B. Thābit, 'a Jew with Two Sidelocks': Judaism and Literacy in Pre-Islamic Medina (Yathrib)," *Journal of Near Eastern Studies* 56, no. 4 (1997): 259–273. For Khazraj-Aws competitions

and Bu`ath, see Al-Samhudi, *Wafa' al-Wafa*, 1:170–173; Tabari, *Tafsir*, 5:653–654, apud Q. 3:103; and Isaac Hasson, "Contributions à l'étude des Aws et des Hazrag," *Arabica* 36, no. 1 (1989): 1–35.

15. The root of the word used for "peace" denotes reconciliation or lack of conflict, and many commentators read it that way. Others construed it as meaning the religion preached by Muhammad, that is, *al-islam*, which, however, does not denote Muhammad's religion in the Qur'an. Some later interpreters said that the implication is that there should be no state of war among the Believers. Those who read it as "peace" vowelled it *silm* or *salm*. Tabari, *Tafsir*, 2:595–602.

16. Ibn Hisham, *Sirat Rasul Allah*, 1:353–354; Ibn Ishaq [Ibn Hisham], *The Life of Muhammad*, 240–241.

17. Ibn Hisham, *Sirat Rasul Allah*, 1:354; Ibn Ishaq [Ibn Hisham], *The Life of Muhammad*, 241; Muhammad ibn Sa`d, *Al-Tabaqat al-Kubra*, 9 vols. (Beirut: Dar Sadir, 1960), 1:502. Cf. G. Stroumsa, *Making of the Abrahamic Religions*, 84, citing the mid-seventh-century *The Secrets of Rabbi Simeon bar Yohai*: "In order to save you from Edom, God raises over the Ishmaelites a prophet according to his will."

18. See S. Schwartz, *Imperialism and Jewish Society*, chap. 4, on how Jews of the pagan Roman Empire joined in many traditionalist practices; and Kahlos, *Debate and Dialogue*, chap. 2, who summarizes findings of scholars of late antiquity about the large number of "in-between" people that she calls *incerti*, who pursued both Christian and pagan practices. Compare what later Muslim sources say of Medina to fourth- and fifth-century Antioch: Kaleres, *City of Demons*, 102–106; Isabella Sandwell, *Religious Identity in Late Antiquity: Greeks, Jews and Christians in Antioch* (Cambridge: Cambridge University Press, 2007); Christine Shepardson, *Controlling Contested Places: Late Antique Antioch and the Spatial Politics of Religious Controversy* (Berkeley: University of California Press, 2014); and Thomas Sizgorich, *Violence and Belief in Late Antiquity: Militant Devotion in Christianity and Islam* (Philadelphia: University of Pennsylvania Press, 2012), chap. 1.

19. Saba Farès, "Christian Monasticism on the Eve of Islam: Kilwa (Saudi Arabia)—New Evidence," *Arabian Archaeology and Epigraphy* 22, no. 2 (2011): 243–252. For evidence of pre-Islamic Arab Christian communities in Northwest Arabia, see Laila Nehmé, "New Dated Inscriptions (Nabataean and Pre-Islamic Arabic) from a Site near al-Jawf,

Ancient Dumah, Saudi Arabia," *Arabian Epigraphic Notes* 3 (2017): 121–164.

20. John Hick, *A Christian Theology of Religion: The Rainbow of Faiths* (Louisville, KY: Westminster John Knox Press, 1995); Alan Race, *Thinking About Religious Pluralism: Shaping Theology of Religion for Our Times* (Minneapolis: Fortress Press, 2015). For application of the typology to the Islamic tradition, see Mohammad Hassan Khalil, *Islam and the Fate of Others: The Salvation Question* (Oxford: Oxford University Press, 2012).

21. For pagan senator and philosopher Themistius's (d. 390) plea with an Arian Christian emperor for pluralism, see Socrates Scholasticus, *The Ecclesiastical History* (1853; reprint, London: George Bell and Sons, 1904), 254 (4.32). See also A. H. Armstrong, "The Way and the Ways: Religious Tolerance and Intolerance in the Fourth Century A.D.," *Vigiliae Christianae* 38, no. 1 (1984): 8–9; and Maijastina Kahlos, *Forbearance and Compulsion: The Rhetoric of Religious Tolerance in Late Antiquity* (London: Duckworth, 2009), 83–87. For Libanius, see Sizgorich, *Violence and Belief*, chap. 3. Modern theologian Hick makes a similar argument for pluralism, though his framework was not Platonic but Kantian. See Ankur Barua, "Hick and Radhakrishnan on Religious Diversity: Back to the Kantian Noumenon," *Sophia* 54, no. 2 (2015): 181–200.

22. Ibn Hisham, *Sirat Rasul Allah*, 303; Ibn Ishaq [Ibn Hisham], *The Life of Muhammad*, 207. Typically, Ibn Hisham asserts that some Muslims did away with the betyl of Manat, but *The Cattle* 6:108 instructs the Believers not to curse the gods and this part of the anecdote seems anachronistic and implausible.

23. Ibn Hisham, *Sirat Rasul Allah*, 355–357; Ibn Ishaq [Ibn Hisham], *The Life of Muhammad*, 242–243.

24. Michael Lecker, "King Ibn Ubayy and the *qussas*," in *Methods and Theories in the Study of Islamic Origins*, ed. Herbert Berg (Leiden: Brill, 2003), 29–71. The later sources say that Abdullah b. Ubayy had been on the verge of becoming a *malik*; while this word can mean "king," it also bore the sense simply of "leader." See Younis al-Shdaifat et al., "An Early Christian Arabic Graffito Mentioning 'Yazid the King,'" *Arabian Archaeology and Epigraphy* 28, no. 2 (2017): 315–324.

25. `Ali ibn Hazm al-Andalusi, *Jamharat Ansab al-`Arab*, ed. `Abd al-Salam Muhammad Harun, 5th printing (Cairo: Dar al-Ma`arif, 1962), 345. Ibn Hisham identified the recalcitrant septs as the Umayya ibn Zayd, Khatma, Wa'il, and Waqif. Ibn Hisham, *Sirat Rasul Allah*, 1:293; Ibn Ishaq [Ibn Hisham], *The Life of Muhammad*, 201. This passage was first discovered and analyzed by Michael Lecker, *Muslims, Jews and Pagans: Studies on Early Islamic Medina* (Leiden: Brill, 1995), chap. 2; cf. al-Faruque, "Emigrants and Helpers."

26. For Ibn al-Aslat, see Al-Samhudi, *Wafa' al-Wafa*, 1:179; Ibn Sa`d, *Al-Tabaqat al-Kubra*, 4:383–384; al-Tabari, *Ta'rikh al-Rusul wa al-Muluk*, 1217; and al-Tabari, *History of al-Tabari*, 6:130. For Abu `Amer, see Ibn Hisham, *Sirat Rasul Allah*, 1:411–412; Ibn Ishaq [Ibn Hisham], *The Life of Muhammad*, 278; and Uri Rubin, "Hanifiyya and Ka`ba: An Inquiry into the Arabian Pre-Islamic Background of din Ibrahim," *JSAI* 13 (1990): 86–89. Some late sources make Abu `Amer a Christian, in what became a general Muslim amnesia about the Sabians. See Ghada Osman, "Pre-Islamic Arab Converts to Christianity in Mecca and Medina: An Investigation into the Arabic Sources," *Muslim World* 95, no. 1 (2005): 67–80.

27. That is, *seb-*, as in *theosebeis*, which some have argued would become the Arabic calque *ṣabi'ū'llāh*. See Alberto Fratini and Carlo Prato, *I Sebomenoi (ton theon): Una risposta all'antico enigma dei Sabei* (Rome: n.p., 1997), http://www.ricerchefilosofiche.it/files/I%20Seb%C3%B2menoi.pdf via http://www.albertofratini.it/en/publications/, English translation at http://www.ricerchefilosofiche.it/files/God-fearers%20sabians%20timlj.pdf. See also Patricia Crone, "Pagan Arabs as God-Fearers," chap. 11 in *The Qur'anic Pagans and Related Matters: Collected Studies* (Leiden: E. J. Brill, 2016), vol. 1. The emphatic *ṣad* combined with the weak ending *hamza* in *ṣaba'a* point to this word being a loan. Those skeptical of such a borrowing from Greek should compare Qur'anic *razaqa*, "to nourish," from the Middle Persian *rōzīg*, or "daily bread," and *kanaza*, "to hoard," based on the Middle Persian *ganj*, or "treasure." See A. Tafazzoli, "Arabic Language II: Iranian Loanwords in Arabic," in *Encyclopaedia Iranica*, http://www.iranica online.org/articles/arabic-ii. The identity of the Sabians has bedeviled scholars for centuries. There has been enormous speculation on the identity of this group, but I concur with the above authors that they

were a branch in Medina of (Damascene?) Hypsistarians or *theosebeis*. For previous theories, that they were Jewish Christians or Manichaeans, see these articles and the works cited: François de Blois, "The 'Sabians' (*sabi'un*) in Pre-Islamic Arabia," *Acta Orientalia* 56 (1995): 39–61; and François de Blois, "Elchasai—Manes—Muhammad. Manichäismus und Islam in religionshistorischem Vergleich," *Der Islam* 81, no. 1 (2004): 31–48.

28. *Repentance* 9:107–110; Muqatil ibn Sulayman [al-Balkhi], *Tafsir*, ed. `Abdallah Mahmud Shihata, 5 vols. (Beirut: Mu'assat al-Ta'rikh al-`Arabi, 2002), 2:195–197, says "the Monk" came back from Syria to lead the prayers at this house of worship, though he makes him Jewish. Michael Lecker, *Muslims, Jews and Pagans: Studies on Early Islamic Medina* (Leiden: Brill, 1995), chap. 4. The tale told in Umayyad and Abbasid sources is that Muhammad had the temple of harm burned down, but the Qur'an simply advises a boycott and elsewhere forbids attacking places of worship. As usual, successive generations militarized a Qur'an verse that on the face of it seems pacific, if firm.

29. Ibn Hisham, *Sirat Rasul Allah*, 341–344; Ibn Ishaq [Ibn Hisham], *The Life of Muhammad*, 231–233. The literature on this document is extensive and is summarized in these recent works: Saïd Amir Arjomand, "The Constitution of Medina: A Sociolegal Interpretation of Muhammad's Acts of Foundation of the 'Umma,'" *IJMES* 41, no. 4 (2009): 555–575; Michael Lecker, *The "Constitution of Medina": Muhammad's First Legal Document* (Princeton, NJ: Darwin Press, 2004); and Munt, *Holy City of Medina*, chap. 2. While this document gives evidence of being early, there are also signs of later redaction, in particular its use of *jihad* to mean fighting for the faith.

30. Arjomand, "Constitution of Medina," 567. This conclusion is disputed by Lecker, *"Constitution of Medina,"* 125–126, who appears to see the passage merely as a warning. That makes no sense to me. Why warn nonsignatories in this document?

31. Arjomand, "Constitution of Medina," 568; Donner, *Muhammad and the Believers*, chap. 2.

32. Ibn Hisham, *Sirat Rasul Allah*, 1:361, 379; Ibn Ishaq [Ibn Hisham], *The Life of Muhammad*, 246, 257.

33. Ibn Hisham, *Sirat Rasul Allah*, 1:343; Ibn Ishaq [Ibn Hisham], *The Life of Muhammad*, 233; Al-Samhudi, *Wafa' al-Wafa*, 1:143; Lecker,

"Constitution of Medina," 79–80, 85–86, esp. 79n148. The treaty gives rights of citizenship in the new polity (*umma*) to the Jews of Banu Awf, then says that the Jews of the Banu Tha`laba have a similar standing. And then it says that another branch of Tha`laba, the Jafna, also have this standing. That the Jafna were Christians is likely the reason for their having been mentioned separately from the rest of the tribe. It is also possible that some clans of the Khazraj or Aws signatories were Christians, while others might have still been pagans.

34. The Qur'an (*The Cow* 2:128) depicts Abraham and Ishmael praying, "Our lord, make us submissive to you and raise from our progeny a devoted nation." See also Carol Bakhos, *The Family of Abraham: Jewish, Christian, and Muslim Interpretations* (Cambridge, MA: Harvard University Press, 2014), chap. 2; and G. Stroumsa, *The Making of the Abrahamic Religions.* For nations and religions, see David G. Horrell, "'Race,' 'Nation,' 'People': Ethnic Identity-Construction in 1 Peter 2.9," *New Testament Studies* 58, no. 1 (2012): 123–143; Judith M. Lieu, *Christian Identity in the Jewish and Graeco-Roman World* (Oxford: Oxford University Press, 2004), chap. 8; and Judith M. Lieu, "The Race of the God-Fearers," *Journal of Theological Studies* 46, no. 2 (1995): 483–501. For this interpretation of the Constitution, see Donner, *Muhammad and the Believers,* 69–74; and Gerald Hawting, "The Religion of Abraham and Islam," in *Abraham, the Nations and the Hagarites: Jewish, Christian, and Islamic Perspectives on Kinship with Abraham,* ed. Martin Goodman et al. (Leiden: Brill, 2010), 485. Hawting doubts direct influence, but it seems clear to me that Muhammad knew passages of the New Testament, as Michel Cuypers has shown.

35. Guy G. Stroumsa, "Religious Dynamics Between Christians and Jews in Late Antiquity (312–640)," in *Cambridge History of Christianity,* ed. A. Casiday and F. Norris (Cambridge: Cambridge University Press, 2007), 2:152, 158; Schäfer, *History of the Jews in the Greco-Roman World,* 190. For endogamy and ethnicity, see, for example, Jessica M. Vasquez, "Disciplined Preferences: Explaining the (Re)Production of Latino Endogamy," *Social Problems* 62, no. 3 (2015): 455–475.

36. Hasson, "Contributions à l'étude," 20.

37. Ibn Hisham, *Sirat Rasul Allah,* 1:385–387; Ibn Ishaq [Ibn Hisham], *The Life of Muhammad,* 261–262.

38. *The Family of Amram* 3:105. See U. Rubin, *Between Bible and Qur'an*, chap. 9, this verse on 209.

39. Cf. Eric Rebillard, *Christians and Their Many Identities in Late Antiquity, North Africa, 200–450 CE* (Ithaca, NY: Cornell University Press, 2012); and Kahlos, *Debate and Dialogue*, chap. 2.

40. Eusebius Pamphilus, "Life of Constantine," in *The Church History of Eusebius*, SLNPNF, n.s. (Oxford: Parker, 1890), 1:554 (4.52); MacMullen, *Christianizing the Roman Empire*, 56–58.

41. Al-Tabari, *Ta'rikh al-Rusul wa al-Muluk*, 1269–1270; al-Tabari, *History of al-Tabari*, 7:14.

42. Al-Tabari, *Ta'rikh al-Rusul wa al-Muluk*, 1268–1267; al-Tabari, *History of al-Tabari*, 7:11–12.

43. Some later Muslim exegetes applied this verse to the Jews of Banu Qaynuqa' or Banu Qurayza (Tabari, *Tafsir*, 11:235ff). Since I maintain that *alladina kafaru* in the Qur'an only means pagans and never applies to Jews or Christians unless they are explicitly specified, and since I maintain that *amana*, or "to believe," is used for the biblical communities as well as for Muslims, I categorically reject this interpretation.

44. Cf. *The Family of Amram* 3:114: "They believe in God and the last day, and enjoin the good and forbid wrongdoing, and hasten to perform charity. Those are the righteous." I am here building on Donner, *Muhammad and the Believers*, 68–82. See also Stephen J. Shoemaker, *The Death of a Prophet: The End of Muhammad's Life and the Beginnings of Islam* (Philadelphia: University of Pennsylvania Press, 2012), 208–209.

45. Justinian, Novella 146, in James Parkes, *The Conflict of the Church and the Synagogue: A Study in the Origins of Antisemitism* (New York: JPS, 1934), 392–393; Willem F. Smelik, "Justinian's Novella 146 and Contemporary Judaism," in *Greek Scripture and the Rabbis*, ed. T. M. Law (Leuven: Peeters Press, 2012), 141–163. For Tabari's recognition of the pluralism implied in *The Cow* 2:62, see Tabari, *Tafsir*, 2:32–46, apud 2:61; Samir Khalil, "Le commentaire de Tabari sur Coran 2.62 et la question du salut des non-musulmans," *Annali: Istituto Orientale di Napoli*, n.s., 40, no. 30 (1980): 555–617; Jane Dammen McAuliffe, *Qur'anic Christians: An Analysis of Classical and Modern Exegesis* (Cambridge: Cambridge University Press, 1991), chap. 3. See also Michel Cuypers, *The Banquet: A Reading of the Fifth Sura of the Qur'an*

(Miami: Convivium Press, 2009), 300–304; and Mahmoud Ayoub, "Religious Pluralism and the Qur'an," in *Islam and Global Dialogue: Religious Pluralism and the Pursuit of Peace*, ed. Roger Boase (Burlington, VT: Ashgate, 2005), 273–282.

46. The Qur'an's *dīn* as "a religion," from the Old Persian *daena* and Middle Persian *dēn,* is an unrelated homonym to the Semitic *"dīn"* with the meaning of "judgment." The fullest recent discussion is Reinhold Glei and Stefan Reichmuth, "Religion Between the Last Judgment, Law and Faith: Koranic Din and Its Rendering in Latin Translations of the Qur'an," *Religion* 42, no. 2 (2012): 247–271. See also Arthur Jeffery, *The Foreign Vocabulary of the Qur'an* (Baroda: Oriental Institute, 1938), 131–132; Wilfred Cantwell Smith, *The Meaning and End of Religion* (1962; reprint, Minneapolis: Fortress Press, 1991), chap. 4, argues that the Manichaeans were the first to refer to the world religions with the term *dēn*, but Zoroastrians surely preceded them. The Persian term was also adopted into Syriac and used by Eastern Christians. See Adam H. Becker, "Martyrdom, Religious Difference, and 'Fear' as a Category of Piety in the Sasanian Empire: The Case of the Martyrdom of Gregory and the Martyrdom of Yazdpaneh," *JLA* 2, no. 2 (2009): 300–336. See also Mansour Shaki, "Dēn," in *Encyclopaedia Iranica Online*, http://www.iranica online.org/articles/den (in print: *Encyclopaedia Iranica*, ed. Ehsan Yarshater, 16 vols. [London: Routledge & Kegan Paul, 1982–2013], 7:279–281); and Allan R. Bomhard and John C. Kerns, *The Nostratic Macrofamily: A Study in Distant Linguistic Relationship* (Berlin: Walter de Gruyter, 1994), 264–265. Although Boyarin points to the use of words such as *eusebeia* (piety) and *threskeia* (worship) to argue that the late eastern Romans had a conception of religion, his examples make it clear that this conception was substantially different from that of the Qur'an in not allowing for the notion of multiple valid religions. Daniel Boyarin, "The Christian Invention of Judaism: The Theodosian Empire and the Rabbinic Refusal of Religion," *Representations* 85 (2004): 21–57; and "Rethinking Jewish Christianity: An Argument for Dismantling a Dubious Category," *Jewish Quarterly Review* 99, no. 1 (2009): 7–36.

47. Ibn Hisham, *Sirat Rasul Allah*, 1:401–411; Ibn Ishaq [Ibn Hisham], *The Life of Muhammad*, 270–277. He makes them from Najran, in keeping

with the mysterious Abbasid fiction that there was no Medinan Christian community.

48. A reference to 3:61, a practice called *mubāhala*.

49. E. W. West, ed., *The Book of the Mainyo-i-khard* (Stuttgart: C. Grüninger, 1871), 4. "Good Religion" here is *weh dēn*. See also Richard E. Payne, *A State of Mixture: Christians, Zoroastrians and Iranian Political Culture in Late Antiquity* (Berkeley: University of California Press, 2015), chap. 1.

50. Cyprian of Carthage (d. 258) and Origen of Alexandria (d. 253 or 254) appear simultaneously to have invented this phrase. See Michel-Yves Perrin, "The Limits of the Heresiological Ethos in Late Antiquity," in *Religious Diversity in Late Antiquity*, ed. David M. Gwynn and Susanne Bangert et al. (Leiden: Brill, 2010), 206; Tom Greggs, "Exclusivist or Universalist? Origen the 'Wise Steward of the Word' (*CommRom.* V.1.7) and the Issue of Genre," *International Journal of Systematic Theology* 9, no. 3 (2007): 319. For the condemnation of Jews who did not accept Jesus at the Parousia, see *Doctrina Jacobi nuper Baptizati*, ed. Vincent Déroche, in G. Dagron and V. Déroche, "Juifs et chrétiens dans l'Orient du VIIe siècle," *Travaux et Mémoires* 11 (1991): 102–103.

51. Justin Martyr, *The Apologies of Justin Martyr*, ed. A. Blunt (Cambridge: Cambridge University Press, 1911), 70; Justin Martyr and Athenagoras, *The Writings of Justin Martyr and Athenagoras*, trans. Marcus Dods et al. (Edinburgh: T. & T. Clark, 1867), 46; Arthur J. Droge, "Justin Martyr and the Restoration of Philosophy," *Church History* 56, no. 3 (1987): 303–319; Bogdan G. Bucur, "Justin Martyr's Exegesis of Biblical Theophanies and the Parting of the Ways Between Christianity and Judaism," *Theological Studies* 75, no. 1 (2014): 34–51; Judith M. Lieu, *Image and Reality: The Jews in the World of the Christians in the Second Century* (Edinburgh: T. & T. Clark, 1996), chap. 4.

52. The term I am translating as *philosophy* is a loan from Aramaic (*melta*) literally meaning "word," which was taken into Qur'anic Arabic as *milla*. Given the context here, of religious pluralism, it is clearly underlain by the Greek conception of the Logos, the Reason that structures reality. Christian Syriac writers sometimes spoke of Moses and Jesus in a positive sense as philosophers. If the Qur'an saw Abraham in those terms as well, it would not be surprising. See Jeffery, *Foreign Vocabulary*

of the Qur'an, 268–269; and F. Buhl and C. E. Bosworth, "Milla," in *Encyclopaedia of Islam*, ed. P. Bearman et al., 2nd ed., http://dx.doi.org .proxy.lib.umich.edu/10.1163/1573-3912_islam_SIM_5199. For *melta* and Logos, see Jacqueline Chabbi, *Le coran décrypté: Figures bibliques en Arabie* (Paris: Fayard, 2008), chap. 13; Adam H. Becker, *Fear of God and the Beginning of Wisdom: The School of Nisibis and the Development of Scholastic Culture in Late Antique Mesopotamia* (Philadelphia: University of Pennsylvania Press, 2013), 135, 133ff (Syriac Christian Neoplatonism), 187 (for Moses and Jesus as philosophers). For the Epistle of James and Abraham, see Roy Bowen Ward, "The Works of Abraham: James 2: 14–26," *Harvard Theological Review* 61, no. 2 (1968): 283–290; and Alexander Stewart, "James, Soteriology, and Synergism," *Tyndale Bulletin* 61, no. 2 (2010): 293–310.

53. Plato, *The Republic*, trans. R. E. Allen (New Haven, CT: Yale University Press, 2006), 124 (4.429d–430b). Likewise, the Stoic emperor-philosopher Marcus Aurelius maintained that the soul is dyed by thoughts and so should be constantly dipped in virtuous ones. Marcus Aurelius, *Meditations*, trans. Maxwell Staniforth (New York: Penguin, 1964), 84 (3.4). For a survey of the controversy, see Sean W. Anthony, "Further Notes on the Word *Sibgha* in Qur'an 2:138," *Journal of Semitic Studies* 59, no. 1 (2014): 117–129.

54. Philo, "De Migratione Abrahami," 70–73, in *Philo in Ten Volumes*, ed. and trans. F. H. Colson and G. H. Whitaker, 10 vols. (1932; reprint, London: Heinemann, 1985), 4:170/171–172/173. See also Annette Yoshiko Reed, "The Construction and Subversion of Patriarchal Perfection: Abraham and Exemplarity in Philo, Josephus, and the Testament of Abraham," *Journal for the Study of Judaism* 40, no. 2 (2009): 193; David Winston, *The Logos and Mystical Philosophy in Philo of Alexandria* (Cincinnati: Hebrew Union College Press, 1985); Phoebe Makiello, "Abraham and the Nations in the Works of Philo of Alexandria," in *Abraham, the Nations and the Hagarites*, ed. Goodman et al., 140–142; Nancy Calvert-Koyzis, *Paul, Monotheism and the People of God: The Significance of Abraham Traditions for Early Judaism and Christianity* (London: T. & T. Clark International, 2004), chap. 3. Philo was anything but obscure; he was so widely cited by Christian authors that he was jokingly called "Bishop Philo." David T. Runia, *Philo in Early Christian Literature: A Survey* (Minneapolis: Fortress Press, 1993).

55. Angelika Neuwirth, "Wissenstransfer durch Typologie: Relektüren des Abrahamsopfers im Koran und im islamischen Kultus," in *Denkraum Spätantike: Reflexionen von Antiken in umfeld des Koran*, ed. in Nora Schmidt, Nora K. Schmid, and Angelika Neuwirth (Wiesbaden: Harrassowitz Verlag, 2016), 195–196; Guy Stroumsa, "Athens, Jerusalem, Mekka: Der Patristische Schmeltztiegel der Abrahamitischen Religionen," ibid., 111; Stroumsa, *Making of Abrahamic Religions*, 193–195. For the issue of Christian appropriation and exclusion, see Jeffrey S. Siker, "From Gentile Inclusion to Jewish Exclusion: Abraham in Early Christian Controversy with Jews," *Biblical Theology Bulletin* 19, no. 1 (1989): 30–36; Calvert-Koyzis, *Paul, Monotheism and the People of God*; Lieu, *Christian Identity*, 77–79, 269–272; and Lieu, *Image and Reality*, 120–123, 136–137.

56. Angelika Neuwirth, "Reclaiming Babylon: The Multiple Languages of the Qur'ān," in *Islamic Thought in the Middle Ages: Studies in Text, Transmission and Translation, in Honour of Hans Daiber*, ed. W. Raven and A. Akasoy (Leiden: Brill, 2008), 565–591; Uri Rubin, "'Become You Apes, Repelled!' (Quran 7:166): The Transformation of the Israelites into Apes and Its Biblical and Midrashic Background," *BSOAS* 78, no. 1 (2015): 25–40. As Rubin points out, the rabbinical tradition says that the Jews wandering in the desert who sought food other than manna were punished with bodily afflictions; the Qur'an says that they were transformed into apes. It is not a general statement about Jews but a midrashic commentary on Numbers 11:19–20.

57. John Wansbrough, *Quranic Studies: Sources and Methods of Scriptural Interpretation* (Oxford: Oxford University Press, 1977), 8–12. For covenants and their invocation in the Qur'an, see Rosalind Ward Gwynne, *Logic, Rhetoric and Legal Reasoning in the Qur'an: God's Arguments* (London: Taylor and Francis, 2004), esp. chap. 1; and Joseph E. B. Lumbard, "Covenant and Covenants in the Qur'an," *JQS* 17, no. 2 (2015): 1–23.

58. Asma Afsaruddin, "The 'Upright Community': Interpreting the Righteousness and Salvation of the People of the Book in the Qur'an," in *Jewish-Muslim Relations in Past and Present: A Kaleidoscopic View*, ed. Joseph Meri (Leiden: Brill, 2017), 48.

59. Afsaruddin, "Upright Community," 56, 66. See also Jarot Wahyudi, "Exegetical Analysis of the 'Ahl al-Kitab' Verses of the Qur'an," *Islamic Studies* 37, no. 4 (1998): 433–436.

60. Wahyudi, "Exegetical Analysis," 425–433.

61. David Novak, *The Image of the Non-Jew in Judaism: An Historical and Constructive Study of the Noahide Laws* (Lewiston, NY: Edwin Mellen, 1983). See also Gilbert S. Rosenthal, "*Hasidei umot ha-olam*: A Remarkable Concept," *Journal of Ecumenical Studies* 48, no. 4 (2013): 467–490; Matthias Morgenstern, "The Quest for a Rabbinic Perception of a Common Humanity," in *The Quest for a Common Humanity: Human Dignity and Otherness in the Religious Traditions of the Mediterranean*, ed. Katell Berthelot and Matthias Morgenstern (Leiden: E. J. Brill, 2011), 41–66; Ruth Langer, "Jewish Understandings of the Religious Other," *Theological Studies* 64, no. 2 (2003): 255–277; and Novak, *Image of the Non-Jew in Judaism*, 14–28.

62. Q. 17:22–35, 25:64–72, and 31:11–18: Angelika Neuwirth, *Scripture, Poetry and the Making of a Community: Reading the Qur'an as a Literary Text* (Oxford: Oxford University Press, 2014), chap. 5. Neuwirth draws on but also much expands on Hartwig Hirscheld, *New Researches into the Composition and Exegesis of the Qoran* (London: Royal Asiatic Society, 1902), 80–82.

63. Hick's schema has been controversial, in part, it seems to me, because he is only speaking of the ideas of salvation or soteriology in each of these rich and varied traditions, whereas they have other dimensions, such as the doctrinal, that his approach ignores. See Lewis E. Winkler, *Contemporary Muslim and Christian Responses to Religious Plurality: Wolfhart Pannenberg in Dialogue with Abdulaziz Sachedina* (Eugene, OR: Pickwick, 2011), chap. 1.

64. Novak, *Image of the Non-Jew in Judaism*, 153–175; Rosenthal, "*Hasidei umot ha-olam*." The Table 5:73 does warn that saying God is "the third of three" is a form of paganizing and would bring torment, but this may be a condemnation of the doctrine of tritheism. See John C. Block, "Philoponian Monophysitism in South Arabia at the Advent of Islam," *Journal of Islamic Studies* 23, no. 1 (2012): 50–75.

CHAPTER 5: JUST WAR

1. The medieval exegete Tabari recounted this narrative about *The Cow* 2:217 from one Muhammad al-San`ani, who said it went back to the prophet Muhammad himself: Tabari, *Tafsir*, 3:655–656. I am

recounting it here because I think it tracks with the Qur'an account much more closely than Ibn Hisham's story.

2. Tabari, *Tafsir*, apud. 2:191; I am using the phrase "coercion of conscience" to translate the capacious Arabic word *fitna*. Some later commentators misinterpreted *fitna* here as paganism or as the turmoil resulting from paganism, and so used the verse to justify violence against them. Reuven Firestone, *Jihad: The Origin of Holy War in Islam* (Oxford: Oxford University Press, 1999), 95. In other words, they read it as saying the opposite of what it does say. For the full range of this word's meanings for this exegete, see Abdulkader Tayob, "An Analytic Survey of al-Tabari's Exegesis of the Cultural Symbolic Construct of Fitna," in *Approaches to the Qur'an*, ed. G. R. Hawting and Abdul-Kader A. Shareef (London: Routledge, 1993), 157–172.

3. `Abd al-Malik ibn Hisham, *Sirat Rasul Allah*, ed. Ferdinand Wüstenfeld, 2 vols. (Gottingen: Dieterichsche Universitäts-Buchhandlung, 1858–1860), 1:423–427; Muhammad ibn Ishaq [`Abd al-Malik ibn Hisham], *The Life of Muhammad*, trans. Alfred Guillaume (1955; reprint, Karachi: Oxford University Press, 2002), 286–289, tells a much more elaborate and implausible version of this story involving a raid on a small caravan carrying leather and raisins, in which the Emigrants desperately wanted to kill some Quraysh and carry off the loot. The incident is improbably sited all the way down south of Mecca at Nakhla on the way to Taif, whereas the Qur'an gives an impression of the Believers being bottled up in Medina and its environs. Since Ibn Hisham admits that this party was sent as reconnoiters, moreover, why did they abruptly alter their mission to a caravan raid? The brief account of the al-Hadrami incident in the letter allegedly written by `Urwa ibn al-Zubayr to Umayyad ruler `Abd al-Malik also does not mention a caravan raid. Muhammad ibn Jarir al-Tabari, *Ta'rikh al-Rusul wa al-Muluk*, ed. M. J. de Goeje (Leiden: E. J. Brill, 1879), 1285; Muhammad ibn Jarir al-Tabari, *The History of al-Tabari (Ta'rikh al-Rusul wa al-Muluk)*, 40 vols. (Albany: SUNY Press, 1989–2007), 7:29.

4. Amaury Levillayer, "Guerre 'juste' et défense de la patrie dans l'Antiquité tardive," *Revue de l'histoire des religions* 227, no. 3 (2010): 320.

5. Firestone, *Jihad*, 73–77; Muhammad Abdel Haleem, *Understanding the Qur'an: Themes and Style* (London: I. B. Tauris, 2010), chap. 5.

6. The word I translated here as "fight...with deadly force" is often rendered in English as the imperative "slay." Logically speaking, however, the Qur'an cannot be using the word precisely in that way since it often (for example, *Repentance* 9:5) goes on to command the Believers to take captives and to offer their foes amnesty if they will repent their aggression. I conclude that in this context, the verb *qatala* has the connotations of unleashing potentially lethal battle rather than of simple killing, a conclusion also reached by Jacqueline Chabbi, *Les trois piliers de l'islam: Lecture anthropologique du Coran* (Paris: Éditions du Seuil, 2016), 201–209, 251–254. It is also possible that it is incorrectly vowelled and should read *qātala*, fight. Some early commentators, as well, read the word as "fight" rather than "kill." Others read such verses as allowing killing only where the enemy had killed a Muslim.

7. Abdel Haleem, *Exploring the Qur'an*, chap. 1.

8. Asma Afsaruddin, *Striving in the Path of God: Jihad and Martyrdom in Islamic Thought* (Oxford: Oxford University Press, 2013), 54.

9. Firestone, *Jihad*, 77–84. For the "utopian tradition" in absolute pacifism, see James Johnson, *The Quest for Peace: Three Moral Traditions in Western Cultural History* (Princeton, NJ: Princeton University Press, 1987), chap. 4.

10. Augustine, *The City of God*, 1:32 (1.21). For the quote from Athanasios, see Athanasius, "Letter to Amoun," quoted in Louis J. Swift, "Early Christian Views on Violence, War, and Peace," in *War and Peace in the Ancient World*, ed. Kurt Raaflaub (Oxford: Blackwell's, 2006), 286.

11. It is obvious that this verse is not about terrorism ("fear," *turhibun*, in this verse is sometimes translated "terror"), despite the appeal made to it by contemporary Muslim extremists and by Islamophobes alike. It is clearly speaking of a battlefield tactic in a formal war of defense, not of using terror to harm and intimidate civilians and accomplish civil, political goals. Moreover, in *The Cow* 2:40, God uses the same root, saying to the Believers, "fear me" (*irhabuni*), which is obviously not a command to be terrorized by the All-Merciful.

12. *The Spoils* 8:7: "Remember when God had promised that one of two bands would be yours, and you had hoped it would be the unarmed group, but God desired to vindicate the truth with his word and completely uproot the pagans?"

13. The verse has *rakb*, which at least in Yemen seems to have meant "camel cavalry." See Iwona Gajda, *Le Royaume de Himyar a l'époque monothéiste* (Paris: Mémoires de l'Académie des Inscriptions et Belles-Lettres, 2009), 219. Most modern translators give it as "caravan," but Ibn Manẓur says *rakb* in this verse could mean horses, or camels, or an army made up of men mounted on both. Muhammad ibn Manẓur, *Lisan al-ʿArab*, 15 vols. (Beirut: Dar al-Sadir, 1956), 1:429.

14. Theophylact Simocatta, *Theophylacti Simocattae historiae*, ed. Peter Wirth and Carl de Boor (Stuttgart: B. G. Teubner, 1972) 138 (3.13); Theophylact Simocatta, *The History of Theophylact Simocatta: An English Translation with Introduction and Notes*, trans. Michael Whitby and Mary Whitby (Oxford: Clarendon Press, 1986), 93–94.

15. David Olster, *Roman Defeat, Christian Response, and the Literary Construction of the Jew* (Philadelphia: University of Pennsylvania Press, 1994), 63, 77–79; Philip Wood, *Crisis of Empire: History and Identity in the Late Antique Near East* (Berkeley: University of California Press, 2013), 98–100; James Howard-Johnston, *Witnesses to a World Crisis: Historians and Histories of the Middle East in the Seventh Century* (Oxford: Oxford University Press, 2010), 447; Tommaso Tesei, "Heraclius' War Propaganda and the Origins of the Qur'ānic Concept of Fighting Martyrdom," forthcoming.

16. Wansbrough, *The Sectarian Milieu*, 25–26. For ʿUrwa's narrative of Badr, see Al-Tabari, *Ta'rikh al-Rusul wa al-Muluk*, 1284–1288; al-Tabari, *History of al-Tabari*, 7:28–32; and Andreas Görke and Gregor Schoeler, *Die ältesten Berichte über das Leben Muḥammads: Das Korpus ʿUrwa ibn az-Zubair* (Princeton, NJ: Darwin Press, 2008), chap. 4.

17. For the peace of God here, see T. Fahd, "Sakina," in *Encyclopaedia of Islam*, ed. P. Bearman et al., 2nd ed., http://dx.doi.org.proxy.lib.umich.edu/10.1163/1573-3912_islam_SIM_6505.

18. Augustine/Boniface, Letter 189, in Augustine, *Political Writings*, ed. E. M. Atkins and R. J. Dodaro (Cambridge: Cambridge University Press, 2004), 216: "You must not think that no one who serves as a soldier, using arms for warfare, can be acceptable to God. The holy David was one such, and the Lord offered a great a witness to him." John Mark Mattox, *Saint Augustine and the Theory of Just War* (London: Continuum, 2006), 20–21; Ambrose, Bishop of Milan, *On the Duties of Clergy*, SLNPNF (New York: Christian Literature, 1890),

10:30 (1.35.177). For Herakleios as David, see Howard-Johnston, *Witnesses to a World Crisis*, 32; Thomas Sizgorich, "Sanctified Violence: Monotheist Militancy as the Tie That Bound Christian Rome and Islam," *Journal of the American Academy of Religion* 77, no. 4 (2009): 906; and Chase Robinson, "Reconstructing Early Islam: Truth and Consequences," in *Method and Theory in the Study of Islamic Origins*, ed. Herbert Berg (Leiden: Brill, 2003), 101–136, esp. 134–136.

19. Andrea Keller, "Cicero: Just War in Classical Antiquity," in *From Just War to Modern Peace Ethics*, ed. H. Justenoven and W. Barbieri (Berlin: De Gruyter, 2012), 9–30; Swift, "Early Christian Views," 279–296.

20. Philip Wynn, *Augustine on War and Military Service* (Minneapolis: Augsburg Fortress, 2013), chap. 2. For other people's wars being holy war but one's own being just war, see Khalid Yahya Blankinship, "Parity of Muslim and Western Concepts of Just War," *Muslim World* 101, no. 3 (2011): 412–426.

21. Augustine, *The City of God*, in *Works of St. Augustine*, ed. Marcus Dods, 15 vols. (Edinburgh: T. & T. Clark, 1871–1876), 2:311 (19.7); Augustine, *Writings on the Old Testament*, trans. Joseph T. Lienhard (Hyde Park, NY: New City Press of the Focolare, 2016), 362–363; Robert Holmes, "St. Augustine and the Just War Theory," in *The Augustinian Tradition*, ed. Gareth B. Matthews (Berkeley: University of California Press, 1999), 330–331.

22. For quotes in this paragraph, see Augustine, *The City of God*, in *Works of St. Augustine*, ed. Marcus Dods, 15 vols. (Edinburgh: T. & T. Clark, 1871–1876), 2:311 (19.7); Augustine, *Writings on the Old Testament*, trans. Joseph T. Lienhard (Hyde Park, NY: New City Press of the Focolare, 2016), 362–363; Robert Holmes, "St. Augustine and the Just War Theory," in *The Augustinian Tradition*, ed. Gareth B. Matthews (Berkeley: University of California Press, 1999), 330–331; Augustine, "To Marcellinus (138)," in *Letters of St. Augustine*, in *Works of St. Augustine*, ed. Dods, 13:205; and Augustine/Boniface, Letter 185, in Augustine, *Political Writings*, 191.

23. Al-Zuhri in Ibn Rashid, *Maghazi*, 76–81; Görke and Schoeler, *Die ältesten Berichte*, chap. 5; Ibn Hisham, *Sirat Rasul Allah*, 1:555–606; Ibn Ishaq [Ibn Hisham], *The Life of Muhammad*, 370–401.

24. Anthony Kaldellis, *The Byzantine Republic: People and Power in New Rome* (Cambridge, MA: Harvard University Press, 2015).

25. Ambrose, Bishop of Milan, *On the Duties of Clergy*, 10:22, 30 (1.27.129, 1.36.179; cf. 3.3.23). See also Swift, "Early Christian Views," 287.

26. For enemies who bow down to created things, see Giorgio di Pisidia, *Carmi*, ed. Luigi Tartaglio (Torino: Editrice Torinese, 1998), 72–74/73–75 (1.1.1–34). For Shahr Varaz's licentiousness, see ibid., 102/103 (2.2.239–243). For God as the commanding general, ibid., 134/135 (2.3.385). For the Roman turn to conceptions of holy war, see Olster, *Roman Defeat*, 53. For Georgios of Pisidia as a source, see Howard-Johnston, *Witnesses to a World Crisis*, chap. 1.

27. Ibn Rashid, *Maghazi*, 82–85; Ibn Hisham, *Sirat Rasul Allah*, 1:669–684; Ibn Ishaq [Ibn Hisham], *The Life of Muhammad*, 450–460; Michael Morony, "Kandaq," in *Encyclopedia Iranica*, http://www.irani caonline.org/articles/khandaq. The Roman military began adopting the trench technique only in the reign of Maurikios, in the late 500s. R. C. Blockley, *The History of Menander the Guardsman: Introductory Essay, Text, Translation and Notes* (Liverpool: Francis Cairns, 1985), 200–201.

28. Alois Musil, *The Manners and Customs of the Rwala Bedouins* (New York: American Geographical Society, 1928), 540–570; William Lancaster and Felicity Lancaster, "Concepts of Tribe, Tribal Confederation and Tribal Leadership," in *Les Jafnides, des rois arabes au service de Byzance (VIe siècle de l'ère chrétienne)*, ed. Denis Genequand and Christian Robin (Paris: De Boccard, 2015), 60–61.

29. This ambiguous verse could say that God "sufficed the believers in the fight," or it could be read, as A. J. Arberry suggested, to say that there was no battle royale. A. J. Arberry, *The Koran Interpreted*, 2 vols. in one (1955; reprint, New York: Macmillan, 1970), 2:133.

30. Theodore Syncellus, *Traduction et commentaire de l'homélie écrite probablement par Théodore le Syncelle sur le siège de Constantinople en 626*, text ed. L. Sternbach, translation from French by Ferenc Makk (Szeged: Acta Universitatis de Attila József Nominatae, 1975), para. 19; cf. *Chronicon Paschale*, ed. and trans. Ludwig Dindorf (Bonn: E. Weber, 1832), 725–726; and *Chronicon Paschale*, trans. Michael Whitby and Mary Whitby (Liverpool: Liverpool University Press, 1989), 180–181. The phrase "fish in a net" is quoted from a sixteenth-century Russian patriarch in Peter Brown, *The World of Late Antiquity* (New York: W. W. Norton, 1989), 172.

31. Bissera V. Pentcheva, "The Supernatural Protector of Constantinople: The Virgin and Her Icons in the Tradition of the Avar Siege," *Byzantine and Modern Greek Studies* 26, no. 1 (2002): 5; Alexei M. Sivertsev, *Judaism and Imperial Ideology in Late Antiquity* (Cambridge: Cambridge University Press, 2011), 96–101.

32. Linguists make a distinction between a general term like *bird* (the hypernym) that serves as a rubric for more specific words, such as *eagle* (the hyponym). Many later Muslim commentators misunderstood this phrase as indicating that all Jews and Christians were somehow being declared infidels. This interpretation cannot stand the test of logic. The very need to identify this subset of paganizers proves that the words for "impious" or "pagan" do not ordinarily refer to Jews and Christians. Moreover, declining to follow Muhammad is hardly the same as participating in pagan worship or joining with hostile pagans to make war on him.

33. *The Gathering* 59:2. For later debates on the meaning of this passage, see Marco Schöller, "Die Palmen (*lina*) der Banu n-Nadir und die Interpretation von Koran 59:5: Eine Untersuchung zur Bedeutung des koranischen Wortlauts in den ersten Jahrhunderten islamischer Gelehrsamkeit," *Zeitschrift der Deutschen Morgenländischen Gesellschaft* 146 (1996): 317–380.

34. Augustine, *The City of God*, in *Works of St. Augustine*, ed. Dods, 2:284 (18.51). For Augustine's change of heart about the desirability of coercing people's consciences, see Augustine/Boniface, Letter 185, in Augustine, *Political Writings*, 189–190; Maijastina Kahlos, *Forbearance and Compulsion: The Rhetoric of Religious Tolerance in Late Antiquity* (London: Duckworth, 2009), 111–125; Michael Gaddis, *There Is No Crime for Those Who Have Christ: Religious Violence in the Christian Roman Empire* (Berkeley: University of California Press, 2005), 128–133; Peter Brown, *Through the Eye of a Needle: Wealth, the Fall of Rome, and the Making of Christianity in the West, 350–550 AD* (Princeton, NJ: Princeton University Press, 2012), chap. 20; and Wynn, *Augustine on War*, chap. 7.

35. Ibn Rashid, *Maghazi*, 90–91; Görke and Schoeler, *Die ältesten Berichte*, chap. 7; Marco Schöller, "Qurayza (Banu al-)," in *EQO*.

36. Ibn Rashid, *Maghazi*, 66–67; Marco Schöller, "In welchem Jahr wurden die Banu l-Nadir aus Medina vertrieben?," *Der Islam* 73 (1996): 1–39;

Marco Schöller, *Exegetisches Denken und Prophetenbiographie: Eine quellenkritische Analyse der Sira-Uberlieferung zu Muhammads Konflikt mit den Juden* (Wiesbaden: Harrassowitz Verlag, 1998), chaps. 6 and 7; Marco Schöller, "Nadir (Banu al)," in *EQO*.

37. Oded Irshai, "Christian Historiographers' Reflections on Jewish-Christian Violence in Fifth-Century Alexandria," in *Jews, Christians, and the Roman Empire: The Poetics of Power in Late Antiquity*, ed. Natalie B. Dohrmann and Annette Yoshiko Reed (Philadelphia: University of Pennsylvania Press, 2013), 137–153; cf. Christine Shepardson, *Controlling Contested Places: Late Antique Antioch and the Spatial Politics of Religious Controversy* (Berkeley: University of California Press, 2014). Peter Sarris notes that seventh-century Greek sources blamed Roman troops or a mixed crowd for an uprising in Antioch in 609, but Theophanes the Confessor, writing some two centuries later, characterized the mob as purely Jewish and said they burned churches. Peter Sarris, *Empires of Faith: The Fall of Rome to the Rise of Islam, 500–700* (Oxford: Oxford University Press, 2011), 240–242.

38. See Jacqueline Chabbi, *Les trois piliers de l'islam: Lecture anthropologique du Coran* (Paris: Éditions du Seuil, 2016), 256–261. Many Muslim biographers of succeeding centuries could no longer imagine the category of neutral or friendly, tolerated pagans and interpreted the verse as a caution against friendly fire among the Believers; one story about this verse has the pagan accosted announce his conversion but be killed anyway. Tabari, *Tafsir*, 4:359. The verse clearly says, however, "You were like them in the past," proving that it is speaking of pagans.

39. Firestone, *Jihad*, chaps. 3–4; Michael Bonner, *Jihad in Islamic History: Doctrines and Practice* (Princeton, NJ: Princeton University Press, 2006), chap. 2; Abdel Haleem, *Exploring the Qur'an*, chap. 1. For the alleged battle of Mu'ta, see David Powers, *Zayd* (Philadelphia: University of Pennsylvania Press, 2014), chap. 3. Powers offers an analysis of conflicting accounts of the battle of Mu'ta in Abbasid authors that raises severe questions about its historicity. I will add another problem: the Abbasids give a welter of dates for the supposed campaign but generally assert that the Believers faced tribal proxies of Herakleios at a time when in fact Iranian General Shahr Varaz still controlled the

Near East (it cannot be assumed that the latter was out before late 629 or even early 630).

40. Augustine, "To Marcellinus (138)," in *Letters of St. Augustine*, in *Works of St. Augustine*, ed. Dods, 13:205.

41. Nicola Bergamo, "Expeditio Persica of Heraclius: Holy War or Crusade?," *Porphyra* 5, no. 12 (2008): 94–107, www.porphyra.it; Yuri Stoyanov, "Apocalypticizing Warfare: From Political Theology to Imperial Eschatology in Seventh- to Early Eighth-Century Byzantium," in *The Armenian Apocalyptic Tradition: A Comparative Perspective*, ed. Kevork B. Bardakjian and Sergio La Porta (Leiden: Brill, 2014), 379–433.

CHAPTER 6: THE HEART OF MECCA

1. Sebeos, *The Armenian History Attributed to Sebeos*, trans. R. W. Thomson (Liverpool: Liverpool University Press, 1999), 79–80.

2. The passage uses four words for religious edifices, two of them typically referring to Christian institutions (one of them a loanword from Aramaic). The other two are vaguer and could refer to Jewish synagogues or Zoroastrian fire temples since the Qur'an is clearly eager that any house of worship dedicated to the one God be protected. Cf. *The Cow* 2:114, which complains about Jews and Christians attacking one another's places of worship, discussed in chapter 3.

3. Wolf Liebeschuetz, *East and West in Late Antiquity: Invasion, Settlement, Ethnogenesis and Conflicts of Religion* (Leiden: Brill, 2015), 249–250.

4. James Howard-Johnston, "Heraclius' Persian Campaigns and the Revival of the East Roman Empire, 622–630," *War in History* 6 (1999): 1–44.

5. Yasht 19 in Prods Oktor Skjaervo, trans., *The Spirit of Zoroastrianism* (New Haven, CT: Yale University Press, 2011), 113–114; Touraj Daryaee, "The Use of Religio-political Propaganda on *Coins of Xusro* II," *Journal of the American Numismatic Society* 7 (1997): 45–46; Abolala Soudavar, *The Aura of Kings: Legitimacy and Divine Sanction in Iranian Kingship* (Costa Mesa, CA: Mazda, 2003), 14, 23. Perhaps the abrupt fall of Khosrow II reminded Iranians of the equally stark decline of the mythical ancient ruler the radiant Jamshid of the good herds.

6. Giorgio di Pisidia, *Carmi*, ed. Luigi Tartaglio (Torino: Editrice Torinese, 1998), 104/105 (2.2.251–55); *Chronicon Paschale*, ed. and trans.

Ludwig Dindorf (Bonn: E. Weber, 1832), 727–728; *Chronicon Paschale*, trans. Michael Whitby and Mary Whitby (Liverpool: Liverpool University Press, 1989), 182–183.

7. Sebeos, *Armenian History*, 83–86; *Histoire nestorienne inédite: (Chronique de Séert)*, ed. and trans. Addaï Scher, 2 vols. (1908; reprint, Turnhout, Belgium: Éditions Brepols, 1983), 2:551–554; Walter E. Kaegi, *Heraclius, Emperor of Byzantium* (Cambridge: Cambridge University Press, 2003), 66–67; and Howard-Johnston, "Heraclius' Persian Campaigns," 5–6. The complicated events in Iran after the execution of Khosrow II are traced in Parvaneh Pourshariati, *Decline and Fall of the Sasanian Empire: The Sasanian-Parthian Confederacy and the Arab Conquest of Iran* (London: I. B. Tauris, 2008), chap. 3.

8. Muhammad ibn Jarir al-Tabari, *Ta'rikh al-Rusul wa al-Muluk*, ed. M. J. de Goeje (Leiden: E. J. Brill, 1879), 1853–1868; Muhammad ibn Jarir al-Tabari, *The History of al-Tabari (Ta'rikh al-Rusul wa al-Muluk)*, 40 vols. (Albany: SUNY Press, 1989–2007), 10:20–38; W. Montgomery Watt, *Muhammad at Medina* (Oxford: Clarendon Press, 1956), 128–130.

9. Ayoub, "Nearest in Amity," 147.

10. Al-Tabari, *Ta'rikh al-Rusul wa al-Muluk*, 958, 1574–1575, 1763, 1851; al-Tabari, *History of al-Tabari*, 5:251–252, 8:113–114; 9:123–124, 10:18; Iwona Gajda, *Le Royaume de Himyar a l'époque monothéiste* (Paris: Mémoires de l'Académie des Inscriptions et Belles-Lettres, 2009), 162; Joseph S. Nye, *Soft Power: The Means to Success in World Politics* (New York: PublicAffairs, 2004).

11. Ibn Rashid, *Maghazi*, 26–50; `Abd al-Malik ibn Hisham, *Sirat Rasul Allah*, ed. Ferdinand Wüstenfeld, 2 vols. (Gottingen: Dieterichsche Universitäts-Buchhandlung, 1858–1860), 1:740–752; Muhammad ibn Ishaq [`Abd al-Malik ibn Ishaq [ibn Hisham], *The Life of Muhammad*, trans. Alfred Guillaume (1955; reprint, Karachi: Oxford University Press, 2002), 499–507; Andreas Görke, "The Historical Tradition About al-Hudaybiyya: A Study of `Urwa ibn al-Zubayr's Account," in *The Biography of Muhammad: The Issue of the Sources*, ed. Harald Motzki (Leiden: Brill, 2000), 240–274; Andreas Görke and Gregor Schoeler, *Die ältesten Berichte über das Leben Muhammads: Das Korpus `Urwa ibn az-Zubair* (Princeton, NJ: Darwin Press, 2008), chap. 8.

12. Tabari, *Tafsir*, 22:571–574, quotes three groups on the meaning of this verse: those who said it pertained to converts to Islam in Mecca who did not emigrate but were now forgiven, those who said it pertained to pagans, and those who said it pertained to all classes of people in Mecca. Al-Tabari prefers the last.

13. `Urwa has them say they are ready to fight if need be, but that vow seems implausible in the circumstances.

14. Al-Tabari, *Ta'rikh al-Rusul wa al-Muluk*, 1009; al-Tabari, *History of al-Tabari*, 5:330.

15. Sohail Hashmi, "The Qur'an and Tolerance: An Interpretive Essay on Verse 5:48," *Journal of Human Rights* 2, no. 1 (2003): 97.

16. R. C. Blockley, *The History of Menander the Guardsman: Introductory Essay, Text, Translation and Notes* (Liverpool: Francis Cairns, 1985), 72–77. The 561–562 treaty was lopsided in requiring the Iranian shah to grant freedom of worship to Christians but laying no obligation on Constantinople to tolerate Zoroastrianism. There is a similar lack of symmetry in some articles of the Treaty of Hudaibiya as it has come down to us. For other points in this paragraph, see G. R. Hawting, "Al-Hudaibiyya and the Conquest of Mecca: A Reconsideration of the Tradition About the Muslim Takeover of the Sanctuary," *JSAI* 8 (1986): 1–23; and Görke, "Historical Tradition About al-Hudaybiyya," 260–268.

17. Pseudo-Callisthenes, *The History of Alexander the Great, Being the Syriac Version*, ed. and trans. Ernest A. Wallis Budge (Cambridge: Cambridge University Press, 1889), 163–200; Kevan van Bladel, "The Alexander Legend in the Qur'an 18:83–102," in *The Qur'an in Its Historical Context*, ed. Gabriel Said Reynolds (New York: Routledge, 2008), 175–202; Tommaso Tesei, "The Prophecy of Dhu-l-Qarnayn (Q 18:83–102) and the Origins of the Qur'anic Corpus," in *Miscellanea Arabica, 2013–2014*, ed. A. Arioli (Ariccia, Rome: Aracne Editrice, 2014), 273–290; G. J. Reinink, *Syriac Christianity Under Late Sasanian and Early Islamic Rule* (Aldershot: Ashgate, 2005), chaps. 3, 6. For later developments in Syriac apocalyptic and "The Alexander Romance" under Muslim rule, see Paul J. Alexander, *The Byzantine Apocalyptic Tradition*, ed. Dorothey F. Abrahamse (Berkeley: University of California Press, 1985); and Marth Himmelfarb, *The Apocalypse: A Brief History* (London: Wiley-Blackwell, 2010), 127–130.

18. Fereydun Vahman, *Arda Wiraz Namag: The Iranian "Divina Comme-dia"* (London: Curzon Press, 1986) 77/191 (my rendering).
19. David P. Melvin, *The Interpreting Angel Motif in Prophetic and Apoca-lyptic Literature* (Minneapolis: Fortress Press, 2013).
20. See Amy C. Merill Willis, *Dissonance and the Drama of Divine Sov-ereignty in the Book of Daniel* (New York: T. & T. Clark, 2010), 118. I wrote that passage in 2016 but before publication was informed by Michael Pregill that the argument had support, pointing to Tommaso Tesei, "An Unusual Hermeneutic of Dan 8 Behind the Epithet of Dhu-l-Qarnayn," international meeting of SBL, Humboldt Univer-sitat, Berlin, August 6–11, 2017. Many thanks to Dr. Tesei for subse-quently sharing a copy of this important work, which is much more grounded in the contemporary Syriac literature than was my own hypothesis.
21. Sidney Griffith, "Christian Lore and the Arabic Qur'an: The 'Com-panions of the Cave' in the Qur'an and in Syriac Christian Tradition," in *The Qur'an in Its Historical Context*, ed. Reynolds, 109–138.
22. C. Hovorun, *Will, Action and Freedom: Christological Controversies in the Seventh Century* (Leiden: Brill, 2008).
23. Al-Tabari, *Ta'rikh al-Rusul wa al-Muluk*, 1634; al-Tabari, *History of al-Tabari*, 8:175; cf. Ibn Hisham, *Sirat Rasul Allah*, 1:802–824; and Ibn Ishaq [Ibn Hisham], *The Life of Muhammad*, 540–555.
24. Many commentators displace verses of *Success* 48 onto the story of the Treaty of Hudaibiya—for example, Tabari, *Tafsir*, 21:238ff. At Hudaibiya, however, the Believers did not reach the heart of Mecca, nor was there a danger out there of harming secret Muslims, as there was inside the city. Most later Muslim narratives call the procession a "raid" and depict the fall of Mecca as a military conquest. Perhaps the Qur'an's alternative view of the matter caused the commenta-tors to apply the decidedly peaceful chapter of *Success* to a different event entirely. It was, however, recognized as being about the fall of Mecca by Hartwig Hirschfeld, *New Researches into the Composition and Exegesis of the Qoran* (London: Royal Asiatic Society, 1902), 127. Although Bell rejected the later Muslim exegetes' assertion that sura 48 is about Hudaibiya, and he acknowledged that some of it must address the fall of Mecca, his conviction that it was earlier than 630 and his continued reliance on the unreliable exegetes misled him

into continuing to apply some verses to Hudaibiya. Richard Bell, *A Commentary on the Qur'an*, ed. C. Edmund Bosworth and M. E. J. Richardson, 2 vols. (Manchester: University of Manchester Press, 1991), 2:281–286.

25. Al-Tabari, *Ta'rikh al-Rusul wa al-Muluk*, 1634–1636; al-Tabari, *History of al-Tabari*, 8:74–76; Görke and Schoeler, *Die ältesten Berichte*, chap. 9. For "al-fath" as "success," see G. R. Hawting, "Al-Hudaybiyya and the Conquest of Mecca," *JSAI* 8 (1986): 3; and Rudi Paret, "Die Bedeutungsentwicklung von arabisch *fath*," in *Orientalia Hispanica*, ed. J. M. Barral (Leiden: Brill, 1974), 1:537–541, https://books.google .com/books?id=NugUAAAAIAAJ&lpg=PA537&ots=p4PGd8EP 0b&dq=Rudi%20Paret%20%22Die%20Bedeutungsentwicklung%20 von%20arabisch%20fath%22&pg=PA537#v=onepage&q.

26. Q. 48:25.

27. Ibid.

28. Arnold M. Goldberg, *Untersuchungen über die Vorstellung von der Schekhinah in der frühen rabbinischen Literatur: Talmud und Midrasch* (Berlin: Walter de Gruyter, 1969), 522–530.

29. Pourshariati, *Decline and Fall of the Sasanian Empire*, 178–179.

30. "A Chronicle Composed in AD 640," in *The Seventh Century in the West-Syrian Chronicles*, trans. Andrew Palmer, Sebastian Brock, and Robert Hoyland (Liverpool: Liverpool University Press, 1993), 13; Sebeos, *Armenian History*, 88.

31. *Success* 48:27.

32. *Success* 48:29. The best reading of this passage is Holger Zellentin, "QS 38, Q48," in *Qur'an Seminar*, ed. Mehdi Azaiez (Berlin: De Gruyter, 2017), 359.

33. Theodoret de Cyr, *Histoire des Moines de Syrie: "Histoire Philothée,"* ed. and trans. Pierre Canivet and Alice Leroy-Molinghen, 2 vols. (Paris: Cerf, 1977–1979), 2:190/191 (26.13); Theodoret of Cyrrhus, *A History of the Monks of Syria*, trans. R. M. Price (Trappist, KY: Cistercian Press, 2008), 166–167. See also Frank R. Trombley, *Hellenic Religion and Christianization, c. 370–529*, 2 vols. (Leiden: Brill, 1993), 2:165–166; and Elizabeth Key Fowden, "Rural Converters Among the Arabs," and Konstantin M. Klein, "How to Get Rid of Venus: Some Remarks on Jerome's Vita Hilarionis and the Conversion of Elusa in the Negev," both in *Conversion in Late Antiquity: Christianity, Islam*

and Beyond, ed. Arietta Papaconstantinou et al. (Farnham: Ashgate, 2015), 175–196 and 241–266, respectively.

34. Jason Moralee, "The Stones of St. Theodore: Disfiguring the Pagan Past in Christian Gerasa," *Journal of Early Christian Studies* 14, no. 2 (2006): 183–215.

35. Cf. Peter Brown, *Authority and the Sacred: Aspects of the Christianisation of the Roman World* (Cambridge: Cambridge University Press, 1995), chap. 3.

36. Muhammad ibn Sa`d, *Al-Tabaqat al-Kubra*, 9 vols. (Beirut: Dar Sadir, 1960), 2:136.

37. H. Munt, "'No Two Religions': Non-Muslims in the Early Islamic Hijaz," *BSOAS* 78, no. 2 (2015): 249–269.

38. Neither the Qur'an nor `Urwa mentions anything about reprisal killings or the handful of executions alleged by later Muslim biographers to have been carried out, and the ebullience of the Qur'an about the lack of bloodshed strongly suggests that these stories were made up out of whole cloth. For the Prophet's gifts to unite the hearts, see Muhammad ibn Habib al-Baghdadi, *Al-Munammaq*, ed. Muhammad Khurshid Fariq (Beirut: `Alam al-Kitab, 1985), 422–423.

39. See the survey in Watt, *Muhammad at Medina*, pt. 4, "The Unifying of the Arabs," and sources cited.

CHAPTER 7: INTO THE WAY OF PEACE

1. Muhammad ibn Jarir Al-Tabari, *Ta'rikh al-Rusul wa al-Muluk*, ed. M. J. de Goeje (Leiden: E. J. Brill, 1879), 1654–1655, 1669–1670; Muhammad ibn Jarir al-Tabari, *The History of al-Tabari (Ta'rikh al-Rusul wa al-Muluk)*, 40 vols. (Albany: SUNY Press, 1989–2007), 9:1–3, 20–21.

2. R. C. Blockley, *The History of Menander the Guardsman: Introductory Essay, Text, Translation and Notes* (Liverpool: Francis Cairns, 1985), 98; Aziz al-Azmeh, *The Emergence of Islam in Late Antiquity: Allah and His People* (Cambridge: Cambridge University Press, 2014), 130.

3. Cf. W. Montgomery Watt, *Muhammad at Medina* (Oxford: Clarendon Press, 1956), 92. Accepting the structural approach of Michel Cuypers, *The Banquet: A Reading of the Fifth Sura of the Qur'an* (Miami: Convivium Press, 2009), to the Qur'an, I will read *Repentance* 9:1–29 as a unified text and come back to pick up further related passages later in the chapter. I believe this initial section of the chapter is all

about pagans reneging on their peace treaties with the prophet and about the lead-up to and the fighting at the Battle of Hunayn.

4. *Repentance* 9:5; Reuven Firestone, *Jihad: The Origin of Holy War in Islam* (Oxford: Oxford University Press, 1999), 84–85; Muhammad Abdel Haleem, *Exploring the Qur'an: Themes and Style* (London: I. B. Tauris, 2010), chap. 1, takes a similar approach to this verse, and this chapter, as do I, though he accepts more of the later Muslim historiographical tradition; his rendering influenced my interpretation of the verse.

5. Tabari, *Tafsir*, 3:293, apud 2:191, which has a similar phrase; cf. Neal Robinson, *Discovering the Qur'an: A Contemporary Approach to a Veiled Text*, 2nd ed. (Washington, DC: Georgetown University Press, 2003), 68. The verse has been mistranslated by Islamophobes to make it sound as though the Qur'an urges civilian Believers to go out and murder any "infidel" they come upon.

6. Justinian, *Corpus iuris civilis: Novellae*, ed. Wilhelm Kroll et al., 3 vols. (Berlin: Weidmann, 1893–1895), 3:688.

7. I should warn readers that I am engaged in a radical act of reinterpretation here. The traditional Muslim interpretation of this verse reads "those given scripture" as modifying "those who do not believe in God and the last day," which would turn it into a complaint about Christians and Jews. That translation makes no logical sense in the context of everything else in the book. The Qur'an repeatedly describes Jews and Christians as believing in God and the last day and includes them in the saved communities on that basis a few passages later (5:69). It cannot here be describing them as atheists or polytheists who do not follow religious law. I am trying to restore some semblance of plausibility to our reading of the verse by having the prepositional phrase *min alladhina utu al-kitab* (from among those given the Book) modify *din* (religion). Another possible resolution of this conundrum is to interpret "given scripture" in the traditional renderings instead as "given a treaty," since that was one meaning of *al-kitab*. Indeed, the Constitution of Medina begins, "*Wa hadha kitab rasul Allah S. bayn al-mu'minin wa ahl Yathrib*": "This is a treaty of the messenger of God between the Believers and the people of Yathrib." This possibility is noted by Paul Heck, "Poll Tax," in *EQO*. Some commenters made this verse refer to the supposed campaign at Tabuk,

because no Christians or Jews (those "given scripture") were involved at Hunayn (Tabari, *Tafsir*, 11:407). In my view, this passage obviously concerns instead the Hawazin pagans against whom the Battle of Hunayn was fought in 630, as *Repentance* 9:25 specifies. Since it begins (9:1–3) with complaints about the pagan tribes not honoring their treaties, that it should mention this fault in 9:29 makes perfect sense. Later Muslims, perhaps in search of income, read *jizya* not as reparations from militant pagans but as a poll tax on non-Muslims, assimilating it to the Sasanian practice of *khak bar sar* or *gazidag*, possibly in part because it sounds like the latter. In the Qur'an, however, the verb *jaza* means "to recompense, reward." For a survey of the traditional view of the Muslim exegetes and some critiques of it, see M. A. S. Abdel Haleem, "The Jizya Verse (Q. 9:29): Tax Enforcement on Non-Muslims in the First Muslim State," *JQS* 14, no. 2 (2012): 72–89; cf. Firestone, *Jihad*, 89–90. For extemporaneous comments of contemporary academics on this verse, see "Q9:29–32," chap. 12 in *Qur'an Seminar*, ed. Mehdi Azaiez (Berlin: De Gruyter, 2017) (unfortunately they join it to 9:30–32 instead of to 9:1–28, but they note, intriguingly, that 9:29 is missing from the Sana`a 1 palimpsest, among the earliest known exemplars of the Qur'an).

8. Abdel Haleem, *Exploring the Qur'an*, chap. 1.

9. *Histoire nestorienne inédite (Chronique de Séert)*, ed. and trans. Addaï Scher, 2 vols. (1908; reprint, Turnhout, Belgium: Éditions Brepols, 1983), 2:579–580. A somewhat garbled account is Sebeos, *The Armenian History Attributed to Sebeos*, trans. R. W. Thomson (Liverpool: Liverpool University Press, 1999), 88–89; Touraj Daryaee, "The Fall of the Sasanian Empire to the Arab Muslims: From Two Centuries of Silence to Decline and Fall of the Sasanian Empire; The Partho-Sasanian Confederacy and the Arab Conquest of Iran," *Journal of Persianate Studies* 3, no. 2 (2010): 239–254, esp. 246–247; Mehdi Malek Hodge and Sarkhosh Curtis Vesta, "History and Coinage of the Sasanian Queen Bōrān (AD 629–631)," *Numismatic Chronicle* 158 (1998): 113–129; Marie Louise Chaumont, "Boran," in *Encyclopedia Iranica Online*, http://www.iranicaonline.org/articles/boran-pers; Parvaneh Pourshariati, *Decline and Fall of the Sasanian Empire: The Sasanian-Parthian Confederacy and the Arab Conquest of Iran* (London: I. B. Tauris, 2008), chap. 3; James Howard-Johnston, "Heraclius' Persian